DATE DUE			

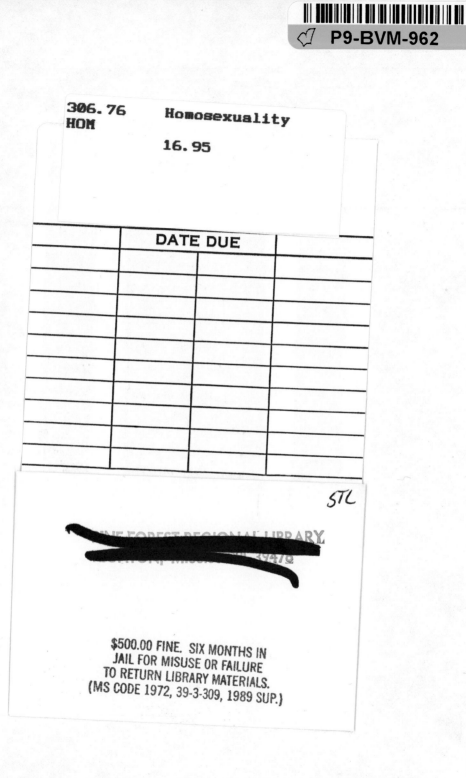

Homosexuality

Contemporary Issues

Series Editors: Robert M. Baird
                      Stuart E. Rosenbaum

Other titles in this series:

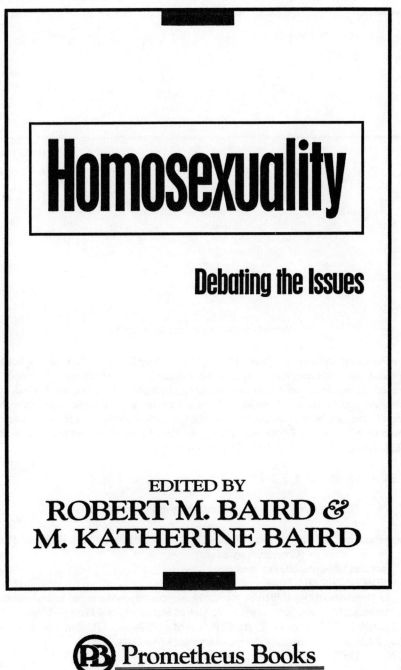

Homosexuality

Debating the Issues

EDITED BY
ROBERT M. BAIRD &
M. KATHERINE BAIRD

Prometheus Books

59 John Glenn Drive
Amherst, New York 14228-2197

Published 1995 by Prometheus Books

99 98 97 96 95   5 4 3 2 1

Library of Congress Cataloging-in-Publication Data

Homosexuality : debating the issues / edited by Robert M. Baird and M. Katherine Baird.
      p.   cm. — (Contemporary issues)
    Includes bibliographical references.
    ISBN 1-57392-003-7 (pbk. : alk. paper)
    1. Homosexuality—United States. 2. Homosexuality—Moral and ethical aspects.
3. Homosexuality—Religious aspects. 4. United States—Armed Forces—Gays.
5. Gay rights—United States. I. Baird, Robert M., 1937–   . II. Baird, M. Katherine
(Mary Katherine) III. Series: Contemporary issues (Amherst, N.Y.)
HQ76.3.U5H673   1995
306.76'6—dc20   95-20281
                                                                                      CIP

Printed in the United States of America on acid-free paper

Contents

6   Contents

Introduction

"Vatican Blasts U.S. Stance on Homosexuality." "Anti-Gay Rights Law Proposed." "Gays Not Allowed to Marry." "Special Rights for Homosexuals—Just Not Fair." "Gay Games Stir Ire." Headlines such as these reflect the passion and, at times, the deep anger generated by the question of homosexuality.

Of all the topics addressed in this Contemporary Issues series, homosexuality is in some ways the most controversial. Unlike abortion, the controversy over homosexuality is such that the very existence of this volume will be objected to by some—and this objection comes from those on both sides of the issue. Some maintain that homosexuality is such an obvious contravention of nature or such a clear violation of God's law that there is nothing to discuss. Indeed, the mere suggestion that the issue is worthy of debate is considered destructive. As one contributor to this volume, Yaakov Levado, puts it, for "many orthodox Jews . . . in the case of homosexuality there is little use for dialogue in the face of such a clear biblical prohibition." On the other side is the claim that homosexuality should be viewed as no more puzzling or objectionable than heterosexuality, and that to publish a book such as this mistakenly suggests the contrary.

As much as some may wish it otherwise, however, the issue is now permanently in the public arena; it is not going away. Therefore, the question remains, will we confront the issue responsibly, and will we establish policies that are wise and just? Our view is that such policies can be established only within a community of civil and informed discussion, and to that end we dedicate this book.

The term 'homosexual' generally refers to individuals sexually attracted to persons of their own sex. This word, therefore, is a label for two phenomena that many insist are quite distinct: male attraction to male and female attraction to female. As the biological and social dimensions of these phenomena are increasingly studied and discussed, it may eventually be discovered that general discussions of homosexuality have to give way to conversations that are gender specific, that is, *either* about women who are lesbian *or* specifically about gay men. While much of the material included in this work addresses the general topic of homosexuality, we need to be constantly alert to the possibility that for that very reason, some crucial distinctions may be being ignored. One of the important consequences of continuing conversation about any issue is the emerging recognition of distinctions that need to be made in order to move the conversation in a more constructive direction. We hope that the selections we have chosen will generate that kind of conversation.

Initial plans for this volume included selections on homosexuality and the family, and homosexuality and education, but we simply did not have the space for those important subtopics. As it is, this work already includes more selections than previous books in this series. Perhaps these other subtopics dealing with homosexuality can be addressed later in a separate collection.

In this volume the opening section serves as an introduction to some of the philosophical issues that undergird more specific points of controversy. The specific areas of controversy that we address are: first, disagreements about the causes of homosexuality; second, disputes about the role the criminal law should play in governing homosexual behavior; third, arguments over the admission of homosexuals into the military; and, finally, disagreements over attitudes religious institutions should take toward homosexuality and individuals who are homosexual.

PART ONE. HOMOSEXUALITY: THE PHILOSOPHICAL DEBATE

From the moment human beings first entered into community, conflict between the individual and the group has been ongoing. This tension is a manifestation of the age-old philosophical problem of the one and the many. Currently, the debate is represented in the conflict between liberalism and communitarianism, between the liberal emphasis on individual freedom and the right to choose one's own way of living, and the communitarian emphasis on community values as the source and *sine qua non* of a constructive and fruitful life. One way to understand the controversy over homosexuality is to see it as another manifestation of this conflict. The homosexual minority advances its arguments for autonomy, respect, and equal rights against what appears to be the larger community's claim that the homosexual lifestyle is destructive of the community's values, inimical to the common good, or contrary to religiously or morally justified standards of sexual behavior.

Precisely the same controversy flared up in England in the late 1950s with the publication of the Report of the Wolfenden Committee (a committee of the British Parliament), which recommended that the British government liberalize laws concerning homosexuality. In the debate that ensued, Sir Patrick Devlin opposed the Wolfenden Report on the grounds that homosexuality was contrary to the established morality essential to social order. The suppression of immoral activity, he argued, is as justified as the suppression of political subversion, and for the same reason—the preservation of community. H. L. A. Hart defended the Wolfenden report, challenging Devlin's claim that individual liberty and personal choices should be limited by the moral feelings of others.

In this first section, as well as throughout this volume, we revisit this conflict. And though the general philosophical issues remain much the same, the current debate has altered, for the discussion is now informed by dramatic developments in science, recent and controversial legal cases, current reflections on the implications of homosexual behavior for social institutions such as the armed forces, and increasing dialogue on the question of homosexuality among practitioners of every major religious community.

Bruce Bawer's article is an appropriate first selection both because his essay provides a historical introduction to the current scene and because he articulates well some of the values that underlie the gay position. "Stonewall" refers to the lesbian and gay riot provoked by the police raid on the Stonewall bar in Greenwich Village, New York, on June 28, 1969. Bawer, in reflecting on this event, which he acknowledges to be the single biggest step in the gay rights movement, argues, nevertheless, that it is time to move beyond the Stonewall mentality. Rather than a defensive and aggressive mode, he proposes a strategy in pursuit of dignity, respect, and equal rights for homosexuals that is appropriate to the current situation.

The material by the Ramsey Colloquium is written by individuals identified with the Jewish or Christian faith. They distinguish among homosexuals who are seeking help in coping with their "problem," those who want to be left alone, and those who aggressively propose changes in what should be considered normative sexual behavior. Concerned with this third group, the colloquium advances moral and religious arguments in opposition to homosexual behavior, and opposes in particular any agenda that seems to undermine heterosexual marriage as the social norm, a norm seen as essential to human fulfillment. The homosexual movement is interpreted by the colloquium as part of a larger sexual agenda rooted in a destructive lack of discipline and restraint.

In the next essay, several members of the National Association of College and University Chaplains object to the Ramsey Colloquium's negative characterization of the homosexual lifestyle. Destructive behavior, they argue, can also be found among heterosexual relationships. The task before us, they argue, is to develop a code of ethics that can serve as a norm for all human relationships regardless of the gender of those involved.

The concluding essay in this section reflects the opposing views of philosopher Martha Nussbaum of Brown University and John Finnis, professor of law at Oxford. Finnis argues against homosexual conduct on the ground that it cannot express commitment to an intelligible common good. The burden of his essay is to show why this is so. He concludes that homosexuality is such a threat to heterosexual marriage (which does involve commitment to a common good) that society ought in every acceptable way possible discourage homosexuality. Nussbaum criticizes the use Finnis makes of the Greek tradition to support his position. Within this tradition, she argues, was a recognition that male-male relationships had the potential for precisely the kind of rich and virtuous life whose existence Finnis wants to deny. Nussbaum is particularly critical of Finnis's claim that the only sexual relationship possible between individuals of the same sex is a selfish, exploitative one. Empirical evidence, she argues, demonstrates this to be false.

PART TWO. HOMOSEXUALITY: EXPLANATIONS AND CAUSES

In a passing reference in his *Nicomachean Ethics* to pederasty, the sexual relationship between an adult male and a boy, Aristotle indicates that in some cases the cause is nature, in others the environment. The nature/nurture debate continues to this day, and is clearly reflected in the selections comprising Part Two of this collection. A careful reading of the essays therein, however, will indicate that even those writers who lean in one direction or the other frequently acknowledge that the causes of homosexuality may be multiple. For example, it may be that a person's genetic disposition is such that given certain environmental conditions he or she might experience sexual attraction to others of his or her own gender. In such a case, biological and psychosocial factors are both involved.

The question of etiology is further complicated by the fact that since the 1948 Kinsey Report, it has been widely agreed that many individuals cannot be categorized as exclusively heterosexual or homosexual. Sexual orientation seems best understood on a continuum ranging from exclusively heterosexual, to predominantly heterosexual, to bisexual, to predominantly homosexual, to exclusively homosexual. These variations suggest a number of complicating causal factors, including the possibility that causal factors operative in one case may not be so in another.

It appears that even if it could be definitively established that homosexuality is genetically or constitutionally determined, the moral and legal debate would still be open. Some would argue that if sexual orientation is genetically determined, moral and legal discrimination against homosexuals would be as inappropriate as discrimination based on race. Others would compare homosexuality to predispositions to alcoholism or kleptomania and argue that such genetically inclined dispositions should be controlled. This issue, too, emerges in the essays in this section.

The opening essay by Joseph Nicolosi advances a neo-Freudian understanding of the development of male homosexuality. At first, the theory goes, children identify with the mother, the earliest nurturer. The developmental task confronting the young male within the first three years of life is to shift from this early identification with the mother to identification with the father. If this transition is successfully achieved, Nicolosi argues, the boy will probably become heterosexual. Problems in the father-son relationship creating alienation from males rather than identification with males may result in homosexuality. Nicolosi discusses several such problems, the most important of which is the boy's experience of male rejection. Nicolosi states unequivocally that "the primary cause of homosexuality is not the absence of a father figure, but the boy's defensive detachment against male rejection."

Neuroanatomist Simon LeVay believes that sexual orientation will eventually be explained biologically, but he also notes that the biological structure of the brain is influenced by "inborn and environmental factors." LeVay first comments on various studies, including recent studies of twins, that suggest a genetic component to homosexuality. He then describes his research showing that in gay men a particular section of the hypothalamus (the INAH 3 nucleus) tends on the average to be smaller than that in heterosexual men and closer in size to that in women. "This finding," concludes LeVay, "suggests that gay and straight men may differ in the central neuronal mechanisms that regulate sexual behavior." It is important, however, to note the qualifications that LeVay introduces concerning his research and his acknowledgment that additional research would be required to determine if the size of the INAH 3 nucleus of the hypothalamus plays a causative role in homosexuality.

Gay activist Darrell Rist is highly critical of the conclusions that LeVay and others draw from such studies. Rist calls into question the methodology or structure of much of the research, but even more fundamentally he calls into question the very categorization of individuals as "gay" and "straight." He is particularly concerned that it is homosexuals themselves "who most often draw the inexorable line and create unbreachable categories of gay and straight." Rist believes that ultimately we must assume "individual responsibility for the construction of sexual desire." An important aspect of Rist's essay is his exploration of the possible motives both openly gay people and avowed heterosexuals have for preferring a "born that way" explanation for homosexuality.

Lindsy Van Gelder also challenges those who argue that gays are "born that way." Whether some are or are not misses the political point, according to Van Gelder, which is that freedom of expression should permit the choice of the gay lifestyle without harassment. In fact, Van Gelder thinks that at least as far as lesbians are concerned, many of them (perhaps 50 percent) are gay by choice.

Michael Bailey and Richard Pillard, like Simon LeVay, have recently made national headlines with research related to the causes of homosexuality. Their work focuses on the study of twins, and they are convinced that their research supports the conclusion that homosexuality is genetically rather than socially determined. Their studies show that the brother of an identical twin who is homosexual is much more likely to be gay himself than is the brother of a fraternal twin who is gay.

Steven Goldberg applauds the work of Bailey and Pillard; he is convinced that their work points to a hereditary component to homosexuality. Goldberg argues, however, that Bailey and Pillard's research also suggests a social or environmental factor in the etiology of homosexuality. A crucial distinction, says Goldberg, must be drawn between a facilitating factor and a physiologically determinative factor. Homosexuality, in his view, appears to be facilitated but not determined by genetics.

The concluding selection in Part Two is a report on the recently released Hamer study, which suggests that homosexual inclinations in males may be the result of the particular nature of the X chromosome. The recognition that homosexuals had more maternal relatives—uncles and cousins—who were gay than gay paternal relatives led Hamer to a study of the X chromosome that is passed from mother to son. His research indicates that the X chromosome of gays showed "different patches of genetic material grouped around a particular area of the X chromosome." The report included here also discusses the social implications of these results.

PART THREE. HOMOSEXUALITY AND THE CRIMINAL LAW

While society debates such finer points as whether lesbians and gay men should be allowed to serve in the military, or adopt children, or be ordained as ministers, some people might be surprised to learn that, in many states, consensual sexual contact between gay men and between lesbians is actually still criminal. The degree to which states have the right to legislate the behavior of Americans in the privacy of their bedrooms is the focus of this section. The resolution of this issue has implications far beyond the question of homosexuality itself. While some believe it is self-evident that individuals should be able to do as they please with their own bodies, others think it is entirely appropriate that states prohibit sexual behavior that the majority judges to be immoral. The result is that different states have a wide variety of laws on the books about sexual behavior—much like the varying state laws about abortion.

The first selection in this section is an edited version of the United States Supreme Court's decision in *Bowers* v. *Hardwick* (1986), which can be thought of as the Court's landmark pronouncement in the area of homosexual rights, just as *Roe* v. *Wade* is the landmark case in the abortion arena. Both opinions continue to be controversial, but for opposite reasons, for, while *Roe* arguably expanded privacy rights, the *Hardwick* decision arguably restricted them.

Hardwick deals with the constitutionality of a Georgia statute criminalizing sodomy. Justice Byron White wrote an opinion for the majority upholding the constitutionality of the statute, on the basis that there is no fundamental constitutional right to engage in homosexual sodomy even in the privacy of one's own home. The majority relied on the "ancient roots" of proscriptions against homosexuality, and found that the Court should exercise restraint with regard to its "authority to discover new fundamental rights imbedded in the [Constitution]." In a dissenting opinion written by Justice Harry Blackmun, the dissenters argued that the case was simply about "the right to be let alone," especially in one's home, and that the majority was wrong in upholding the constitutionality of the statute. *Hardwick* was decided on the basis of a 5-4 vote.

The next piece provides a rare "behind-the-scenes" perspective on the Supreme Court's decision-making process in *Hardwick*. Taken from John J. Jeffries, Jr.'s, recent biography, *Justice Lewis F. Powell, Jr.*, this selection provides interesting information about the underlying facts in the *Hardwick* case. It also describes the soul-searching and tortuous process that Justice Powell went through with his law clerks (one of whom, unbeknown to the Justice, was gay) in finally casting the deciding vote to uphold the constitutionality of Georgia's anti-sodomy statute. Jeffries, who evidently disagrees with the majority decision in *Hardwick*, argues that Powell "failed" with regard to "one of the most crucial constitutional issues of his time."

The brief essay by Stuart Taylor, Jr., is an opinion piece about what the courts should (and shouldn't do) with regard to gay rights. While cautioning against an activist role by the courts with respect to the issues of gays in the military, Taylor unabashedly calls for *Hardwick* to be overruled. His position is that laws punishing people for intimate associations that do not harm others should not be countenanced in our society.

In a letter critical of Taylor's position, attorney George Weaver defends the reasoning of *Hardwick* as sound despite that opinion's acknowledged unpopularity. Weaver, in language evocative of the majority opinion in *Hardwick* itself, cautions against an expansive reading of the Constitution. A brief reply to the letter by Taylor follows, in which he argues that his own view of the privacy issues is shared by five current members of the Supreme Court.

The next selection moves away from the United States Supreme Court's treatment of this issue and focuses on the state court arena, with an edited version of the Kentucky Supreme Court's decision in *Commonwealth* v. *Wasson*. In that case Kentucky's highest state court struck down a statute prohibiting homosexual sodomy on the ground that it violated Kentucky's *state* constitution. Relying heavily on the libertarian views of the nineteenth-century English philosopher John Stuart Mill, the majority argued that Kentucky has been "in the forefront" in recognizing the right of privacy and held that the state law violated that right, as well as homosexuals' right to equal protection. A dissenting opinion is also included, which argues strongly for the right of legislative prerogative and which reasons that the application of Mill's libertarian view "would necessarily result in the eradication of numerous other criminal statutes."

A brief case note from the *Harvard Law Review* critiquing *Wasson* concludes this section. The writer points out weaknesses in the majority's reasoning and concludes that *Wasson* will probably have a limited impact on the effort to expand homosexual rights at the state level.

PART FOUR. HOMOSEXUALITY AND THE MILITARY

In the 1992 presidential campaign, candidate Bill Clinton promised, if elected, to rescind the policies and to alter the practices of the United States Department of Defense toward homosexuals. It was one of the first issues he addressed after assuming office, and, as a result, his administration was immediately embroiled in controversy. In fact, the controversy became so intense that the policy finally agreed upon by the administration and the Department of Defense was a compromise that left many on both sides of the dispute dissatisfied. With the exception of the first selection, the essays in this section are related to Clinton's initiative. The controversy can again be interpreted as opposition between the alleged rights of the individual and the alleged well-being of the group; it is a conflict between those who defend the right of the individual who is homosexual to serve and those who argue that to admit acknowledged homosexuals into the military will undermine the effectiveness of the United States Armed Forces.

The opening selection is taken from Randy Shilts's final work, *Conduct Unbecoming: Lesbians and Gays in the U.S. Military, Vietnam to the Persian Gulf.* Shilts vividly presents what he calls "intransigent facts" about the United States Armed Forces: the extensive presence of gays in the military, the significant roles they have played, and the pervasive hostility toward them.

This is followed by a statement of the current Department of Defense Policy on Homosexuality growing out of President Clinton's directive. It declares that sexual *orientation* is a private matter and will not serve as a bar to admission into the armed forces or as grounds for dismissal. On the other hand, homosexual *conduct* will be considered grounds for barring and/or dismissing a person from military service. This is the highly publicized "don't ask, don't tell, don't pursue" policy. If a person acknowledges that he or she is homosexual, that will be considered grounds for assuming that that person engages in or intends to engage in homosexual behavior; however, the service member will have the opportunity to present evidence that such is not the case.

Prior to issuing the revised policy statement on homosexuality as requested by President Clinton, the Secretary of Defense appointed a task force, the Military Working Group, to discuss the issues involved and, within certain constraints, to make a policy recommendation. This section's third selection is a summary report of that recommendation.

The *New York Times* editorial included in this section is highly critical of the new Department of Defense policy on homosexuality, particularly of what the writer describes as President Clinton's sacrificing principle to political expediency. While acknowledging that the policy makes minor advances over the previous one, the editorial charges that, in effect, the revised policy only codifies the military's discriminatory treatment of homosexuals.

R. D. Adair and Joseph Myers advance arguments against integrating homosexuals into the military. It should be noted that this article predates the policy decision issued by Secretary of Defense Les Aspin. In opposition to such a policy as eventually announced by Aspin, Adair and Myers enumerate a series of unfortunate consequences that they are convinced would accompany the integration of homosexuals into the military. Among their concerns are issues of health and privacy. More fundamentally, they raise the question of the morality of homosexuality. If it is immoral, they argue, no concession should be made. If it is morally permissible, on the other hand, they ask why the military should have *any* restrictions on gays and their lifestyle.

Conservative Senator (now retired) Barry Goldwater, who chaired the Armed Services Committee from 1982 to 1986, unreservedly supports lifting the ban on gays in the military. Included in this *Washington Post* editorial is the widely published expression of Goldwater's own view. While the piece does not contain extended arguments, it does emphatically indicate the direction in which such arguments could be taken.

This section's concluding essay is Robert Stone's review of Shilts's *Conduct Unbecoming*. Not only does Stone recount important dimensions of Shilts's studied advocacy of gays in the military, but he also uses the occasion to address additional issues related to the question.

PART FIVE. HOMOSEXUALITY AND RELIGION

The book *The Churches Speak on Homosexuality* includes a brief and helpful history of the gay church in America. In 1946 George Hyde founded the Eucharistic Catholic Church in Atlanta, Georgia, possibly the first church created for homosexuals. This was followed by the development of other gay churches, "but none became as significant to the homosexual community as the Universal Fellowship of Metropolitan Community Churches" initiated by Troy Perry, a Pentecostal minister.[1] Today Metropolitan Community churches are found throughout the United States.

The creation of churches comprised predominantly of members of the homosexual community dramatically underscores the difficulties gays and lesbians have had being accepted by traditional religious institutions. Every major religious denomination in the United States is currently struggling with the homosexuality question. The issue concerns not only open acceptance of gays and lesbians, but also their ordination as ministers. Indeed, the gay and lesbian demand for the right of ordination has been particularly controversial. Within the last few years, the Evangelical Lutheran Church in America, the Episcopal Church, the United Methodist Church, the Presbyterian Church (U.S.A.), the American Baptist Church, the Southern Baptist Convention, and the Roman Catholic Church have addressed some aspect of the issue. While an increasing number of churches have opened membership to acknowledged homosexuals, a 1993 Associated Press release reported that "the United Church of Christ is the only major Protestant denomination to permit the ordination of homosexuals."

The basic conflict that emerges is between those who maintain that homosexuality is proscribed by Scripture and by God's design for human sexuality and those who argue that the love of God surely must embrace the lifestyle of those who discover that by nature they are homosexuals. This conflict is expressed in a variety of ways in the essays comprising this section. In several of them the distinction between homosexuality *as a condition of sexual predispositions* and homosexual *behavior* becomes important.

The opening selection, a letter to the bishops of the Catholic Church, sets forth the Church's official position on homosexuality. Its opposition to homosexual behavior is rooted in the interpretation of Scripture as unequivocally viewing homosexuality as immoral and is founded on the conviction that the only moral use of sex is within the context of the procreative goal of marriage between a man and a woman. The letter is aimed at countering developing movements within the Church to foster a more tolerant view of homosexual activity. The letter encourages pastoral concern for those who have a homosexual orientation, but it calls on such persons to wholly abstain from homosexual activity.

John Quinn's defense of the "Letter to the Bishops" emphasizes that the document represents the official teaching of the Holy Church and thus carries its authority. Quinn's positive appraisal of the letter attempts to counter much of the negative reaction the letter has received in the Catholic community. He underlines the reasons why the letter was written and calls attention to the positive and compassionate attitude it exhibits toward those who have a homosexual orientation.

Margaret Thompson expresses the view of a Catholic feminist angry at the Church because of the letter. She is also a college teacher who listens to the struggles of her students, many of whom have difficulty with the Church's attitude toward homosexuality. Thompson reflects on these experiences with her students, and she expresses her conviction that profitable answers to questions raised about faith and homosexuality are more likely to be found in God than in the male hierarchy of the Church.

While the date of the essay by Carlyle Marney (1966) might suggest that it is outdated, its challenge to the Christian community seems to us timeless. Influenced by Jean-Paul Sartre's philosophical analysis, Marney argues that the major problem with the Church's response to homosexuals is the distinction drawn between "us" and "them." Once the tendency to objectify (to make a thing of) the other is replaced by graceful identification with the other, the Christian community can begin to respond constructively to the homosexual community.

The material by Paul Duke is taken from a pastoral conversation he had with his congregation on the subject of homosexuality. It expresses his feelings and thoughts about the church's need to respond with compassion and grace to individuals who are homosexual. In the process, he discusses such issues as the continuum between homosexual and heterosexual predispositions, feelings, and behaviors; the dishonest and destructive tendency to associate all homosexuals with the most demeaning and exploitative expressions of homosexuality; and the pastoral word that needs to be addressed to parents of homosexual children and young persons who have doubts about their own sexual identities. Duke also includes a brief summary of James Nelson's analysis of the four ways heterosexual persons tend to respond to individuals who are homosexual.

The title of Stanton Jones's essay, "The Loving Opposition," captures the two dimensions of his argument: The church should express Christ's love and compassion toward homosexual persons, but should also uphold "the Christian vision for sexuality and marriage." Homosexual behavior must be rejected as immoral, Jones argues, because it is at odds with God's purpose for sexual union, a purpose which is revealed in Scripture. Jones defends a "high view" of Scripture which, he argues, explicitly condemns homosexuality and establishes heterosexual marriage as God's standard.

The first essay by Yaakov Levado (a pseudonym) is a first-person account of what it is like to discover that one is gay. Since Levado is a rabbi, his struggle is to understand his homosexuality not only within the framework of the Jewish religion, but also as a leader in that community. He focuses on the deepest spiritual and emotional problem he faces: the role of the gay person in a religious community that emphasizes reproduction and parenting as crucial dimensions of the covenant relationship with God. Levado appeals to texts from Isaiah to support a broader understanding of the covenant itself.

Reuven Kimelman, also writing from a Jewish perspective, suggests that the controversy over homosexuality is more likely to be resolved by moving the issue from the sphere of private morality to the realm of public policy. At the level of policy, Kimelman argues that Judaism must oppose homosexuality, which by its very nature is at odds with the norm of the procreative family, a norm which is Judaism's "major contribution to the civilization of humanity." The essay is an effort to make explicit this "civilizing" role of heterosexual marriage, a role recognized, emphasized, and sanctified by biblical religion. Any behavior—and this, for Kimelman, certainly includes homosexual behavior—that undermines, "intentionally or not, the primacy of the family is *eo ipso* inimical to the interests of religion and its vision of redemption."

Levado's second piece concludes this section by directly challenging Kimelman's claim that acceptance of homosexuality endangers heterosexual marriage and, thereby, the family. Levado argues that most gays are themselves committed to the value of family, and he encourages the Jewish community to recapture a more biblical and a more expansive understanding of family, an understanding that would provide some creative options for homosexuals. The family-values argument fails logically, concludes Levado, but it succeeds emotionally by appealing to a variety of fears among heterosexuals about homosexuality.

Having completed the essays in this volume, the reader may conclude that once again we are faced with an insoluble conflict. If one means by this that there are strong arguments on both sides of the issue and that we are unlikely to arrive at unanimity of opinion, that is surely correct. The issues are indeed complex; facts are often hard to come by; and compelling arguments lead to different conclusions. That is the essence of a controversial matter. However, in the face of such controversy, the only reasonable response for a democratic community is civil conversation aimed at a resolution that is fair to all sides. The purpose of this volume is to encourage that kind of conversation.

NOTE

1. J. Gordon Melton, ed. *The Churches Speak on Homosexuality: Official Statements from Religious Bodies and Ecumenical Organizations* (Detroit: Gale Research Inc., 1991), p. xviii.

Part One

Homosexuality:
The Philosophical Debate

1

Notes on Stonewall

Bruce Bawer

Twenty-five years ago, in the early morning hours of June 28, 1969, several patrons at the Stonewall bar in Greenwich Village, many of them flamboyant drag queens and prostitutes, refused to go quietly when police carried out a routine raid on the place. Their refusal escalated into five days of rioting by hundreds of people. Though it wasn't the first time anyone had contested the right of the state to punish citizens just for being gay, that rioting marked a pivotal moment because news of it spread in every direction and sparked the imaginations of countless gay men and lesbians around the world. It made them examine, and reject, the silence, shame, and reflexive compliance with prejudice to which most of them had simply never conceived a realistic alternative.

There is something wondrous about Stonewall, and it is this: that a mere handful of late-night bar patrons, many of them confused, lonely individuals living at the margins of society, started something that made a lot of lesbians and gay men do some very serious thinking of a sort they had never quite done before—thinking that led to action and to a movement. It was the beginning of a revolution in attitudes toward homosexuality. How odd it is to think that those changes could all be traced back to a drunken riot at a Greenwich Village bar on a June night in 1969. But they can. And that's why Stonewall deserves to be commemorated.

Today, however, Stonewall is not only commemorated but mythologized. Many gay men and lesbians routinely speak of it as if it was a sacred event that lies beyond the reach of objective discourse. They talk as if there was no gay rights activism at all before Stonewall, or else they mock pre-Stonewall activists as Uncle Toms. They recite the name "Stonewall" itself with the

From *The New Republic*, June 13, 1994. Reprinted by permission of the author.

same reverence that American politicians reserve for the names of Washington and Lincoln. And indeed the word is perfectly suited to the myth, conjuring as it does an image of a huge, solid barrier separating the dark ages prior to the day that Judy Garland died from the out-loud-and-proud present. Every year, on what has long since become an all-purpose gay holiday—a combination of Independence Day, May Day, Mardi Gras, and, since the advent of HIV, Memorial Day as well—millions ritualistically revisit the raucous, defiant marginality of Stonewall in marches around the world. This year [1994] in New York, on the twenty-fifth anniversary, the ritual will reach a climax. For many, Stonewall has already become a Platonic model of gay activism—and, indeed, a touchstone of gay identity.

A few weeks ago, in a sermon about an entirely different subject, the rector of the Episcopal church I belong to in New York used the phrase "the politics of nostalgia." The phrase has stuck in my mind, for it seems to me that both sides of the gay rights struggle are trapped in what may well be characterized as a politics of nostalgia. Many of those who resist acceptance of homosexuality and reject equal rights for gay men and lesbians know on some level that they are wrong, but they cling to old thinking because a change, however just, seems to them a drastic departure from the comfortable words of "don't ask, don't tell." Some gay people, likewise, cling to what might be called the Stonewall sensibility, reacting defensively and violently, as if to some horrendous blasphemy or betrayal, even to the hint that perhaps the time has come to move in some way beyond that sensibility. Such people often declare proudly that they have been "in the trenches" for twenty-five years, which is to say that in a way they have been reliving Stonewall every day since June 1969.

Yet every day *can't* be Stonewall—or shouldn't. And in fact the time *has* come to move beyond the Stonewall sensibility. For, thanks largely to developments that can trace their inspiration to that barroom raid, some things *have* changed since 1969. Levels of tolerance have risen; gay rights laws have been passed; in the last quarter-century, and especially recently, gay Americans have come out of the closet in increasing numbers. As a result, it has become clear to more and more heterosexuals that gay America is as diverse as straight America—that many of the people who were at the Stonewall bar on that night twenty-five years ago represent an anachronistic politics that largely has ceased to have salience for gay America today. To say this is not to condemn people who consider themselves members of that fringe or to read them out of the gay community. It is simply to say that for gay America to continue to be defined largely by its fringe is a lie, and that this lie, like all lies about homosexuality, needs to be countered vigorously. The Stonewall sensibility—like the Stonewall myth—has to be abandoned.

On May 6[, 1994,] *The New York Times* described the arguments among gay leaders about the planning of Stonewall 25, the forthcoming New York event that will culminate in a march on the United Nations. Some of these leaders worried that Stonewall 25 wouldn't focus enough on the fact that many of the Stonewall heroes were transvestite and transsexual hustlers. One woman wanted, in her words, to "radicalize" Stonewall 25. "Stonewall," she told the *Times,* "was a rebellion of transgender people, and this event has the potential to reduce our whole culture to an Ikea ad."

It is strange to read the words of those who speak, on the one hand, as if Stonewall, in and of itself, achieved something once and for all time that gay Americans are now free to celebrate, and, on the other, as if the kind of growing acceptance that is represented by the depiction of a middle-class gay couple in a furniture commercial on network TV is bad news, a threat to a Stonewall-born concept of gay identity as forever marginal. It would almost seem as if those leaders don't realize that Stonewall was only part of a long, complex process that is still proceeding, and that the best way to honor it is to build upon it by directing that process as wisely and responsibly as we can.

In the May 3[, 1994,] issue of the gay magazine *The Advocate,* activist Torie Osborn wrote that thirty-nine gay leaders, whom she described as "our community's best and brightest," had gathered recently to discuss the state of the movement and "retool [it] to match the changing times." The group, she wrote, "had a collective 750 years of experience in gay rights or other political work." But even as she wrote of seeking "common ground" and "common vision" among the gay leaders, Osborn reaffirmed the linking of gay rights to "other progressive movements with which many of us identify."

In other words, she embraced the standard post-Stonewall practice of indiscriminately linking the movement for gay equal rights with any left-wing cause to which any gay leader might happen to have a personal allegiance. That practice dates back to 1969, when radical activists, gay and straight, were quick to use the gay rights movement as a way to prosecute their own unrelated revolutionary agendas. Such linkages have been a disaster for the gay rights movement; not only do they falsely imply that most gay people sympathize with these so-called progressive movements, but they also serve to reinforce the idea of homosexuality itself as a "progressive" phenomenon, as something that is essentially political in nature. Osborn wrote further that she and the other gay leaders at the summit "talked about separating strategic thinking into two discrete areas: our short-term political fights and the long-term cultural war against systematic homophobia." And she added that "we have virtually no helpful objective data or clear strategy on the long-term war, which grapples with deep-seated sexphobia as well as heterosexism." Her conclusion (my emphasis): *"We need to start working on this problem."*

With all due respect to Osborn and her fellow gay leaders, it seems to me more than a bit astonishing that in spite of their collective 750 years of experience, at least some of them only now have begun to realize that homosexuals should be giving thought to something other than short-term political conflicts. At the same time, those leaders still can't quite understand the long-term challenge as anything other than, in Osborn's words, a "war." Nor can they see that achieving real and lasting equality is a matter not of changing right-wingers into left-wingers, or of emancipating Americans from "sexphobia," but of liberating people from their discomfort with homosexuality, their automatic tendency to think of homosexuals in terms of sex, and their often bizarre notions of who gay people are, what gay people value, and how gay people live.

Perhaps, at the threshold of the second generation of the post-Stonewall gay rights movement, it behooves us to recall that, as I've noted, there *was* at least some species of gay activism prior to Stonewall. Years before those patrons at the Stonewall bar hurled garbage, beer bottles, feces, and four-letter words at the policemen who had come to arrest them, a few small groups of men in business suits and women in dresses staged sober, orderly marches at which they carried signs that announced their own homosexuality and that respectfully demanded an end to anti-homosexual prejudice. Those people were even more radical than the rioters at Stonewall, and—dare I say it?—perhaps even more brave, given how few they were, how premeditated their protests, and how much some of them had to lose by publicly identifying themselves as gay. They were heroes, too; they won a few legal battles, and they might have won more. Sure, Stonewall was, without question, an important step—indeed, the biggest single step the gay rights movement has taken. But that's all it was: a step, the first big one in a long, difficult journey. It was a reaction to intolerance, and it set us on the road to tolerance. The next road leads to acceptance—acceptance not only of gay people by straight people, but an easier acceptance by young gay people of their own sexuality. It's a different road—and, in a way, a harder one.

First-generation post-Stonewall gay activists saw themselves as street combatants in a political war. Second generation activists would better see themselves as participants in an educational program of which the expressly political work is only a part. Getting America to accept homosexuality will first be a matter of education. The job is not to shout at straight Americans, "We're here, we're queer, get used to it." The job is to do the hard, painstaking work of *getting* straight Americans used to it. This isn't dramatic work; nor is it work that provides a quick emotional release. Rather, it requires discipline, commitment, responsibility.

In some sense, of course, most straight Americans *are* used to the idea of people being gay. The first generation of the post-Stonewall gay rights movement has accomplished that. At the same time, it has brought us to a place where many straight Americans are sick and tired of the very word "gay." They've heard it a million times, yet they don't understand it nearly well enough. They still feel uncomfortable, confused, threatened. They feel that the private lives of homosexuals have been pushed "in their faces," but they don't really know about those private lives.

And why should they be expected to? Yes, at Gay Pride Day marches, some gay men and lesbians, like the Stonewall rioters, have exposed America to images of raw sexuality—images that variously amuse, titillate, shock, and offend while revealing nothing important about who most of those people really are. Why, then, do some people do such things? Perhaps because they've been conditioned to think that on that gay high holy day, the definitively gay thing to do is to be as defiant as those heroes twenty-five years ago. Perhaps they do it because they can more easily grasp the concept of enjoying one day per year of delicious anarchy than of devoting 365 days per year to a somewhat more disciplined and strategically sensible demonstration designed to advance the causes of respect, dignity, and equality.

And perhaps they do it because, frankly, it is relatively easy to do. Just as standing up at a White House press conference and yelling at the president can take less courage than coming out to your parents or neighbors or employers, so taking off your pants or your bra for a Gay Pride Day march in the company of hundreds of thousands of known allies can be easier than taking down your defenses for a frank conversation with a group of colleagues at an office lunch about how it feels to grow up gay. For an insecure gay man or lesbian, moreover, explaining can feel awfully close to apologizing, and can open one up to charges of collaboration with the enemy by those who join the author Paul Monette in seeing America as the "Christian Reich" and themselves as members of the queer equivalent of the French resistance.

As a friend said to me recently, building acceptance of homosexuals is like teaching a language. When gays speak about themselves, they are speaking one language; when most straight people speak about gays, they are speaking another. Most heterosexuals look at gay lives the way I look at a page of German. I may be able to pick out a few familiar words, but I feel awkward when I use them, and if I try to put together a sentence I'm likely to find myself saying something I don't mean at all, perhaps even something offensive or hurtful. There's only one way to get past that feeling of confusion: tireless, meticulous dedication to study. You can't learn a foreign language overnight, and you can't teach it by screaming it at people. You teach it word by word, until, bit by bit, they feel comfortable speaking it and can find their way around the country where it's spoken. That's the job of the second generation of post-Stonewall gay activism: to teach those who don't accept us the language of who gay people are and where gay people live. Indeed, to the extent that professional homophobes have stalled progress in the movement toward legal and social parity for gay men and lesbians, it is not because those homophobes are so crafty, and certainly not because they are right. It is because they have spoken to straight America in its own language and addressed its concerns, whereas gay Americans, more often than not, out of an understandable fear and defensive self-righteousness, haven't.

Some reviewers in the gay press read the title of my book, *A Place at the Table: The Gay Individual in American Society,* as a sign that I, personally, long to sit at a dinner table with people like Pat Buchanan and Jerry Falwell—that this book is my attempt to indicate to them that I'm a nice, well-mannered gay man and that I, along with the other nice, well-mannered gay men, should be allowed at the table while the "bad," ill-mannered gays are excluded. Some other gay press reviewers have understood that I don't mean that at all, and that I feel everyone should be welcome at the American table, but they have angrily rejected the idea: "Why," one critic wrote, "should I want to sit at that table?" A writer for the gay magazine *Out* dismissed the book in one line: "Bruce Bawer has written a book about the gay individual in American society entitled *A Place at the Table*. Some will prefer take-out."

What these reactions signify to me is a powerful tendency among some homosexuals to recoil reflexively from the vision of an America where gays live as full and open members of society, with all the rights, responsibilities, and opportunities of heterosexuals. Many gay people, indeed, have a deep, unarticulated fear of that metaphorical place at the table. This is understandable: gay people, as a rule, are so used to minimizing their exposure to homophobia, by living either in the closet or on the margins of society, that for someone—even a fellow gay person—to come along and invoke an image of gay America sitting openly at a table with straight America can seem, to them, like a hostile act. This sense of threat—this devotion to the margin—may help explain the gay activist rancor toward the movie *Philadelphia*. But most gay men and lesbians were happy to see a movie that showed homosexuality as part of the mainstream, just as most are pleased by the new tendency to depict gay life, in everything from Ikea ads to movies like *Four Weddings and a Funeral*, in a matter-of-fact way, as an integrated part of society.

Am I attacking radicalism? No. I'm saying that the word "radical" must be defined anew by each generation. In the late twentieth century, when radicalism has often been viewed as a fashion choice, it's easy to lose sight of what real radicalism is. It's not a matter of striking a defiant pose and maintaining that pose over a period of years; it's not a matter of signing on to a certain philosophy or program and adhering to it inflexibly for the rest of your life. And it's not always a matter of manning barricades or crouching in trenches. It's a matter of honest inquiry, of waking up every morning and looking at the social circumstances in which you find yourself and having the vision to perceive what needs to be done and the courage to follow up on that vision, wherever it may take you. It's a matter of going to the root of the problem, wherever that root may lie.

And going to the root of this particular problem means going to the root of prejudice. It means probing the ignorance and fear that are responsible for the success of anti-gay crusaders. It means seriously addressing those opponents' arguments against gay rights, in which they combine a defense of morality and "family values" with attacks on homosexuality as anti-God, anti-American, and anti-family. Too often, the first generation of the post-Stonewall gay movement has responded to such rhetoric by actually saying and doing things that have only reinforced the homophobes' characterization of homosexuality. The second generation of the movement would do well to respond not by attacking the American values and ridiculing the religious faith that these people claim as a basis for their prejudice, but by making it clear just how brutal, how un-American, and how anti-religious their arguments and their prejudice are.

And there are a *lot* of untruths out there to overcome. More and more people understand that homosexuals are no more likely to be child molesters than heterosexuals are, but there remains on the part of many people a lingering discomfort about such notions, and anti-gay crusaders exploit that discomfort with ambiguous, dishonest rhetoric suggesting that homosexuals are (to quote a recent statement published in *The Wall Street Journal* by a group of religious figures calling itself the Ramsey Colloquium) a threat to the "vulnerabilities of the young." That's a lie. But how can homosexuals help heterosexuals understand it's a lie so long as some gay political leaders, in the best Stonewall tradition, feel more comfortable condemning the Log Cabin Republicans than they do condemning the North American Man-Boy Love Association?

Likewise, more and more people understand that homosexuals' lives are no more about sex than their lives are, but there are many who still *don't* understand that, and the anti-gay crusaders exploit their ignorance by saying (again in the words of the Ramsey Colloquium) that gay people "define" themselves by their "desires alone," that they seek "liberation from constraint," from obligations to the larger society and especially to the young, and from all human dignity. *That's* a lie. But how can gays help straights understand it's a lie so long as a few marchers on Gay Pride Day feel the best way to represent all gay men and lesbians is to walk down the avenue in their underwear?

Anti-gay propagandists shrewdly exploit the fact that we live in times when there's ample reason for concern about children. American children today grow up in an often uncivil and crime-ridden society, and with a pop culture that is at best value-neutral and at worst aggressive and ugly. Altogether too many of those kids grow up inured to the sight of beggars sleeping on the sidewalk, of condoms and hypodermic needles in the gutter, of pornographic magazines on display at streetcorner kiosks. Anti-gay propagandists routinely link homosexuality to these phenomena, seeing homosexual orientation, and gay people's openness about it, and gay people's desire for equal rights and equal respect, as yet more signs of the decline of morals, of the family, of social cohesion and stability, and of civilization generally.

One of Stonewall's legacies is that gay leaders have too often accepted this characterization of the conflict and see any attempt to correct it as "sex-negative." The second generation of post-Stonewall gay activism has to make it clear that that's not the way the sides break down at all, and that when it comes to children, the real interests of parents and of gay people (many of whom are themselves parents, of course) are not unalterably opposed, but are, in fact, perfectly congruent. Gay adults care about children, too; and they know from experience something that straight parents can only strive to understand—namely, what it's like to grow up gay.

Homosexuals, of course, are *not* a threat to the family; among the things that threaten the family are parents' profound ignorance about homosexuality and their reluctance to face the truth about it. In the second generation of the post-Stonewall gay rights movement, gay adults must view it as an obligation to ensure that parents understand that truth—and understand, too, that according equal rights to homosexuals and equal recognition to same-sex relationships (and creating an atmosphere in which gay men and lesbians can live openly without fear of losing their jobs or homes or lives) would not threaten the institution of the family but would actually strengthen millions of American families.

It is ironic that, to a large extent, what perpetuates Stonewall-style antagonism between gay and straight are not our differences, really, but traits that we all share as human beings. We all, for instance, fear the unknown. To most straight people, homosexuality is an immense unknown; to gay people, a society that would regard sexual orientation indifferently and grant homosexuals real equality is also an immense unknown. But it is also our humanity that makes most of us long to know and live with the truth, even in the wake of a lifetime of lies. The greatest tribute we can pay to the memory of Stonewall is to work in our own homes and workplaces to dismantle, lie by lie, the wall of lies that has divided the families of America for too long.

2

The Homosexual Movement

The Ramsey Colloquium*

I. THE NEW THING

Homosexual behavior is a phenomenon with a long history, to which there have been various cultural and moral responses. But today in our public life there is something new, a *novum,* which demands our attention and deserves a careful moral response.

The new thing is a movement that variously presents itself as an appeal for compassion, as an extension of civil rights to minorities, and as a cultural revolution. The last of these seems to us the best description of the phenomenon; indeed, that is what its most assertive and passionate defenders say it is. *The Nation,* for example, asserts (May 3, 1993): "All the crosscurrents of present-day liberation struggles are subsumed in the gay struggle. The gay moment is in some ways similar to the moment that other communities have experienced in the nation's past, but it is also something more, because sexual identity is in crisis throughout the population, and gay people—at once the most conspicuous

*Hadley Arkes, Amherst College; Matthew Berke, *First Things*; Gerard Bradley, Notre Dame Law School; Rabbi David Dalin, University of Hartford; Ernest Fortin, Boston College; Jorge Garcia, Rutgers University; Rabbi Marc Gellman, Hebrew Union College; Robert George, Princeton University; The Rev. Hugh Haffenreffer, Emanuel Lutheran Church, Hartford, Conn.; John Hittinger, College of Saint Francis; Russell Hittinger, Catholic University of America; Robert Jenson, St. Olaf College; Gilbert Meilaender, Oberlin College; Jerry Muller, Catholic University of America; Fr. John Neuhaus, Institute on Religion and Public Life; Rabbi David Novak, University of Virginia; James Nuechterlein, *First Things*; Max Stackhouse, Princeton Theological Seminary; Philip Turner, Berkeley Divinity School (Yale University); George Weigel, Ethics and Public Policy Center; Robert Wilken, University of Virginia.

From *First Things: A Monthly Journal of Religion and Public Life,* No. 41 (March 1994). FIRST THINGS is a monthly journal published in New York City by the Institute on Religion and Public Life. Reprinted by permission.

subjects and objects of the crisis—have been forced to invent a complete cosmology to grasp it. No one says the changes will come easily. But it's just possible that a small and despised sexual minority will change America forever."

Although some date "the movement" from the "Stonewall Riot" of June 1969, we have more recently witnessed a concerted and intense campaign, in the media and in leading cultural institutions, to advance the gay and lesbian cause. Despite the fact that the Jewish and Christian traditions have, in a clear and sustained manner, judged homosexual behavior to be morally wrong, this campaign has not left our religious communities unaffected. The great majority of Americans have been surprised, puzzled, shocked, and sometimes outraged by this movement for radical change. At the same time, the movement has attracted considerable support from heterosexual Americans who accept its claim to be the course of social justice and tolerance.

We share a measure of ambivalence and confusion regarding this remarkable insurgency in our common life. We do not present ourselves as experts on the subject of homosexuality. We are committed Christians and Jews and we try to be thoughtful citizens. In this statement, we do our best to respond to the claims made by the gay and lesbian movement and to form a moral judgment regarding this new thing in our public life.

We are not a "representative group" of Americans, nor are we sure what such a group would look like. No group can encompass the maddening and heartening diversity of sex, race, class, cultural background, and ideological disposition that is to be found among the American people. We are who we are. As such, we offer this product of our study, reflection, and conversation in the hope that others may find it helpful.

Our aim is to present arguments that are public in character and accessible to all reasonable persons. In doing so, we draw readily on the religious and moral traditions that have shaped our civilization and our own lives. We are confident that arguments based, *inter alia,* on religious conviction and insight cannot legitimately be excluded from public discourse in a democratic society.

In discussing homosexuality, homosexuals, and the gay and lesbian movement, it is necessary to make certain distinctions. Homosexuality is sometimes considered a matter of sexual "orientation," referring to those whose erotic desires are predominantly or exclusively directed to members of the same sex. Many such persons live lives of discipline and chastity. Others act upon their homosexual orientation through homogenital acts. Many in this second group are "in the closet," although under the pressure of the current movement, they may be uneasy about that distinction between public and private. Still another sector of the homosexual population is public about its orientation and behavior and insists that a gay "lifestyle" be not simply tolerated but affirmed. These differences account for some of the tensions within the "movement." Some aim at "mainstreaming" homosexuality, while others declare their aim to be cultural, moral, and political revolution.

We confront, therefore, a movement of considerable complexity, and we must respect the diversity to be found among our homosexual fellow citizens and fellow believers. Some want no more than help and understanding in coping with what they view as their problem; others ask no more than that they be left alone.

The new thing, the *novum,* is a gay and lesbian movement that aggressively proposes radical changes in social behavior, religion, morality, and law. It is important to distinguish public policy considerations from the judgment of particular individuals. Our statement is directed chiefly to debates over public policy and what should be socially normative. We share the uneasiness of most Americans with the proposals advanced by the gay and lesbian movement, and we seek to articulate reasons for the largely intuitive and pre-articulate anxiety of most Americans regarding homosexuality and its increasing impact on our public life.

II. NEW THING/OLD THING: THE SEXUAL REVOLUTION

While the gay and lesbian movement is indeed a new thing, its way was prepared by, and it is in large part a logical extension of, what has been called the "sexual revolution." The understanding of marriage and family once considered normative is very commonly dishonored in our society and, too frequently, in our communities of faith. Religious communities and leaderships have been, and in too many cases remain, deeply complicit in the demeaning of social norms essential to human flourishing.

Thus moral criticism of the homosexual world and movement is unbalanced, unfair, and implausible if it is not, at the same time, criticism of attitudes and behaviors that have debased heterosexual relations. The gay and lesbian insurgency has raised a sharp moral challenge to the hypocrisy and decadence of our culture. In the light of widespread changes in sexual mores, some homosexuals understandably protest that the sexual license extended to "straights" cannot be denied to them.

We believe that any understanding of sexuality, including heterosexuality, that makes it chiefly an arena for the satisfaction of personal desire is harmful to individuals and society. Any way of life that accepts or encourages sexual relations for pleasure or personal satisfaction alone turns away from the disciplined community that marriage is intended to engender and foster. Religious communities that have in recent decades winked at promiscuity (even among the clergy), that have solemnly repeated marriage vows that their own congregations do not take seriously, and that have failed to concern themselves with the devastating effects of divorce upon children cannot with integrity condemn homosexual behavior unless they are also willing to reassert the heterosexual norm more believably and effectively in their pastoral care. In other words, those determined to resist the gay and lesbian movement must be equally concerned for the renewal of integrity, in teaching and practice, regarding "traditional sexual ethics."

It is a testimony to the perduring role of religion in American life that many within the gay and lesbian movement seek the blessing of religious institutions. The movement correctly perceives that attaining such formal approbation—through, for example, the content and style of seminary education and the ordination of practicing homosexuals—will give it an effective hold upon the primary institutions of moral legitimation in our popular culture. The movement also correctly perceives that our churches and synagogues have typically been inarticulate and unpersuasive in offering reasons for withholding the blessing that is sought.

One reason for the discomfort of religious leaders in the face of this new movement is the past and continuing failure to offer supportive and knowledgeable pastoral care to persons coping with the problems of their homosexuality. Without condoning homogenital acts, it is necessary to recognize that many such persons are, with fear and trembling, seeking as best they can to live lives pleasing to God and in service to others. Confronted by the vexing ambiguities of eros in human life, religious communities should be better equipped to support people in their struggle, recognizing that we all fall short of the vocation to holiness of life.

The sexual revolution is motored by presuppositions that can and ought to be effectively challenged. Perhaps the key presupposition of the revolution is that human health and flourishing require that sexual desire, understood as a "need," be acted upon and satisfied. Any discipline of denial or restraint has been popularly depicted as unhealthy and dehumanizing. We insist, however, that it is dehumanizing to define ourselves, or our personhood as male and female, by our desires alone. Nor does it seem plausible to suggest that what millennia of human experience have taught us to regard as self-command should now be dismissed as mere repression.

At the same time that the place of sex has been grotesquely exaggerated by the sexual revolution, it has also been trivialized. The mysteries of human sexuality are commonly reduced to matters of recreation or taste, not unlike one's preferences in diet, dress, or sport. This peculiar mix of the exaggerated and the trivialized makes it possible for the gay and lesbian movement to demand, simultaneously, a respect for what is claimed to be most importantly and constitutively true of homosexuals, and tolerance for what is, after all, simply a difference in "lifestyle."

It is important to recognize the linkages among the component parts of the sexual revolution. Permissive abortion, widespread adultery, easy divorce, radical feminism, and the gay and lesbian movement have not by accident appeared at the same historical moment. They have in common a declared desire for liberation from constraint—especially constraints associated with an allegedly repressed culture and religious tradition. They also have in common the presuppositions that the body is little more than an instrument for the fulfillment of desire, and that the fulfillment of desire is the essence of the self. On biblical and philosophical grounds, we reject this radical dualism between the self and the body. Our bodies have their own dignity, bear their own truths, and are participant in our personhood in a fundamental way.

This constellation of movements, of which the gay movement is part, rests upon an anthropological doctrine of the autonomous self. With respect to abortion and the socialization of sexuality, this anthropology has gone a long way toward entrenching itself in the jurisprudence of our society as well as in popular habits of mind and behavior. We believe it is a false doctrine that leads neither to individual flourishing nor to social well-being.

III. THE HETEROSEXUAL NORM

Marriage and the family—husband, wife, and children, joined by public recognition and legal bond—are the most effective institutions for the rearing of children, the directing of sexual passion, and human flourishing in community. Not all marriages and families "work," but it is unwise to let pathology and failure, rather than a vision of what is normative and ideal, guide us in the development of social policy.

Of course many today doubt that we can speak of what is normatively human. The claim that all social institutions and patterns of behavior are social constructions that we may, if we wish, alter without harm to ourselves is a proposal even more radical in origin and implication than the sexual revolution. That the institutions of marriage and family are culturally conditioned and subject to change and development no one should doubt, but such recognition should not undermine our ability to discern patterns of community that best serve human well-being. Judaism and Christianity did not invent the heterosexual norm, but these faith traditions affirm that norm and can open our eyes to see in it important truths about human life.

Fundamental to human life in society is the creation of humankind as male and female, which is typically and paradigmatically expressed in the marriage of a man and a woman who form a union of persons in which two become one flesh—a union which, in the biblical tradition, is the foundation of all human community. In faithful marriage, three important elements of human life are made manifest and given support.

1. *Human society extends over time; it has a history.* It does so because, through the mysterious participation of our procreative powers in God's own creative work, we transmit life to those who will succeed us. We become a people with a shared history over time and with a common stake in that history. Only the heterosexual norm gives full expression to the commitment to time and history evident in having and caring for children.

2. *Human society requires that we learn to value difference within community.* In the complementarity of male and female we find the paradigmatic instance of this truth. Of course, persons may complement each other in many differ-

ent ways, but the complementarity of male and female is grounded in, and fully embraces, our bodies and their structure. It does not sever the meaning of the person from bodily life, as if human beings were simply desire, reason, or will. The complementarity of male and female invites us to learn to accept and affirm the natural world from which we are too often alienated.

Moreover, in the creative complementarity of male and female we are directed toward community with those unlike us. In the community between male and female, we do not and cannot see in each other mere reflections of ourselves. In learning to appreciate this most basic difference, and in forming a marital bond, we take both difference and community seriously. (And ultimately, we begin to be prepared for communion with God, in Whom we never find simply a reflection of ourselves.)

3. *Human society requires the direction and restraint of many impulses.* Few of those impulses are more powerful or unpredictable than sexual desire. Throughout history societies have taken particular care to socialize sexuality toward marriage and the family. Marriage is a place where, in a singular manner, our waywardness begins to be healed and our fear of commitment overcome, where we may learn to place another person's needs rather than our own desires at the center of life.

Thus, reflection on the heterosexual norm directs our attention to certain social necessities: the continuation of human life, the place of difference within community, the redirection of our tendency to place our own desires first. These necessities cannot be supported by rational calculations of self-interest alone; they require commitments that go well beyond the demands of personal satisfaction. Having and rearing children is among the most difficult of human projects. Men and women need all the support they can get to maintain stable marriages in which the next generation can flourish. Even marriages that do not give rise to children exist in accord with, rather than in opposition to, this heterosexual norm. To depict marriage as simply one of several alternative "lifestyles" is seriously to undermine the normative vision required for social well-being.

There are legitimate and honorable forms of love other than marriage. Indeed, one of the goods at stake in today's disputes is a long-honored tradition of friendship between men and men, women and women, women and men. In the current climate of sexualizing and politicizing all intense interpersonal relationships, the place of sexually chaste friendship and of religiously motivated celibacy is gravely jeopardized. In our cultural moment of narrow-eyed prurience, the single life of chastity has come under the shadow of suspicion and is no longer credible to many people. Indeed, the nonsatisfaction of sexual "needs" is widely viewed as a form of deviance.

In this context it becomes imperative to affirm the reality and beauty of sexually chaste relationships of deep affectional intensity. We do not accept the notion that self-command is an unhealthy form of repression on the part of single people, whether their inclination be heterosexual or homosexual. Put differently, the choice is not limited to heterosexual marriage on the one hand, or relationships involving homogenital sex on the other.

IV. THE CLAIMS OF THE MOVEMENT

We turn our attention now to a few of the important public claims made by gay and lesbian advocates (even as we recognize that the movement is not monolithic). As we noted earlier, there is an important distinction between those who wish to "mainstream" homosexual life and those who aim at restructuring culture. This is roughly the distinction between those who seek integration and those who seek revolution. Although these different streams of the movement need to be distinguished, a few claims are so frequently encountered that they require attention.

Many gays argue that they have no choice, that they could not be otherwise than they are. Such an assertion can take a variety of forms—for example, that "being gay is natural for me" or even that "God made me this way."

We cannot settle the dispute about the roots—genetic or environmental— of homosexual orientation. When some scientific evidence suggests a genetic predisposition for homosexual orientation, the case is not significantly different from evidence of predispositions toward other traits—for example, alcoholism or violence. In each instance we must still ask whether such a predisposition should be acted upon or whether it should be resisted. Whether or not a homosexual orientation can be changed—and it is important to recognize that there are responsible authorities on both sides of this question—we affirm the obligation of pastors and therapists to assist those who recognize the value of chaste living to resist the impulse to act on their desire for homogenital gratification.

The Kinsey data, which suggested that 10 percent of males are homosexual, have now been convincingly discredited. Current research suggests that the percentage of males whose sexual desires and behavior are exclusively homosexual is as low as 1 percent or 2 percent in developed societies. In any case, the statistical frequency of an act or desire does not determine its moral status. Racial discrimination and child abuse occur frequently in society, but that does not make them "natural" in the moral sense. What is in accord with human nature is behavior appropriate to what we are meant to be—appropriate to what God created and calls us to be.

In a fallen creation, many quite common attitudes and behaviors must be straightforwardly designated as sin. Although we are equal before God, we are not born equal in terms of our strengths and weaknesses, our tendencies and dispositions, our nature and nurture. We cannot utterly change the hand we have been dealt by inheritance and family circumstances, but we are responsible for how we play that hand. Inclination and temptation are not sinful, although they surely result from humanity's fallen condition. Sin occurs in the joining of the will, freely and knowingly, to an act or way of life that is contrary to God's purpose. Religious communities in particular must lovingly support all the faithful in their struggle against temptation, while at the same time insisting that precisely for their sake we must describe as sinful the homogenital and extramarital heterosexual behavior to which some are drawn.

Many in our society—both straight and gay—also contend that what people do sexually is entirely a private matter and no one's business but their own. The form this claim takes is often puzzling to many people—and rightly so. For what were once considered private acts are now highly publicized, while, for the same acts, public privilege is claimed because they are private. What is confusedly at work here is an extreme individualism, a claim for autonomy so extreme that it must undercut the common good.

To be sure, there should in our society be a wide zone for private behavior, including behavior that most Americans would deem wrong. Some of us oppose anti-sodomy statutes. In a society premised upon limited government there are realms of behavior that ought to be beyond the supervision of the state. In addition to the way sexual wrongdoing harms character, however, there are often other harms involved. We have in mind the alarming rates of sexual promiscuity, depression, and suicide and the ominous presence of AIDS within the homosexual subculture. No one can doubt that these are reasons for public concern. Another legitimate reason for public concern is the harm done to the social order when policies are advanced that would increase the incidence of the gay lifestyle and undermine the normative character of marriage and family life.

Since there are good reasons to support the heterosexual norm, since it has been developed with great difficulty, and since it can be maintained only if it is cared for and supported, we cannot be indifferent to attacks upon it. The social norms by which sexual behavior is inculcated and controlled are of urgent importance for families and for the society as a whole. Advocates of the gay and lesbian movement have the responsibility to set forth publicly their alternative proposals. This must mean more than calling for liberation from established standards. They must clarify for all of us how sexual mores are to be inculcated in the young, who are particularly vulnerable to seduction and solicitation. Public anxiety about homosexuality is preeminently a concern about the vulnerabilities of the young. This, we are persuaded, is a legitimate and urgent public concern.

Gay and lesbian advocates sometimes claim that they are asking for no more than an end to discrimination, drawing an analogy with the earlier civil rights movement that sought justice for black Americans. The analogy is unconvincing and misleading. Differences of race are in accord with—not contrary to—our nature, and such differences do not provide justification for behavior otherwise unacceptable. It is sometimes claimed that homosexuals want only a recognition of their status, not necessarily of their behavior. But in this case the distinction between status and behavior does not hold. The public declaration of status ("coming out of the closet") is a declaration of intended behavior.

Certain discriminations are necessary within society; it is not too much to say that civilization itself depends on the making of such distinctions (between, finally, right and wrong). In our public life, some discrimination is in order— when, for example, in education and programs involving young people the intent is to prevent predatory behavior that can take place under the guise of supporting young people in their anxieties about their "sexual identity." It is necessary to discriminate between relationships. Gay and lesbian "domestic partnerships," for example, should not be socially recognized as the moral equivalent of marriage. We note again that marriage and the family are institutions necessary for our continued social well-being and, in an individualistic society that tends to liberation from all constraint, they are fragile institutions in need of careful and continuing support.

V Conclusion

We do not doubt that many gays and lesbians—perhaps especially those who seek the blessing of our religious communities—believe that theirs is the only form of love, understood as affection and erotic satisfaction, of which they are capable. Nor do we doubt that they have found in such relationships something of great personal significance, since even a distorted love retains traces of love's grandeur. Where there is love in morally disordered relationships we do not censure the love. We censure the form in which that love seeks expression. To those who say that this disordered behavior is so much at the core of their being that the person cannot be (and should not be) distinguished from the behavior, we can only respond that we earnestly hope they are wrong.

We are well aware that this declaration will be dismissed by some as a display of "homophobia," but such dismissals have become unpersuasive and have ceased to intimidate. Indeed, we do not think it a bad thing that people should experience a reflexive recoil from what is wrong. To achieve such a recoil is precisely the point of moral education of the young. What we have tried to do here is to bring this reflexive and often pre-articulate recoil to reasonable expression.

Our society is, we fear, progressing precisely in the manner given poetic expression by Alexander Pope:

> Vice is a monster of so frightful mien,
> As to be hated needs but to be seen;
> Yet seen too oft, familiar with her face,
> We first endure, then pity, then embrace.

To endure (tolerance), to pity (compassion), to embrace (affirmation): that is the sequence of change in attitude and judgment that has been advanced by the gay and lesbian movement with notable success. We expect that this success will encounter certain limits and that what is truly natural will reassert itself, but this may not happen before more damage is done to innumerable individuals and to our common life.

Perhaps some of this damage can be prevented. For most people marriage and family is the most important project in their lives. For it they have made sacrifices beyond numbering; they want to be succeeded in an ongoing, shared history by children and grandchildren; they want to transmit to their children the beliefs that have claimed their hearts and minds. They should be supported in that attempt. To that end, we have tried to set forth our view and the reasons that inform it. Whatever the inadequacies of this declaration, we hope it will be useful to others. The gay and lesbian movement, and the dramatic changes in sexual attitudes and behavior of which that movement is part, have unloosed a great moral agitation in our culture. Our hope is that this statement will contribute to turning that agitation into civil conversation about the kind of people we are and hope to be.

3

Response to the Ramsey Colloquium

Members of the National Association
of College and University Chaplains*

As members of the National Association of College and University Chaplains (NACUC), we want to offer a response to the article "The Homosexual Movement: A Response by the Ramsey Colloquium" (March [1994]).† Since this essay sets out to "form a moral judgment regarding this new thing in our public life," namely, "The Homosexual Movement," it seems imperative that other scholars and clergy make their response to the Ramsey Colloquium. As chaplains in colleges and universities across the country whose ministry is with and among all students, faculty, and staff, including lesbians and gay men, we offer the following response.

The members of the Ramsey Colloquium assert that they (and presumably all people) simply "are who they are" and that our bodies "participate in our personhood in a fundamental way"; they then continue and write of one's sexual orientation as though it were governed by whim or fad—a "movement," a

*Joan Austin, Elizabethtown College; James P. Breeden, Dartmouth College; Martha Cash Burless, Mount Union College; Deene Clarke, Amherst College; John Colatch, Ferrum College; Janet Cooper Nelson, Brown University; Ben Curry; Ron Flowers, Wesley Foundation at Georgia State University; Jan Fuller Carruthers, Hollins College; Peter J. Gomes, Harvard University and the Divinity School; Larry Green; David Harper, Dickinson College; Donovan E. Hull, Hamline University; Robert L. Johnson, Cornell University; Stanley B. Johnson, University of Pennsylvania; Rabbi Joseph H. Levine, DePauw University; Stuart C. Lord, DePauw University; Tom Modd, University of Texas Medical Branch, Texas A&M (Galveston), Galveston College; C. Jay Pendleton, Pfeiffer College; Janna Roche, Hamilton College; Frederick J. Streets, Yale University; Cynthia A. Terry, Yale University; Charlie Wallace, Willamette University; Joseph C. Williamson, Princeton University; D. Darrell Woomer, Lebanon Valley College.

†See chapter 2 in this volume.

From *First Things: A Monthly Journal of Religion and Public Life,* No. 45 (August/September 1994). FIRST THINGS is a monthly journal published in New York City by the Institute on Religion and Public Life. Reprinted by permission.

matter of "recreation or taste, not unlike one's preference in diet, dress, or sport
... simply a difference in lifestyle"—a lifestyle that they judge to be in the
same category with alcoholism and violence.

It seems extraordinary to us that a group of eminent scholars, writing in
1994, could write in such a superficial and impersonal manner about an aspect
of human nature that, in their own words, defines one's personhood "in a fundamental way"; they clearly overlook the growing body of scholarly, religious
work about sexuality and religion. Further, it seems to us that the writers challenge their own logic when they treat sexual orientation as though it were a
mere fad or "movement" but then go on to acknowledge that "some scientific
evidence suggests a genetic predisposition for homosexual orientation."

The writers of the Ramsey Colloquium article declare that "it is dehumanizing to define ourselves or our personhood as male or female by our
desires alone," suggesting that lesbians and gay men have so defined themselves. It is, however, the Ramsey Colloquium members themselves who so
dehumanize everyone of homosexual orientation, without distinction, precisely by defining them exclusively according to their desires. There is no reference to the long-time commitment, loving-kindness, and caring unto death
demonstrated by many gay and lesbian people. There is no reference to the
many stable, two-parent lesbian and gay families in which children are being
raised. There is no reference to the ways in which families are destroyed when
parents and siblings "disown" their gay and lesbian family members. And there
is no reference to the contributions that gays and lesbians make to family life.

Instead, the writers repeatedly allude to the effects of those desires in an
exclusively negative manner with assertions of "sexual promiscuity, depression and suicide . . . within the homosexual subculture," as well as "seduction
and solicitation." Has evidence of these been the prevailing discovery of the
writers concerning the gay men and women whom they number among their
friends, colleagues, and families? Are such friends and colleagues "doing
damage to innumerable individuals and to our common life"? While the
authors focus on the so-called sexual revolution, we suggest that the sexual
revolution should be viewed with the concurrent civil rights movement;
together these movements helped foster justice and integrity in all human
relationships, be they sexual or not. The writers, however, focus only on the
sexual revolution and put gay and lesbian sexuality in the same category with
"permissive abortion, widespread adultery, easy divorce, radical feminism" as
well as "predatory behavior." One might gather a long list of dehumanizing,
manipulative, often violent behaviors demonstrated by persons of heterosexual orientation, such as rape, wife-battering, child molestation, incest, and murder, stories about which we read in each day's newspapers; would that be sufficient evidence to judge all heterosexual people as moral threats to society?

What is more helpful to and supportive of all people, regardless of sexual
orientation, is the development of sexual ethics that apply to all relationships.
Such ethics include the qualities of love, trust, mutuality, justice, monogamy,

and covenant, along with many others. The witness of countless lesbian and gay relationships proves that these qualities can and do exist in intimate, loving relationships between members of the same sex; likewise, those qualities can and do exist in relationships between members of the opposite sex. The gender of the individuals in any given relationship is not the defining characteristic of what makes the relationship good or bad, healthy or unhealthy, life-giving or destructive.

In the words of the Ramsey Colloquium, we wholeheartedly affirm that "Our bodies have their own dignity, bear their own truths, and are participant in our personhood in a fundamental way." We affirm this truth for all people, straight, lesbian, and gay.

4

Is Homosexual Conduct Wrong?
A Philosophical Exchange

John Finnis and Martha Nussbaum

DISINTEGRITY

The underlying thought is on the following lines. In masturbating, as in being masturbated or sodomized, one's body is treated as instrumental for the securing of the experiential satisfaction of the conscious self. Thus one disintegrates oneself in two ways, (1) by treating one's body as a mere instrument of the consciously operating self, and (2) by making one's choosing self the quasi-slave of the experiencing self which is demanding gratification. The worthlessness of the gratification, and the disintegration of oneself, are both the result of the fact that, in these sorts of behavior, one's conduct is not the actualizing and experiencing of a real common good. Marriage, with its double blessing—procreation and friendship—is a real common good. Moreover, it is a common good that can be both actualized and experienced in the orgasmic union of the reproductive organs of a man and a woman united in commitment to that good. Conjugal sexual activity, and—as Plato and Aristotle and Plutarch and Kant all argue—*only* conjugal activity is free from the shamefulness of instrumentalization that is found in masturbating and in being masturbated or sodomized.

At the very heart of the reflections of Plato, Xenophon, Aristotle, Musonius Rufus, and Plutarch on the homoerotic culture around them is the very deliberate and careful judgment that homosexual *conduct* (and indeed all extramarital sexual gratification) is radically incapable of participating in, or actualizing, the

---

*Editors' note: the following arguments are taken from two legal depositions in the recently concluded trial in Denver, Colorado, [which concluded in 1993] on the constitutionality of Amendment 2, which bars local ordinances protecting homosexuals and lesbians from discrimination.

common good of friendship. Friends who engage in such conduct are following a natural impulse and doubtless often wish their genital conduct to be an intimate expression of their mutual affection. But they are deceiving themselves. The attempt to express affection by orgasmic nonmarital sex is the pursuit of an illusion. The orgasmic union of the reproductive organs of husband and wife really unites them biologically (and their biological reality is part of, not merely an instrument of, their *personal* reality); that orgasmic union therefore can actualize and allow them to experience their real common good—their marriage with the two goods, children and friendship, which are the parts of its wholeness as an intelligible common good. But the common good of friends who are not and cannot be married (man and man, man and boy, woman and woman) has nothing to do with their having children by each other, and their reproductive organs cannot make them a biological (and therefore a personal) unit. So their genital acts together cannot do what they may hope and imagine.

In giving their considered judgment that homosexual conduct cannot actualize the good of friendship, Plato and the many philosophers who followed him intimate an answer to the questions why it should be considered shameful to use, or allow another to use, one's body to give pleasure, and why this use of one's body differs from one's bodily participation in countless other activities (e.g., games) in which one takes and/or gets pleasure. Their response is that pleasure is indeed a good, when it is the experienced aspect of one's participation in some intelligible good, such as a task going well, or a game or a dance or a meal or a reunion. Of course, the activation of sexual organs with a view to the pleasures of orgasm is sometimes spoken of as if it were a game. But it differs from real games in that its point is not the exercise of skill; rather, this activation of reproductive organs is focused upon the body precisely as a source of pleasure for one's consciousness. So this is a "use of the body" in a strongly different sense of "use." The body now is functioning not in the way one, as a bodily person, acts to instantiate some other intelligible good, but precisely as providing a service to one's consciousness, to satisfy one's desire for satisfaction.

This disintegrity is much more obvious when masturbation is solitary. Friends are tempted to think that pleasuring each other by some forms of mutual masturbation could be an instantiation or actualization or promotion of their friendship. But that line of thought overlooks the fact that if their friendship is not marital . . . activation of their reproductive organs cannot be, in reality, an instantiation or actualization of their friendship's common good. In reality, whatever the generous hopes and dreams with which the loving partners surround their use of their genitals, *that* use cannot express more than is expressed if two strangers engage in genital activity to give each other orgasm, or a prostitute pleasures a client, or a man pleasures himself. Hence, Plato's judgment, at the decisive moment of the *Gorgias,* that there is no important distinction in essential moral worthlessness between solitary masturbation, being sodomized as a prostitute, and being sodomized for the pleasure of it. . . .

Societies such as classical Athens and contemporary England (and virtually every other) draw a distinction between behavior found merely (perhaps extremely) offensive (such as eating excrement) and behavior to be repudiated as destructive of human character and relationships. Copulation of humans with animals is repudiated because it treats human sexual activity and satisfaction as something appropriately sought in a manner that, like the coupling of animals, is divorced from the expressing of an intelligible common good—and so treats human bodily life, in one of its most intense activities, as merely animal. The deliberate genital coupling of persons of the same sex is repudiated for a very similar reason. It is not simply that it is sterile and disposes the participants to an abdication of responsibility for the future of humankind. Nor is it simply that it cannot *really* actualize the mutual devotion that some homosexual persons hope to manifest and experience by it; nor merely that it harms the personalities of its participants by its disintegrative manipulation of different parts of their one personal reality. It is also that it treats human sexual capacities in a way that is deeply hostile to the self-understanding of those members of the community who are willing to commit themselves to real marriage [even one that happens to be sterile] in the understanding that its sexual joys are not mere instruments or accompaniments to, or mere compensation for, the accomplishments of marriage's responsibilities, but rather are *the actualizing and experiencing* of the intelligent commitment to share in those responsibilities. . . .

This pattern of judgment, both widespread and sound, concludes as follows. Homosexual orientation—the deliberate willingness to promote and engage in homosexual acts—is a standing denial of the intrinsic aptness of sexual intercourse to actualize and give expression to the exclusiveness and open-ended commitment of marriage as something good in itself. All who accept that homosexual acts can be a humanly appropriate use of sexual capacities must, if consistent, regard sexual capacities, organs, and acts as instruments to be put to whatever suits the purposes of the individual "self" who has them. Such an acceptance is commonly (and in my opinion rightly) judged to be an active threat to the stability of existing and future marriages; it makes nonsense, for example, of the view that adultery is per se (and not merely because it may involve deception), and in an important way, inconsistent with conjugal love. A political community that judges that the stability and educative generosity of family life is of fundamental importance to the community's present and future can rightly judge that it has a compelling interest in denying that homosexual conduct is a valid, humanly acceptable choice and form of life, and in doing whatever it properly can, as a community with uniquely wide but still subsidiary functions, to discourage such conduct.

John Finnis

INTEGRITY

Finnis's arguments against homosexuality set themselves in a tradition of "natural law" argumentation that derives from ancient Greek traditions. The term "law of nature" was first used by Plato in his *Gorgias*. The approach is further developed by Aristotle, and, above all, by the Greek and Roman Stoics, who are usually considered to be the founders of natural law argumentation in the modern legal tradition, through their influence on Roman law. This being so, it is worth looking to see whether those traditions did in fact use "natural law" arguments to rule homosexual conduct morally or legally substandard.

Plato's dialogues contain several extremely moving celebrations of male-male love, and judge this form of love to be, on the whole, superior to male-female love because of its potential for spirituality and friendship. The *Symposium* contains a series of speeches, each expressing conventional views about this subject that Plato depicts in an appealing light. The speech by Phaedrus points to the military advantages derived by including homosexual couples in a fighting force: because of their intense love, each will fight better, wishing to show himself in the best light before his lover. The speech of Pausanias criticizes males who seek physical pleasure alone in their homosexual relationships, and praises those who seek in sex deeper spiritual communication. Pausanias mentions that tyrants will sometimes promulgate the view that same-sex relations are shameful in order to discourage the kind of community of dedication to political liberty that such relations foster. The speech of Aristophanes holds that all human beings are divided halves of formerly whole beings, and that sexual desire is the pursuit of one's lost other half; he points out that the superior people in any society are those whose lost "other half" is of the same sex—especially the male-male pairs—since these are likely to be the strongest and most warlike and civically minded people. Finally, Socrates's speech recounts a process of religious-mystical education in which male-male love plays a central guiding role and is a primary source of insight and inspiration into the nature of the good and beautiful.

Plato's *Phaedrus* contains a closely related praise of the intellectual, political, and spiritual benefits of a life centered around male-male love. Plato says that the highest form of human life is one in which a male pursues "the love of a young man along with philosophy," and is transported by passionate desire. He describes the experience of falling in love with another male in moving terms, and defends relationships that are mutual and reciprocal over relationships that are one-sided. He depicts his pairs of lovers as spending their life together in the pursuit of intellectual and spiritual activities, combined with political participation. (Although no marriages for these lovers are mentioned, it was the view of the time that this form of life does not prevent its participants from having a wife at home, whom they saw only rarely and for procreative purposes.)

Aristotle speaks far less about sexual love than does Plato, but it is evident that he too finds in male-male relationships the potential for the highest form of friendship, a friendship based on mutual well-wishing and mutual awareness of good character and good aims. He does not find this potential in male-female relationships, since he holds that females are incapable of good character. Like Pausanias in Plato's *Symposium,* Aristotle is critical of relationships that are superficial and concerned only with bodily pleasure; but he finds in male-male relationships—including many that begin in this way—the potential for much richer developments.

The ideal city of the Greek Stoics was built around the idea of pairs of male lovers whose bonds gave the city rich sources of motivation for virtue. Although the Stoics wished their "wise man" to eliminate most passions from his life, they encouraged him to foster a type of erotic love that they defined as "the attempt to form a friendship inspired by the perceived beauty of young men in their prime." They held that this love, unlike other passions, was supportive of virtue and philosophical activity.

Furthermore, Finnis's argument, in his article against homosexuality, is a bad moral argument by any standard, secular or theological. First of all, it assumes that the purpose of a homosexual act is always or usually casual bodily pleasure and the instrumental use of another person for one's own gratification. But this is a false premise, easily disproved by the long historical tradition I have described and by the contemporary lives of real men and women. Finnis offers no evidence for this premise, or for the equally false idea that procreative relations cannot be selfish and manipulative. Second, having argued that a relationship is better if it seeks not casual pleasure but the creation of a community, he then assumes without argument that the only sort of community a sexual relationship can create is a "procreative community." This is, of course, plainly false. A sexual relationship may create, quite apart from the possibility of procreation, a community of love and friendship, which no religious tradition would deny to be important human goods. Indeed, in many moral traditions, including those of Plato and Aristotle, the procreative community is ranked beneath other communities created by sex, since it is thought that the procreative community will probably not be based on the best sort of friendship and the deepest spiritual concerns. That may not be true in a culture that values women more highly than ancient Greek culture did; but the possibility of love and friendship between individuals of the same sex has not been removed by these historical changes.

Martha Nussbaum

Part Two

Homosexuality:
Explanations and Causes

5

The Importance of the
Father-Son Relationship

Joseph Nicolosi

Homosexuality is a developmental problem that is almost always the result of problems in family relations, particularly between father and son. As a result of failure with father, the boy does not fully internalize male gender identity, and develops homosexually. This is the most commonly seen clinical model.

THE DEVELOPMENT OF GENDER IDENTITY

As very young infants, both boys and girls are first identified with the mother, who is the first and primary source of nurturance and care. However, whereas the girl *maintains* primary identification with the mother, the boy later has the additional developmental task of shifting identification from the mother to the "second other" (Greenspan 1982). It is through his relationship with father that the boy will change to a masculine identification, which is necessary if he is to develop a normally masculine personality (Sears et al. 1957). This additional developmental task for boys explains why they have more difficulty than girls in developing gender identity (LaTorre 1979) and may also explain the higher ratio of male to female homosexuality (Lynn 1961).

AGE OF GENDER IDENTIFICATION

In the course of the child's life, every significant developmental lesson has its critical periods of receptivity. These periods of heightened awareness appear

From Joseph Nicolosi, Ph.D., *Reparative Therapy of Male Homosexuality: A New Clinical Approach* (Northvale, N.J.: Jason Aronson, Inc., 1991). Copyright © 1991 by Jason Aronson, Inc. Reprinted by permission.

to have a biological basis. There is a particular period of openness to language, which is best taught during the first three years, after which time it is exceedingly difficult to acquire. Receptivity to gender identity also has a critical period, after which the lesson will not be easily learned. Most researchers agree that the critical period for gender identification occurs before the third year (Greenacre 1966, Kohlberg 1966, LaTorre 1979, Moberly 1983, Money and Ehrhardt 1972, Socarides 1968, Stoller 1968). Within that period, the time of greatest receptivity appears to be the second half of the second year.

The child has some sense of the father from the very early months (Loewald 1951, Mahler et al. 1975), in fact, perhaps as early as four months of age (Abelin 1975). By eighteen months he can differentiate pictures of boys and girls, men and women (LaTorre 1979). On a social level, he himself is increasingly being treated as a male. During this time, the acquisition of language further reinforces the basic division of people as either male or female.

The boy gradually develops a need to move away from mother. He develops an intense intuition based on a bodily sense that he is not only *separate* from mother—in the way sister experiences her individuation—but also *different from* mother, and this new and exciting difference is somehow like father. He gradually begins to view father as a self-like object. Now open and receptive to maleness, he will "exhibit a special interest in his father; he would like to grow like him and be like him . . ." (Freud 1921: 105). The boy does not yet understand that his emerging interest in father comes from a primal affinity based in their shared masculinity. Nor does he realize that father is the embodiment of what he himself is destined to be. Yet somehow there is a familiarity and a charismatic power.

Now with the boy's emerging sense of being like father, a dependency arises. He desires to be received and accepted by his father, and that fragile emerging masculine identity, receiving its only impetus from instinct, must be reflected in their relationship.

Father needs to mirror and affirm the boy's maleness. As Payne explains, "The masculinity within is called forth and blessed by the masculinity without" (1985: 13). This beautiful and mysterious match is the union of an inner need and an outer reality. The boy seeks to take in what is exciting, fun, and energizing about his father. There is a freedom and power to outgrowing mother—and this power is personified by the father.

If father is warm and receptive, the boy will be encouraged to dis-identify from the feminine and enter into the masculine sphere. He will then become masculine-identified and most probably heterosexual. If both parents encourage the boy this way, he will be well on his way to fulfilling his male gender-identification and heterosexuality.

FATHER'S INFLUENCE IN SEPARATION FROM MOTHER

One of father's most significant tasks during this period is to protect the child against mother's impulses to prolong the mother-infant symbiosis (Stoller 1979). This intimacy between mother and son is so primal, complete, and exclusive that the father's presence may have to be almost traumatic to disrupt it (Freud 1910). Through his example, the father demonstrates to the boy that it is possible to maintain an intimate but autonomous relationship with the mother.

This triangular relationship of parents and son helps the boy clarify his separateness and his differentness from his mother. It is in this triangular relationship that the homosexual's family background is commonly faulty. Typically there is an overly close relationship between mother and son, with the father distant from both of them. Ideally, the mother and father should work together to assist the boy in the identification shift from feminine to masculine. However, if a too-close mother discourages this gender-identification shift, a father who conveys dominance and nurturance can counteract her regressive influence.

Perhaps one significant factor is the availability of mother when the boy of two or three is experiencing problems with the father. A receptive and over-sympathetic mother might provide such a haven of emotional security that the boy would find it easy to disengage totally from such a father. If the mother tended to be less emotionally available, the boy might be more inclined to tolerate the frustrations of a difficult father.

Many writers recognize the importance of the father in helping the boy individuate from mother (Abelin 1971, 1975; APA Panel 1978; Greenson 1968; Loewald 1951; Ross 1977, 1979). Mahler (1955) describes the importance of a "renunciation of the mother" and believes that a stable image of the father may be necessary to neutralize the threat of reengulfment by the mother.

It is important that the father commit himself to the development of maleness in his son. For this purpose, it is not necessary for the father himself to be very masculine. An effeminate father apparently has no adverse effects upon the boy's gender identity; in fact, many quite effeminate homosexual men have raised heterosexual sons. Once the boy identifies with maleness, he is open to models in other men.

RENUNCIATION OF THE FEMININE

"The first order of business in being a man is: don't be a woman" (Stoller 1985: 183).

In very early childhood, many boys imagine that they need not give up one sex to claim the other. However, reality eventually forces the healthy child to renounce the feminine and surrender its privileges. Yet many homosexual men still hold onto this wish to be both male and female, expressing it through androgyny and occasionally bisexuality. There is sometimes an idealization of women celebrities—Judy Garland, Barbra Streisand, Marilyn Monroe, and Bette Midler, for instance—and even an impersonation of such women in a humorous projection of a particular man's feminine ideal.

Heterosexual men maintain a vigilance against this pull to return to symbiosis with the feminine (Stoller and Herdt 1981). For them, heterosexual pairing is a resolution to this conflict. Through sexual and emotional intimacy with his wife, a man is free to merge with the feminine, but in complementary form—without his masculinity being engulfed by the feminine.

IDENTIFICATION WITH FATHER

For many years, psychoanalytic child-development literature paid little attention to the role of the father. Recently, there has been increasing acknowledgment of the emotional intensity of the father-son relationship—and in particular, of father's contribution to the boy's gender-identity formation (Greenspan 1982; Herzog 1982; Liddicoat 1957; Miller 1958; Mussen and Distler 1960; Tyson 1985, 1986; West 1959).

We know that the child attempts to mold his own ego after the person he has taken as a model, introjecting many of father's personality traits, values, and behaviors. This primal need of the boy has been referred to as "father hunger" (Herzog 1982) and "father thirst" (Abelin 1975). Usually it is the father who is the most significant male figure in the life of the boy during his early development. However, it could be any available male: grandfather, older brother, neighbor, uncle. Usually he is the man who is emotionally involved with mother.

Early psychoanalytic attempts to understand *how* the boy identifies with the father placed the emphasis on the theory of identification with the aggressor. In classic psychoanalytic theory of the oedipal conflict, the boy perceives the father as punitive, threatening, and castrating, and identifies with him out of fear. Later theorists referred to such a process as defensive identification. This concept remains significant to us because it represents the boy's earliest experience of competition with another male for the acquisition of his own masculinity. Indeed, resolution of competition with another male is central to the formation of masculine identity. However, in recent years it has become clear that there is much more to identification development.

Since Freud's time, more recent theorists have expanded our understanding of identification by recognizing the significance not only of punitiveness and limit-setting, but also of positive features of the relationship, such as the father's warmth, affection, and involvement (Brim 1958, Parsons 1955). In fact, paternal qualities of warmth and nurturance seem necessary for male gender identification (Mowrer 1950, Mussen and Distler 1959–1960, Mussen and Rutherford 1963, Payne and Mussen 1956). Five-year-old boys with warm and affectionate fathers have shown stronger father identification than boys with "cold" fathers (Sears 1953). Similar results have been found with adolescent boys (Payne and Mussen 1956). Mussen and Distler (1959) conclude: "Young boys are more likely to identify strongly with their fathers, and thus to acquire masculine interests, if they perceive their fathers as highly nurturant and rewarding" (p. 353). The same researchers found a connection between high masculinity and a boy's perception of his father as both nurturant and punitive.

Failure to gender-identify through relationship with father may be due to many influences, including the following:

1. *More Rewarding Relationship with Mother.* Learning theory shows us how rewards (i.e., nurturance and positive regard) play an important role in the identification process. We can see how the boy would be reluctant to surrender identification with mother, if father was the less rewarding parent.

2. *Lack of a Salient Father.* The father's ability to elicit masculine identification in the son is dependent upon two factors—first, his presence as a strong influence within the household, and second, his warmth, availability, and empathy (Ross 1979). Perhaps the best word to describe this combination of qualities is "salience." In fact the very definition of salience—"something that projects outward or upward from its surroundings"—offers a metaphor for masculinity. Dominance plus nurturance equals father salience.

Dominance refers to the following: in the early psychoanalytic literature, the boy is seen as identifying with the father out of fear. This is known as "identification with the aggressor" (A. Freud 1946). The father upsets the comfortable, nurturing, symbiotic relationship the boy has with the mother. The boy must face this challenge, because the rewards father offers—nurturance, high regard, even material possessions—are dependent upon his responsiveness. The father has to be a strong and attractive-enough parent to induce the son to leave the comfortable relationship and original identification with mother.

Nurturance is defined as: warmth, acceptance, presence and availability, caring and physical display of affection for the boy. The nurturance of the mother is more likely to be unconditional; however, since the father mediates between the boy and reality, his nurturance is more likely to be conditional.

3. *Failure to Encourage Autonomy.* The toddler undertakes two major tasks during the same developmental period: autonomous identity formation (including the development of a sense of personal power) and gender identification. Particularly for the boy, these two tasks are highly interdependent—for personal power reinforces the sense of maleness, and maleness reinforces the sense of personal power.

Some fathers use nurturance of the son as a way of satisfying their own narcissistic needs, loving the child in a way that is controlling and self-centered. Nurturance is not sufficient if the father fails to encourage the boy's own masculine autonomy. When love is used as leverage against the boy's masculine strivings, both personal power and gender development are sabotaged.

Masculine autonomy can be thwarted by both *overprotection* and *over-domination.* Friedberg (1975) made the observation: "Children who become homosexuals are those who have been either pampered or who have found themselves to be in a hopelessly inferior position" (p. 202).

4. *Father Absence.* A number of studies show that father absence in boys may result in dependency, lack of assertion, and/or weaker masculine identity (Apfelberg 1944; Bach 1946; Badaines 1976; Biller 1968, 1969; Hetherington 1966; Santrock 1970). In a study of eighty children of Norwegian sailors away from home for long periods of time, boys showed general immaturity, poorer peer adjustment, and stronger strivings toward father identification (Lynn and Sawrey 1959).

There is clear evidence that boys with absent fathers are capable of het-erosexual adjustment if they have not experienced emotional rejection from a significant male figure. Without the impulse to guard against hurt, they can grow up with a trusting and receptive attitude toward masculine figures. For the primary cause of homosexuality is not the absence of a father figure, but the boy's defensive detachment against male rejection. As long as the boy remains open to masculine influence, he will eventually encounter some father-figure who will fulfill his needs. Every male has a healthy need for inti-macy with other males. This desire emerges in early childhood and is satisfied first with the father, then later with male peers. When this drive is frustrated, homosexual attraction emerges as a "reparative striving" (Moberly 1983: ix).

There are many factors influencing the boy's failure to identify with father. Mother dominance, a more rewarding mother, and the narcissistic needs of either parent are among the contributing influences. Yet the pivotal factor remains the father—and whether he is able to create a relationship sufficiently salient to encourage the development of gender identification.

FATHER AS THE REALITY PRINCIPLE

The mother's relationship to the infant, as we have described, is usually sym-biotic and unconditionally accepting. It is not until he reaches out to the ear-liest symbol of the outside world—his father—that the boy encounters his first real challenge for acceptance. The father symbolizes strength, independence, and mastery of the environment.

Mastery of the father-son relationship is crucial. Where there is traumatic failure in relationship with father, the boy will be deeply handicapped. Rela-tionship with father represents the lifelong task of balancing internal needs with external expectations and requirements. Relationship with father rein-forces the Reality Principle (Freud 1949) for the boy.

PHYSICAL NATURE OF THE FATHER-SON RELATIONSHIP

During their son's infancy, most fathers have felt ill-at-ease handling and caring for a fragile newborn boy. Then as the boy enters the toddler stage of reckless exploration of the environment, his high activity level offers a common ground through which he and his father will be drawn together. Free to venture farther and farther from mother, the boy discovers that Dad has a particular appeal distinct from mother—"Dad does things." There is a physical boldness, a masculine energy about the father that the boy finds exciting.

Father-son relationships have always been based upon the sharing of physical activity. In fact, the boy's "need to be shown how" is characteristic of his relationship with his father during the pre-oedipal period (Herzog 1980). A behavioral, bodily phenomenon of identification seems to result from father and son "doing" together. As one of his son's first play partners, father challenges the boy with his masculine form of interaction. At the same time he is setting reasonable boundaries, the father encourages the boy's youthful energy and optimism. From the father, the boy learns that danger can be fun and exciting.

Not only in toddlerhood but on into adulthood, doing things together characterizes the way males relate to each other. Men tend to view their bodies in terms of strength, agility, and action, and they need to relate on a physical level. Unlike men, most women can relate in a static manner by sitting and talking face-to-face. Similarly, while men view their bodies in terms of how they function, women are inclined to view their bodies in terms of how they look as static objects (Franzoi 1989). And so the task for the developing boy is to find the normal masculine, action-oriented way of perceiving his own body, and to engage it in his relationships with other males.

Boys with gender-identity confusion are often excited about dressing up and being pretty, while not at all interested in (in fact, quite resistant to) doing things with their fathers. While not all prehomosexual boys evidence such effeminate behavior, still they often missed this "doing" dimension of development in the early father-son relationship. Later in life, they are often particularly drawn to the mystique of masculine boldness, strength, and power.

In previous generations, it was the day-to-day labor that unified father and son. Traditionally, they had a functional relationship grounded in shared tasks. The son saw his father confront the challenges of life. He witnessed his father struggle with the soil, with the crops, with tools, and with the weather. Or perhaps father had a small business in which the boy could help. He was able to gain a sense of his father's work, and thus to envision his own place in the male world.

Today's technology and division of labor have eroded the common ground upon which the father-son bond was formed. Today, the boy often doesn't understand his father's work. It is typically away from home and is often technical and beyond the boy's comprehension. Because father's work is detached from home life, men today are detached from their own sons. Today it is the mother who mediates between the father and the son, and consequently the boy now sees father through feminine eyes. The link between the father and the son has become distorted and diluted by this feminine perspective. Mother tells the boy who Dad is, what he is about, and what he is feeling. Today we must often artificially create activities fathers and sons can share, such as Little League, Boy Scouts, and camping trips. Arranged as such activities may be, they are nevertheless an important medium for the male bonding that lays the groundwork for masculine identification.

MASCULINE INITIATION

Throughout world history, the transformation from boy to man has required the challenge of an initiation ritual. These trials have always been an important part of human consciousness for males (Bly 1990, Campbell 1971). The masculine-initiation ritual involves death of the boy's premasculine self and rebirth into manhood. With the elements of danger, vulnerability, and the symbolic threat of annihilation, the boy undergoes a trial to determine whether he is strong enough and wise enough to be worthy of the status of a man.

The first initiatory trial occurs during the separation-individuation phase, when the infant begins to see himself as a separate person and reaches out to the father. As he grows and their relationship develops, he eventually learns that his father—who represents the realities of the outside world—will make demands he must meet. For father's love is not unconditional: the boy must work to come to accord with father.

All rites of initiation into manhood involve some personal trial in which an adult male participates. If the boy is successful, the rite culminates with acknowledgment from that man, who passes on the transforming power of masculine energy. This initiation is played out on a dramatic level in cultures such as the Sambia Tribe of New Guinea (Stoller and Herdt 1981). There is great value placed on masculinity in that culture. Sambian men believe their son's masculinity is threatened by too much intimacy from the mother. During the rite of passage into manhood, boys are taken from their mothers and sisters into the forest. In a ritual that is sometimes brutalizing and frightening, the boy is resocialized into manhood so that he will be brave, manly, a husband and a father.

The Sambian rite of initiation illustrates these points:

1. prolonged identification with mother is a threat to a boy's masculinity;

2. masculinity can only be transmitted by other men; and

3. masculinity is a prized commodity to be achieved, not simply acquired.

Where there is a good fight with the experience of acknowledgment, we have full masculinity and heterosexuality. This is not so with homosexuality. There is no direct struggle, no confrontation or competition. Even where there is hostility with the father, it is never a "fair and square" competition with the possibility of the boy being successful. Rather, we see competition with these father figures as indirect and undermining, particularly in the boy's subversive alignment with mother. The boy conspires with the mother to erode, dismiss, or mock the father.

Homosexuality is an alienation from males—in infancy from father, and in later life from male peers. By eroticizing what he feels disenfranchised from, the homosexual man is still seeking this initiation into manhood through other males.

REFERENCES

Abelin, E. (1971). "The Role of the Father in the Separation-Individuation Process." In *Separation-Individuation: Essays in Honor of Margaret S. Mahler,* ed. J. B. McDevitt and C. F. Settlage, pp. 229–52. New York: International Universities Press.
———. (1975). "Some Further Observations and Comments on the Earliest Role of the Father." *Journal of the American Psychoanalytic Association* 56:293–306.
APA Panel (1978). "The Role of the Father in the Preoedipal Years." *Journal of the American Psychoanalytic Association* 26:143–61.
Apfelberg, B., C. Sugar, and A. Pfeffer (1944). "A Psychiatric Study of 250 Sex Offenders." *American Journal of Psychiatry* 100:762–70.
Bach, G. (1946). "Father-Fantasies and Father-Typing in Father-Separated Children." *Child Development* 17:63–80.
Badaines, J. (1976). "Identification, Imitation, and Sex-Role Preference in Father-Present and Father-Absent Black and Chicano Boys." *Journal of Psychology* 92:14–24.
Biller, H. (1968). "A Note on Father-Absence and Masculine Development in Young Lower-Class Negro and White Boys." *Child Development* 39:1003–1006.
———. (1969). "Father Absence, Maternal Encouragement, and Sex-Role Development in Kindergarten Age Boys." *Child Development* 40:539–46.
Bly, R. (1990). *Iron John: A Book about Men.* Reading, Mass.: Addison-Wesley.
Brim, O. (1958). "Family Structure and Sex-Role Learning by Children." *Sociometry* 21:1–16.
Campbell, J. (1971). *The Hero with a Thousand Faces.* Princeton, N.J.: Princeton University Press.
Franzoi, S. (1989). "*The Beauty Bind,* by P. Calistro." *Los Angeles Times Magazine,* May 28, p. 34.
Freud, A. (1946). "The Ego and the Mechanisms of Defense." In *The Writings of Anna Freud,* vol. 11. New York: International Universities Press, 1968.
Freud, S. (1910). "Leonardo da Vinci and a Memory of His Childhood." *Standard Edition,* 11:59–138.
———. (1921). "Group Psychology." *Standard Edition,* 18:67–145.
———. (1949). *An Outline of Psychoanalysis.* New York: W. W. Norton.
Friedberg, R. (1975). "Early Recollections of Homosexuals as Indicators of their Life Styles." *Journal of Individual Psychology* 13:196–204.
Greenacre, P. (1966). "Problems of Overidealization of the Analyst and of Analysis: Their Manifestations in the Transference and Countertransference Relationship." In *Emotional Growth,* pp. 743–61. New York: International Universities Press.
Greenson, R. (1968). "Disidentifying from Mother: Its Special Importance for the Boy." *International Journal of Psychoanalysis* 49:370–74.
Greenspan, S. (1982). " 'The Second Other': The Role of the Father in Early Personality Formation and the Dyadic-Phallic Phase of Development." In *Father and Child,* ed. S. Cath. Boston: Little, Brown.

Herzog, J. (1980) "Sleep Disturbance and Father Hunger in 18–28-Month Boys: The Erlkonig Syndrome." *Psychoanalytic Study of the Child* 35: 219–33. New Haven: Yale University Press.

———. (1982). "On Father Hunger: The Father's Role in the Modulation of Aggressive Drive and Fantasy." In *Father and Child,* ed. S. Cath. Boston: Little, Brown.

Hetherington, E. (1966). "Effects of Paternal Absence on Sex-Typed Behaviors in Negro and White Preadolescent Males." *Journal of Personality and Social Psychology* 4:87–91.

Kohlberg, L. (1966). "A Cognitive-Developmental Analysis of Children's Sex-Role Concepts and Attitudes." In *The Development of Sex Differences,* ed. E. Maccoby. Stanford, Calif: Stanford University Press.

LaTorre, R. (1979). *Sexual Identity.* Chicago: Nelson-Hall.

Liddicoat, R. (1957). "Homosexuality." *British Medical Journal* 9:1110–11.

Loewald, H. (1951). "Ego and Reality." *International Journal of Psychoanalysis* 41:16–33.

Lynn, D. (1961). "Sex Differences in Identification Development." *Sociometry* 24:373–83.

Lynn, D., and W. Sawrey (1959). "The Effects of Father-Absence on Norwegian Boys and Girls." *Journal of Abnormal and Social Psychology* 59:258–62.

Mahler, M., and R. Gosliner (1955). "On Symbiotic Child Psychosis: Genetic, Dynamic and Restitutive Aspects." *Psychoanalytic Study of the Child* 10:195–212. New York: International Universities Press.

Mahler, M., F. Pine, and A. Bergman (1975). *The Psychological Birth of the Human Infant.* New York: Basic Books.

Miller, P. R. (1958). "The Effeminate, Passive, Obligatory Homosexual." *AMA Archives of Neurology and Psychiatry* 80:612–18.

Moberly, E. (1983). *Homosexuality: A New Christian Ethic.* Greenwood, S.C.: Attic Press.

Money, J., and A. Ehrhardt (1972). *Man and Woman, Boy and Girl.* Baltimore, Md.: Johns Hopkins University Press.

Mowrer, O. (1950). *Learning Theory and Personality Dynamics.* New York: Ronald Press.

Mussen, P., and L. Distler (1959). "Masculinity, Identification and Father-Son Relationships." *Journal of Abnormal Social Psychology* 59:350–56.

———. (1960). "Child-Rearing Antecedents of Masculine Identification in Kindergarten Boys." *Child Development* 31:89–100.

Mussen, P., and E. Rutherford (1963). "Parent-Child Relations and Parental Personality in Relation to Young Children's Sex-Role Preferences." *Child Development* 34:589–607.

Parsons, T. (1955). "Family Structure and Socialization of the Child." In *Family, Socialization and Interaction Process,* ed. T. Parsons and R. Bales. Glencoe, Ill.: Free Press.

Payne, D., and P. Mussen (1956). "Parent-Child Relations and Father Identification among Adolescent Boys." *Journal of Abnormal and Social Psychology* 52:358–62.

Payne, L. (1985). *Crisis in Masculinity.* Westchester, Ill.: Crossway Books.

Ross, J. (1977). "Toward Fatherhood: The Epigenesis of Paternal Identity during a Boy's First Decade." *International Review of Psycho-Analysis* 4:327–47.

———. (1979). "Fathering: A Review of Some Psychoanalytic Contributions on Paternity." *International Journal of Psycho-Analysis* 60:317–20.

Santrock, J. W. (1970). "Paternal Absence, Sex-Typing and Identification." *Developmental Psychology* 2:264–72.

Sears, R. (1953). "Child-Rearing Factors Related to the Playing of Sex-Typed Roles." *American Psychologist* 8:431.

Sears, R., E. McCabe, and H. Levin (1957). *Patterns of Child Rearing.* Evanston, Ill.: Rowe, Peterson and Co.

Socarides, C. (1968a). "A Provisional Theory of Etiology in the Male Homosexual: A Case of Preoedipal Origin." *International Journal of Psychiatry* 49:27–37.

———. (1968b). *The Overt Homosexual.* New York: Grune and Stratton.

Stoller, R. (1968). *Sex and Gender.* New York: Science House.

Stoller, R. (1979). "A Contribution to the Study of Gender Identity: Follow-Up Interview." *International Journal of Psycho-Analysis* 60:433–41.

———. (1985). *Presentations of Gender.* New Haven, Conn.: Yale University Press.

Stoller, R., and G. Herdt (1981). "The Development of Masculinity: A Cross-Cultural Contribution." *Journal of the American Psychology Association* 30:29–59.

Tyson, P. (1985). "The Role of the Father in Gender Identity, Urethral Erotism and Phallic Narcissism." In *Father and Child: Developmental and Clinical Perspectives,* ed. S. Cath, pp. 175–87. Boston: Little, Brown.

———. (1986). "Male Gender Identity: Early Developmental Roots." *Psychoanalytic Review* 73:1–21.

West, D. J. (1959). "Parental Figures in the Genesis of Male Homosexuality." *International Journal of Social Psychiatry* 5:85–97.

6

Sexual Orientation and Its Development

Simon LeVay

. . . I do not know—nor does anyone else—what makes a person gay, bisexual, or straight. I do believe, however, that the answer to this question will eventually be found by doing biological research in laboratories and not by simply talking about the topic, which is the way most people have studied it up to now.

Believing in a biological explanation for sexual orientation is not the same thing as insisting that sexual orientation is inborn or genetically determined. Our entire mental life involves biological processes. We know that our sexual orientation, like our tastes in music and our memory of our last vacation, is engraved in some morphological or chemical substrate in the brain. It is not maintained solely by the brain's actual activity, whether electrical or metabolic. This activity can be brought to a complete stop, for example by cooling the brain to near the freezing point. Yet, once restarted, we regain our original sexual feelings, we still prefer the same composers, and our memories are unimpaired, except for events immediately prior to losing consciousness. So both inborn and environmental factors influence us by influencing the anatomical or chemical structure of the brain. . . .

Homosexuality runs in families. Many gay men and lesbian women have at least one brother or sister or other close relative who is also homosexual. From statistical studies (especially one carried out by Richard Pillard and James Weinrich at Boston University) it emerges that having a gay brother increases your own chances of being gay severalfold: about 25 percent of all the brothers of gay men are themselves gay, whereas in the general male population the incidence of homosexuality is probably under 10 percent. . . . The

From Simon LeVay, *The Sexual Brain* (Cambridge, Mass.: MIT Press, 1993). © 1993 Massachusetts Institute of Technology. Reprinted by permission.

studies on women are less extensive, but it is believed that about 15 percent of the sisters of lesbian women are themselves lesbian, a figure that is also well above the incidence in the general population. There are conflicting data on whether the grouping of homosexual individuals crosses the sex lines: that is, whether having a gay brother increases a woman's chance of being lesbian, and vice versa. The weight of the evidence is that it does not, or does so only weakly. This suggests that the factors influencing sexual orientation in men may be different from those operating in women. This is reasonable enough, given that "homosexuality" is just a label for two phenomena that are really different things in the two sexes: being attracted to men in one case and being attracted to women in the other.

Such family grouping by itself does not distinguish between the effects of nature and nurture. If parents treated one child in such a way as to make him or her homosexual, they might well treat another child in the same way. More telling evidence for an inborn component comes from the studies of twins, especially from a comparison of monozygotic (identical) twins, who share the same genes, and dizygotic (fraternal) twins, who are no more closely related than non-twin siblings.

Pairs of monozygotic twins, both of whom were homosexual, were described already by [Magnus] Hirschfeld at the turn of the century. Since then there have been a number of studies, some claiming almost total concordance (both twins gay), others noting substantial numbers of discordant pairs (one gay and one straight twin). Two recent studies (one by Michael Bailey of Northwestern University and Richard Pillard; the other by Fred Whitam and colleagues at Arizona State University) have reported that having a gay monozygotic twin makes your own likelihood of being gay about 50–65 percent, while having a gay dizygotic twin makes your chances of being gay only about 25–30 percent. In a comparable study of female twins, Bailey, Pillard, and Yvonne Agyei reported that 48 percent of the monozygotic twin sisters of lesbian women were also lesbian, while only 16 percent of the dizygotic twin sisters were lesbian, about the same as the rate for non-twin sisters of lesbian women.

These studies are of course beset by problems that might have distorted the estimates of heritability in one direction or another. The subjects who volunteered for the study might not have been representative of the entire population, or the causes of homosexuality among twins might be different from those operating among singletons. Such factors could have inflated the estimates of heritability. Alternatively, the fact that some of the twins studied were quite young might have led to an underestimate of heritability, since some individuals do not acknowledge their own homosexuality till quite late in life.

The best available model for distinguishing inborn from postnatal environmental factors is the case of identical twins separated at birth and raised separately. Unfortunately, such twin pairs are difficult to locate and study, and the additional requirement that at least one of the twins be gay makes the search even harder. Thomas Bouchard and his colleagues at the University of

Minnesota have for many years studied twins raised apart. They identified two cases of male identical twins where one of the twins was gay. In one case, the co-twin was also gay. In fact the pair (neither of whom knew he had a twin brother) met after one was mistaken for his twin at a gay bar, and they subsequently became lovers. The other case was more equivocal: one twin considered himself gay, but had had some heterosexual experience; the other considered himself completely heterosexual, but had had a three-year homosexual relationship as a teenager. The Minnesota group also identified three female pairs where one twin was lesbian. In all three of these cases, the co-twin was entirely heterosexual.

All in all, these twin studies point to a strong but not total genetic influence on sexual orientation in men, and a substantial but perhaps somewhat weaker genetic influence in women. Clearly, some nongenetic factors make a contribution. Ideally, study of the discordant identical twin pairs would allow one to identify these factors, but in practice this has proved very difficult. Identical twins generally are treated very similarly by their parents and siblings, and the life experiences of the two twins do not give obvious clues as to their ultimate sexual orientation. Indeed, sometimes these experiences are the opposite of what one might expect. For example, it has often been claimed that sexual molestation of girls contributes to homosexuality in adulthood. Yet in one discordant female pair in the Minnesota study (one heterosexual, one bisexual) the heterosexual woman, and not her co-twin, was sexually molested as a child.

One should bear in mind that nongenetic factors can operate before birth as well as after birth. . . . Even identical twins do not necessarily share an identical prenatal environment: the blood supply of one twin may be better than the other's, for example, and this in turn may lead to a difference in the twins' birth weights.

Also pointing to a genetic factor is a special case, that of men with an extra X chromosome. These XXY individuals are men because . . . it is a gene on the Y chromosome that confers maleness; the number of X chromosomes is irrelevant. Nevertheless, the possession of an extra X chromosome does influence development: these individuals tend to be taller and less intelligent than XY men, and their testes fail to produce sperm—the so-called Klinefelter's syndrome. There have been numerous reports over the years of differences in sexual behavior between XXY and XY men, but the interpretation has been problematic because the individuals were often identified through special circumstances such as their being confined to prisons or mental hospitals. A recent U.S.-Danish study solved this problem by "brute force": the researchers simply karyotyped (counted the chromosomes of) every male resident of Copenhagen who filled certain age and height criteria. Out of thousands of men examined, they identified sixteen XXY men and compared their sex histories with those of control men matched for height, age, IQ, and socioeconomic status. There was a highly significant excess of homosexuality among the XXY men compared with the control men.

Of course, an extra X chromosome is very uncommon and is certainly not the usual cause of homosexuality. But this study is important in showing unequivocally that genetic factors *can* influence sexual orientation. The exact mechanism by which the extra X chromosome has its effect remains unclear. XXY men have in general slightly lower testosterone levels in their blood than do XY men. It is conceivable that testosterone levels were also lower during a developmental period critical for the determination of sexual orientation. . . .

Are there differences in the anatomical or chemical structure of the brain between homosexual and heterosexual individuals? As I stated at the beginning . . . the answer to this question must in principle be yes, because a person's sexual orientation remains unaltered after all brain activity and metabolism have been temporarily halted. So the practical question is: Are the structural differences scattered through a million widely dispersed, anonymous synapses in the cerebral cortex (as the structural differences representing preference for different musical composers presumably are) or are they concentrated at a key location, where they so dominate the cellular landscape as to make themselves evident to an anatomist's inspection?

My own research suggests that there is at least one such key location, the medial preoptic region of the hypothalamus. . . . [T]his region of the brain is believed to be involved in the regulation of male-typical sexual behavior, and it contains at least four small groups of neurons termed the interstitial nuclei of the anterior hypothalamus (INAH). One of these, named INAH 3, is bigger on average in men than women. The others either show no sex differences (INAH 1 and 4) or show equivocal differences that may be limited to certain age ranges (INAH 2). I obtained the brains of gay men (all of whom had died of AIDS) as well as the brains of heterosexual men who had also died of AIDS (these were intravenous drug abusers) and of presumably heterosexual men who had died of a variety of other causes. In addition, I obtained the brains of several women, presumably heterosexual ("presumably" means simply on the basis of the preponderance of heterosexual women in the population: a woman's sexual orientation is rarely if ever noted in her medical records). I was not able to obtain the brains of any women known to have been lesbian.

I processed and analyzed the hypothalamic tissue from these brains "blind," that is, not knowing which specimen came from which group of subjects. After decoding the results, I obtained two significant results. First, INAH 3 was on average two- to threefold bigger in the presumed heterosexual men (whether or not they died of AIDS) than in the women. This result confirmed that of Laura Allen and colleagues at UCLA. Second, in the gay men INAH 3 was on average the same size as in the women, and two to three times smaller than in the straight men. It should be emphasized that these differences were in the *averages*: some of the women and gay men had a large INAH 3, and some of the presumed heterosexual men had a small one. None of the other three nuclei showed any differences between groups.

This finding suggests that gay and straight men may differ in the central neuronal mechanisms that regulate sexual behavior. Although the data described only the size of the nuclei, not the numbers of neurons within each nucleus, it is very likely that there are fewer neurons in INAH 3 of gay men (and women) than in straight men. To put an absurdly facile spin on it, gay men simply don't have the brain cells to be attracted to women.

Several important qualifications have to be made. All the gay men in my sample died of AIDS. Was the disease rather than their sexual orientation responsible for the small size of INAH 3? After all, we know that AIDS and its complications can devastate the brain. My reasons for thinking that the disease was not responsible were fivefold. First, the control group of AIDS patients who were heterosexual had a large INAH 3. Second, none of the other three nuclei showed differences between groups as they might well have done if the disease was destroying neurons nonselectively in this region of the brain. Third, there was no correlation between the length of the patients' illness, or the complications that occurred, and the size of INAH 3. Fourth, there were no dying cells, inflammatory reactions, or other signs of a pathological process at work. Lastly, after publication of my study I obtained the brain of one gay man who died of a disease other than AIDS (he died of lung cancer). I examined this brain "blind" along with three other brains from presumably heterosexual men of similar ages. Already during the analysis I correctly guessed which was the hypothalamus of the gay man; INAH 3 was less than half the size of the nucleus in the other three men.

Even if, as I believe, AIDS was not the reason for the difference in the size of INAH 3, the use of brains from AIDS patients does raise other problems. Are gay men who die of AIDS representative of gay men as a whole, or are they atypical, for example in preferring receptive anal intercourse (the major risk factor in homosexual sex) or in having unusually large numbers of sexual partners (another risk factor)? It is difficult to answer these questions decisively. However, HIV infection is now so widespread in the gay community that it is unrealistic to imagine a group to be highly atypical simply because they died of AIDS.

To many people, finding a difference in brain structure between gay and straight men is equivalent to proving that gay men are "born that way." Time and again I have been described as someone who "proved that homosexuality is genetic" or some such thing. I did not. My observations were made only on adults who had been sexually active for a considerable period of time. It is not possible, purely on the basis of my observations, to say whether the structural differences were present at birth, and later influenced the men to become gay or straight, or whether they arose in adult life, perhaps as a result of the men's sexual behavior.

In considering which of these interpretations is more likely, one is thrown back on . . . animal research. . . . [T]he sexually dimorphic nucleus of the medial preoptic area in rats (which may or may not correspond to INAH 3 in humans) is highly susceptible to modification during a critical period that

lasts for a few days before and after the rat's birth. After this time, it is difficult to change the size of the nucleus by any means. Even castrating adult rats
(which removes the rat's source of androgens and greatly impairs the rat's sexual behavior) has at most a very slight effect on the size of the nucleus. If the
same is true for INAH 3 in humans, it would seem likely that the structural differences between gay and straight men come about during the initial period of
sexual differentiation of the hypothalamus. If this is the case, it is possible that
these differences play some role in determining a person's sexual orientation.
However, we cannot exclude the possibility that in humans, with their longer
lifespan and better developed cerebral cortex, gross changes in the size of
INAH 3 might come about as a result of adult behavior.

The ideal experiment would of course be to measure the size of INAH 3
in newborn infants by some scanning technique, to wait twenty years, and then
to inquire about their sexual orientation. If the size of the nucleus at birth were
to any extent predictive of the person's ultimate sexual orientation, one could
argue more strongly that the size of the nucleus might play some kind of
causative role. This experiment is not possible, at the moment at least, as scanning techniques capable of imaging INAH 3 in living people do not yet exist.

In the rat research, the major factor influencing the size of the sexually
dimorphic nucleus has been shown to be the levels of circulating androgens,
which act on the neurons of the nucleus during the critical period to promote
their survival. This suggests two possible developmental mechanisms by
which the different size of INAH 3 in gay and straight men might come about.
One would be that there are differences between "gay" and "straight" fetuses
in the levels of circulating androgens during the critical period for the development of INAH 3. The other would be that the levels of androgens are the
same, but that the cellular mechanisms by which the neurons of INAH 3
respond to the hormones are different. These possibilities will be discussed further below.

More recently, another difference in brain structure between gay and
straight men has been described, this time by Allen and [Roger] Gorski at
UCLA. They found differences in the anterior commissure, which . . . is an
axonal connection between the left and right sides of the cerebral cortex and is
generally larger in women than men. Allen and Gorski's finding (which like my
work was made on autopsied brains, many from AIDS patients) was that the
anterior commissure is on average larger in gay men than in straight men. In
fact they found it to be larger in gay men even than in women, but after correction for overall brain size the size of the structure was about the same in gay
men and in women. (As in my study, Allen and Gorski were unable to determine the sexual orientation of the women from their medical records; presumably the majority of them were heterosexual.)

This finding is interesting for several reasons. First, it strengthens the
notion that the brains of gay and straight men are indeed different. Second, it
may relate to some of the cognitive differences mentioned above: if cerebral

functions are less strongly lateralized in gay men than in straight men, there may be greater need to interconnect the two hemispheres. Finally, the very fact that the anterior commissure is *not* involved in the regulation of sexual behavior makes it highly unlikely that the size differences *result* from differences in sexual behavior. Much more probably, the size differences came about during the original sexual differentiation of the anterior commissure, either under the direct influence of gonadal steroids or as a consequence of developmental events in the cortical regions that it interconnects. Thus, whatever the functional significance of the size of the commissure may be, it may serve as an independent label for processes that went forward differently in "gay" and "straight" fetuses or young children.

Unlike INAH 3, which is far too small to be imaged in a living person's brain by any available scanning technique, the anterior commissure can be seen, although not terribly clearly, in magnetic resonance images (MRI scans). Modest improvements in technique might allow the commissure to be measured accurately in living persons. This would allow the issue of brain structure and sexual orientation to be extended to women, and it would also allow one to obtain a detailed sex history, including details of preferred erotic roles, childhood characteristics, and so on, from the same individuals whose brain structures were measured.

The other major connection between the two cerebral hemispheres, the corpus callosum, is also sexually dimorphic, being relatively larger in women than in men. . . . In a preliminary study in which I and my colleagues at UCSD [University of California at San Diego] have been involved, we failed to find significant differences in the size or shape of the corpus callosum between gay and straight men. This issue needs to be investigated further, but it may well be that the corpus callosum mediates sex-differentiated functions that are not atypical, or not markedly so, in gay men. . . .

. . . [I]t is not unrealistic to expect a gene or genes influencing sexual orientation to be identified within the next few years, since there are at least three laboratories in the United States alone that are working on the topic. If such genes are found, it will be possible to ask where, when, and how these genes exert their effects, and hence to gain a much more basic understanding of the biological mechanisms that make us straight or gay. Of course such work, like all the research currently devoted to the human genome, carries with it the likelihood of major social consequences: the revision of the public's views about the nature of homosexuality, and the development of screening tests that might give an indication of whether a person (or fetus) is more or less likely to be (or become) gay. All science fiction at present, but perhaps not so far off from becoming scientific reality. Certainly it is not too early to begin thinking about what should or should not be done with this kind of information.

If there are genes that influence people to become homosexual, why do such genes exist and why have they been perpetuated? A number of sociobiologists, including G. E. Hutchinson, E. O. Wilson, J. D. Weinrich, and

Michael Ruse, have speculated on this issue, and the following discussion is based on their writings.

On the face of it, evolutionary processes would strongly select against a gene that induced nonprocreative sexual behavior. One possibility is that, during much of human evolution, societal pressures forced men and women to procreate regardless of their sexual orientation. If this was the case, "gay genes" might be maintained because of some other, beneficial traits associated with homosexuality (say increased verbal ability), or because homosexual behavior itself confers some benefit, for example by promoting mutually beneficial cooperation between persons of the same sex.

On the whole, this explanation seems to me unlikely. There is evidence even from preliterate societies that homosexuality is associated with decreased reproduction. Given the intense selection pressures that act on sexual behavior, it is improbable that a lack of sexual attraction to the opposite sex could be sufficiently compensated by purely social forces. . . .

According to . . . [the sociobiological theory of kin selection], gay genes reduce the direct reproductive success of the individual possessing them, but cause that individual to promote the reproductive success of his or her close relatives. As a specific example, let us think of a man who would otherwise have fathered two children, but on account of his gay genes fathered none. If this man promoted the reproductive interests of his siblings to the extent that they successfully reared four more children than they otherwise would have done, his genes have had the same reproductive success as if he had had two children of his own, because his siblings' children are half as closely related to himself as his own children are. If the gay man does have some direct reproductive success (fathering one child, for example) then of course he only has to help his siblings produce two extra children for his gayness to be "worthwhile."

It is not hard to think of ways in which a gay man might help his siblings produce and successfully rear extra children. The main problem is that this theory does not account for homosexuality, it only accounts for the lack of heterosexuality. To put it crudely, why do gay men waste so much time cruising each other, time that according to this theory would be better spent baby-sitting their nephews and nieces?

Another theory is the so-called sickle-cell model for homosexuality. Sickle-cell anemia is a recessive trait: the disease occurs in individuals that are homozygous for the sickle-cell gene, that is, carry copies of it on both homologous chromosomes. Individuals who are heterozygous (i.e., carry just one copy of the gene) do not suffer from the disease, but have slight differences in their red blood cells that confer a resistance to malaria. In areas where malaria is endemic, this advantage to the heterozygous individuals is sufficient to keep the gene in the population. The homozygous condition is just an unwanted byproduct, occurring in some of the offspring of matings between heterozygous individuals. The same could be true of a gay gene: it might be preserved in the population because individuals who are heterozygous for the gene, besides not being gay, have some other advantage that improves their reproductive success. This theory, which brands gay men and lesbian women as the losers in a genetic roulette game, may not appeal to many gay men or lesbian women—it certainly doesn't appeal to me—but it nevertheless has some plausibility.

A final possibility is that gay genes *are* in fact deleterious from the point of view of reproductive success, and do tend to get eliminated from the population, but that for some reason the variant genes are recreated at a high rate, so that the genes that are eliminated are replaced by new ones. To evaluate this possibility would require identifying the genes that are involved.

To sum up . . . I should emphasize first that the factors that determine whether a person becomes heterosexual, bisexual, or homosexual are still largely unknown. Yet there are indications that sexual orientation is strongly influenced by events occurring during the early developmental period when the brain is differentiating sexually under the influence of gonadal steroids. From family and twin studies, it is clear that genes play a major role, but it remains to be seen whether these genes operate by influencing the level of sex steroids before birth, by influencing the way in which the brain responds to these steroids, or by other means. Environmental factors must also play a role: these could include maternal stress or other environmental influences occurring prenatally, parental and sibling interactions during childhood, or social and sexual interactions at adolescence or in adulthood. None of the proposed nongenetic factors are as yet well supported by scientific evidence. Given the evidence that some brain structures differ between gay and straight individuals and that childhood traits are to some extent predictive of a person's sexual orientation in adulthood, it would seem that environmental factors operating very early in life are better candidates than those operating later. Further progress in this field will most likely come from the identification of the genes that influence sexual orientation, and the mechanisms by which these genes exert their effects. Once these mechanisms have been clarified, it will be much easier to study how environmental processes can interact with them to modify the final outcome.

7

Are Homosexuals Born That Way?

Darrell Yates Rist

Was Schubert Gay? If He Was, So What? Debate Turns Testy
—*The New York Times,* February 4[, 1992]

Aside from abortion, few social issues—not the nation's illiteracy or poverty or crumbling health care system—rouse such persistent, angry interest among the American populace as questions of homosexuality. Nor is it only on the vulgar hustings—like the "family values" Republican convention in August [1992]—that the discourse on same-sex love makes people mad. Just this past February, for example, according to a report in *The New York Times,* even so sober an event as the annual weeklong Schubertiade at New York City's 92nd Street Y turned vitriolic when an assertion of the master's same-sex libido and its effect on his music was made. While noted feminist musicologist Susan McClary merely argued for the "possible homosexual character" of the second movement of the "Unfinished Symphony," an even more strident propagandist in the audience declared that "heterosexuals are more repressed than homosexuals." One disgusted participant felt at last compelled to ask whether Schubert's short, fat stature had in any way influenced his music—a response I am enormously in sympathy with.

In their own way, debates like these over the artistic stamp of Schubert's homosexuality disturb me more than all the weird ranting over moral decline from the likes of Pat Robertson, Pat Buchanan, Dan Quayle, and George Bush. These arguments among intellectuals—whether art critics or political philosophers or, say, research scientists—treat homosexuality more polemically than it deserves and, under the guise of being socially progressive, go a

Darrell Yates Rist, "Are Homosexuals Born That Way?" Reprinted with permission from *The Nation* magazine. © 1992 The Nation Company, L.P.

long way in darkening our already benighted, though deeply believed, sexual thinking. In the end, such "liberated" views continue to imprison desire in the dark cells of "gay" and "straight," rather than freeing our hearts and genitals to the fullest expression of human affection, which ought to be the unabashed ideal of any sexual liberation movement.

This Schubert debate, for example, cannot pass merely for an innocent argument to establish a biographical fact—that Schubert was known to favor men in his erotic pursuits. Rather, in the hands of a certain brand of homosexual ideologue, it is intended to feed the ridiculous and dangerous assumption that there is such a thing as a "homosexual character" in art and in life, a particular sensibility welling up from the homosexual soul, embedded in the genes. Behind it is the devout belief that homosexuals are constitutionally different.

This dogma is by no means new. As John Lauritsen and David Thorstad relate in *The Early Homosexual Rights Movement (1864–1935),* when a new penal code criminalizing sex between men (women's sexuality has almost always been treated as trivial) was proposed for Prussia in the 1860s, one Hungarian activist doctor, under the pseudonym K. M. Kertbeny, sent an open letter to the Minister of Justice decrying the German state's barbaric intrusion into all-male bedrooms. Kertbeny justified his position by arguing that homosexuality, a term he devised, is an "inborn, and therefore irrepressible, drive," consequently incapable of seducing the majority of men—those born with "normal sexualism"—because it is naturally alien to them. The pseudonymous Kertbeny's musings were, of course, egregiously political. As Lauritsen and Thorstad epitomize Kertbeny's argument: "If homosexuality is inborn . . . it cannot be regarded as a punishable offense by rational persons who respect the mysterious laws of nature."

In the end, this convenient theory failed to convince enough of Prussia's lawmakers. In 1871, the legal ban on male homosexual acts was accepted by the Reichstag with no debate as the cruel Paragraph 175 of the Second Reich's new penal code—which some sixty years later became the cornerstone of the Nazi crusade to exterminate homosexuals.

Nevertheless, activists persevered, albeit with a more baroque sexual theory than even Kertbeny had proposed. As early as 1862, Karl Heinrich Ulrichs, an acquaintance of Kertbeny's, had begun to call the homosexually inclined, whether male or female, "Uranians," after the muse of same-sex love in Plato's *Symposium.* That idea, which soon gained wide currency in the fight for the right of homosexual expression both on the Continent and in England, "embodied the notion," as Lauritsen and Thorstad explain, "that homosexuals were a 'third sex'—a woman's mind in a man's body, and *vice versa* for women."

Who could be surprised that activists—desperate in every age to achieve their ends through any trick of thinking—would embrace such a cockamamie idea as a hybrid sex with a misplaced brain to justify same-sex longing? What should give pause, though, is that such a quaint concept continues to attract large numbers of believers, even to this day. In nearly two decades of involvement in gay politics, I have known very few gay male activists, and certainly no more than a scattering of gay men-on-the-street, who *don't* subscribe to much the same kind of thinking the German third-sexers employed. Most claim to remember some early sensation—the seductive feel of their father's beard, an interest in dolls or their mother's high heels, an aversion to football or to pulling the wings off butterflies—that they now define as "gay." Never mind that plenty of men exclusively heterosexual in adulthood have felt the same things; it is such sensibilities and behaviors that gave these disciples of homosexualism a sense of "difference" so early in their existence that they feel it *had* to have been from conception. That is the premise, after all, underlying the oft-parroted article of faith among gay partisans (I proclaimed it myself, in my more orthodox days) that, throughout history and across cultures, one in ten men and women has been homosexual—a consistency only the laws of genetics can provide.

To be sure, at some desperate moment in my own "coming out" process, I told my grieving parents that I was "born that way." I think the claim was an olive branch of sorts for my parents, who, like most, wanted to exonerate themselves for creating a home that might be thought by some to have contributed to perversion. But beyond that, I suspect that I, like perhaps most other homosexually desirous men who say they believe in the destiny of biology, was grasping for some explanation—*any* device that carried with it the sound of reason—for contrary sexual desires that I certainly knew I did not *choose* to feel by any commonly understood process of human decision.

The power that can be wielded—if not politically, then personally—by the assertion of genetic determinism was poignantly brought home to me in a recent conversation I had with a young man whom I first met while journeying across the continent some years earlier to discover the lives of America's gay men. After years of enmity, Chris Yates had only recently reconciled with his parents, Pentecostal ministers who had tortured his adolescence with Christian cures for sexual perversity. Shock and aversion therapies under born-again doctors and gruesome exorcisms of sexual demons by spirit-filled preachers had culminated in a plan to have him castrated by a Mexican surgeon who touted the procedure as a way to make the boy, if not straight, at least sexless. Only then had the terrified son rebelled. Nothing more could be said between him and his parents. To his folks' mind, Chris's deviancy was willful and wicked.

Then, in the summer of 1991, the journal *Science* reported anatomical differences between the brains of homosexual and heterosexual men (again, forget women). The euphoric media—those great purveyors of cultural myths—drove the story wildly. Every major paper in the country headlined the discovery smack on the front page, along with more eminent news like the breakup of the Soviet Union. Reporters seized triumphantly on the renewed presumption that we humans are not responsible for our sexual choices any more than for whatever else we choose to do, that we are chromosomally driven to everything. But what was by far most ecstatically reassuring—at least to many—was that what had sometimes seemed a fuzzy line between gay and straight was now certified as biologically inviolable. America's men—both gay and straight—need no longer worry.

Nor America's parents: Like many others, I suspect, Chris Yates's family saw in this newly reported sexual science a way out of its wrenching impasse. After years of virtual silence between them and their son, Chris's parents drove several hundred miles to visit him and ask for reconciliation. Whatever faded guilt they might have felt for the family's faulty genes was nothing next to the reassurance that neither by a perverse upbringing nor by his own iniquity was Chris or the family culpable for his urges and actions. "We could never have condoned this," they told him, "if you could do something to change it. But when we finally understood that you were *born* that way, we knew we'd been wrong. We had to ask your forgiveness."

The beauty of a family's reconciliation with a prodigal son is nothing to be scoffed at. But something is *still* wrong here. Had the report indicated that the condition could be reversed through genetic engineering, would they then have tried to force him into the lab of a Dr. Frankenstein? Or worse, what if the study had found that, by some subtle pattern of erotic choices from childhood on, men like Chris defiantly nurture a kind of desire, possible in every man, that might otherwise lie dormant—what then? Would his family have continued to despise his sexuality and seek to have him turned into a eunuch?

I find such contingencies all the more disturbing, given that the substance of the *Science* report was in fact quite meager. Simon LeVay, a neuroanatomist at the Salk Institute, sliced open the brains of forty-one corpses and determined that among the male subjects thought to be heterosexual the size of the hypothalamus, a microscopic part of the brain associated with sexual behavior, was two times larger than in the corpses of assumed homosexual men or of women of undetermined sexual attractions. What could be more straightforward? Gay men were hermaphrodites of sorts, sporting feminine brains in masculine bodies—that old German idea of homosexual men, *Warmbrüder,* as the third sex. There was, of course, a degree of skepticism within the scientific community about LeVay's research, some of which he referred to in the article, if only to preempt it. It now seems well established, for example, that the brain is a plastic thing, its structure and chemistry metamorphosing in accordance with external stimuli. So certain sexual habits alone—say, consistent passivity in intercourse or a preference for mutual masturbation rather than intercourse—might in the end account for a shrinkage in the hypothalami of LeVay's tiny homosexual sampling.

Then there are the glaring exceptions in LeVay's findings—presumed heterosexual men with small hypothalami, presumed homosexual men with big ones—that the scientist is wont to dismiss. While conceding that these might cast some doubt on strict genetic theories of homosexuality, he seems to suggest that the contradictions are due to possible "technical shortcomings or to misassignment of subjects to their subject groups."

It's this second possibility that is by far the more distressing, though the researcher himself seems not at all to see it that way. What criteria, other than self-identification, could LeVay possibly have relied on to categorize his cadavers? How did he account for the frequent dissonance between sexual self-definitions and what men actually want and do? In the best of circumstances, how would he measure degrees of desire and draw the inexorable line between gay and straight? Does he actually believe that most American men (including his study's presumed heterosexuals) will confess to homoerotic urges? Or that self-defined gay men, by nature, experience no heterosexual longing? All these men, alas, were *dead* by the time he met them!

Despite these questions, scientists such as LeVay remain addicted to the idea of finding the virtual "cause" of homosexuality, forever distinguishing same-sex love from the love of "normal" men. This past summer *The Proceedings of the National Academy of Sciences* reported a new idiosyncrasy in the brains of men categorized as homosexual. This time the anterior commissure, a cord of nerve fibers believed to allow the two halves of the brain to integrate sensory information, was reported to be larger in the cadavers of homosexually identified men than in the corpses of either presumed heterosexual men or of women whose sexual self-identification was unknown. A devastating weakness in this study—which at least does not exist in LeVay's—is the nearly universal presumption among neuroanatomists that the anterior commissure has no direct influence on sexual behavior. In addition, all the problems that plague LeVay's research in regard to sexual identities persist. Likewise, there were inconsistencies in the size of the brain structure being measured within the study's separate categories. The scientists' findings were based on distinctions in the *average* dimensions of the commissures within the sample groups, and wild variations existed within each group. (The largest of the dead women's commissures was three times the size of the smallest, while the "homosexual" men's were only 34 percent larger, on average, than the "straight" men's.)

There were also the nagging criticisms of experts in neuroanatomy and psychiatry. Like LeVay, the researchers relied on the remains of "homosexual" men who died of HIV disease, which is known to attack brain cells. "I don't think that we can rule out that this is having an effect," Robert Cabaj, a University of California psychiatrist, told *The New York Times*. More astutely, though, Dr. William Byne, of the Columbia University College of Physicians and Surgeons, assessed: "There's really a trend in this area for each paper to be just another statistical fluke. I just don't think sexual orientation is going to be represented in any particular brain structure. It's like looking in the brain for your political party affiliation."

LeVay, of course, had nothing but praise for the work. With tendentious humility, he told the *Times,* "It's such a clear result, and in a sense it's more important than my own finding." And his enthusiasm was matched in the gay political world by that of Robert Bray, head of public information for the

National Gay and Lesbian Task Force, who effused, "It points out that gay people are made this way by nature. It strikes at the heart of people who oppose gay rights and who think we don't deserve our rights because we're choosing to be the way we are."

Of course, nothing will daunt the true believer. But what belies the fantasies of such activists—and LeVay's and all similar scientific prying into the homing instincts of our genitalia—is sex itself. A little sharp-eyed observation of actual human eroticism—and some academic reading—reveals the fatal flaw in such theoretical ejaculations. For however much our own psychiatrically intimidated culture has deluded us about the nature of our sexuality, there are, and have been historically, countless societies in which the rigid categories of gay and straight do not hold.

In a telephone interview last fall, in fact, I asked LeVay about the ubiquitous homosexuality of some tribal peoples that was uncovered in the fieldwork of pioneering anthropologists like Margaret Mead and Tobias Schneebaum—and Walter Williams, whose *The Spirit and the Flesh* examined the same-sex erotic tradition of berdaches and warriors in Native American cultures. "I'm not tremendously familiar with that list," LeVay reported. Similarly, he did not know Yale historian John Boswell's myth-shattering tome *Christianity, Social Tolerance, and Homosexuality*. But he nonetheless dismissed Boswell's descriptions, as I repeated them to him, of nearly universal male-to-male love-making among the citizen classes in some periods of ancient Greece and Rome. Were LeVay properly to acquaint himself with such scholarship, he'd presumably also have to argue that all the great men of classical antiquity had undersized hypothalami.

But ancients and tribes aside, there is reasonable evidence that even in sex-frightened America most men, though perhaps in spite of themselves, engage in same-sex lust at some point in their lives, whatever the birth weight of their hypothalami. As long ago as 1948, when Alfred Kinsey published his *Sexual Behavior of the Human Male,* as many as 50 percent of American men were found to have indulged in some "overt or psychic" homoeroticism during their mature lifetime, and a full 30 percent confessed "at least incidental homosexual experience or reactions" between the ages of sixteen and fifty-five. Given the power of repression to control our behavior and our minds, those percentages are probably egregiously low. It's not farfetched to assume that in the darkness of the 1940s many fewer men would have admitted to such reactions than actually experienced them—even had they recognized their interest in other men for what it really was and ever acted upon it. In reality, men exclusively "straight" throughout their lives, both in thought and deed, are probably as rare as those Kinsey found to be exclusively "gay"—about 4 percent. Both categories probably amount to sexual perversities, if not merely rarities of the natural world, and ought to be the subject of intense psychological study and possibly treatment.

Human beings, of course, often believe what isn't true. But the irony of attempts at airtight groupings into gay and straight is that it is homophobes who are less likely to make them, for intrinsic to diatribes against homosexuality—by everyone from Dan Quayle and Pat Buchanan to panic-stricken Mel Gibson—is the repugnant knowledge that the taste for same-sex copulation is corrupting, that it can be spread. Nor is their antagonism essentially a fear of the alien—that of blacks or Jews invading white Christian neighborhoods, for example—but rather a terrified recognition that the subversive kernel of same-sex love, like murder and mayhem and every other sin, lies waiting to bloom in all of us under proper watering.

A woman I met on a journey to the outback of Alaska put it more benignly. Having been in a longtime same-sex relationship when we were introduced, she insisted that throughout her adolescence and early adulthood she had never had the slightest attraction to anyone but men—not even, she said, an infrequent libidinous dream full of secret, vulval icons—until she met an interested woman in a nurturing environment that suspended moral judgments about homosexual love. She had not been tortured by desire; she was not "closeted." "It just wasn't something that ever occurred to me," she explained. "It didn't *exist*! Girls liked boys. That was it. You only want what you know can maybe happen. I didn't know anything else."

Her statement was not atypical of the woman-loving women I've known, whose sexual identities and behaviors are in general far more fluid than those of my gay-identified male friends. This seems more true of women's perspective in general, in fact. Women, after all, are granted far greater latitude in showing affection among themselves than is socially permissible among men. The line dividing "lesbians" from "straight" women is vaguer, and transgressing it is less catastrophic. As Roseanne Arnold recently told the gay weekly *QW,* "I think we probably all are [attracted to other women] somewhere in there. I think part of all women is lesbian, definitely. Also I think there's a political aspect to it."

To be sure, there is—and one far subtler in its psychological shading than the viscerally simplistic sin- and machismo-based construction of sexual choice espoused by homophobes. Still, both this feminine perspective and that of the crazies emphasize the affectional possibilities that offer themselves in differing degrees to all of us. And it is curious, indeed, that it should ever be gay activists and their sympathizers in medical research, psychiatry, and progressive politics who argue otherwise. For theirs is a constituency whose ostensibly tolerant agenda presumably stands most to gain from the acknowledgment of a universal polymorphous perversity. Nonetheless, it is most often they—those who pretend to promote tolerance—who piously propagate the gene-based theory of "one-in-ten." It is they who most often draw the inexorable line and create unbreachable categories of gay and straight.

Part of the ploy is no doubt pragmatic—the political expectation that courts and legislatures will react as Chris Yates's parents did. As LeVay, who is himself gay, told me, "If it's shown that that's the way we're born, it would undercut the idea that we're just misbehaving. I'm shocked to find how many people believe it's a matter of choice."

But his, like all such research, is a futile attempt to convince people who intuitively know better that under no circumstances can their children be lured by queer ideas if the urge is not embedded in their brains from birth; nor will husbands be seduced from their wives. I have found that even many of my most unbiased straight friends grow skittish with my homosexual candor—say, kissing my mate—when their children are around. For underneath it all, they too understand that sexually free ideas are infectious and that, once introduced to the suggestion of same-sex love, their kids might just try it and like it. The model of my open sexuality offers to their children that sense of possibility that my Alaskan acquaintance had only discovered relatively late in life.

And yet, in spite of all their intuitions, they are as likely as their homosexually identified friends to parrot the gene theory. Part of their conflicted thinking no doubt derives from a genuine desire to protect their sexually defiant friends politically and socially, in the most expedient way possible. But it also occurs to me that, having embraced, in theory at least, a greater range of acceptable eroticism, these allies of same-sexers do not merely risk the imputation of homosexuality by association, but they are perhaps in more imminent danger of falling into the abyss themselves, of becoming one of the constitutionally alien creatures they consider same-sex practitioners to be. Their dilemma is circular, a double bind. They are left looking for a preponderance of proof—an early enthusiasm for baseball, a penchant for maiming butterflies—that, regardless of an occasional, discomfiting same-sex urge, they were not born like gays. Their shallow belief in the blood-borne theory is their protection.

In the end, science may well discover some way to describe intricate play of genes and environment that entices any of us to make the subtle choices throughout our lives that lead us to our particular expressions, sexual or otherwise, in a conformity-laden culture. Fine. Ultimately, though, it seems to me cowardly to abnegate our individual responsibility for the construction of sexual desires. Rather, refusing the expedient lie and insisting instead on the right to fulfill ourselves affectionally—in whatever direction our needs compel us, however contrary to the social norm they may be—is both honest and courageous, an act of utter freedom.

Nor is the issue simply one of psychic or behavioral constraint, though that would be enough for those of us who loathe such enforced, artificial limits on human possibilities. In a day when physical brutality against the homosexually identified is epidemic, many gay activists vacuously continue to rely on sensitizing heterosexuals to the "native" differences of gays and on encouraging them to accept the "gay community" as a constitutional minority, innocuously akin to Jews and blacks. But the ruse won't fly. As long as we are inculcated with the terror of our own secret desires, we will try to beat them out of others when we cannot kill them in ourselves. Until men and women can at last learn to respect the fullness of their sexuality, whether they choose to act on it or not, the violence will only increase against our lives—and against our social and spiritual liberties.

The photographer Nan Goldin recently published in *Mother Jones* a body of work that both investigates the construction of personal identity and simultaneously undermines it; that focuses on the radically transformative power of our affections, portraying them as a vehicle for personal renewal and change. In comments about her own perspective, she told reviewer Carole Naggar, "My dream was that you slept with people you liked and would not know about their sex until you undressed them." In a democratic society, the fact that our affectional urges are diverse and that we choose to fulfill them comfortably—all of us to our own degree—ought to be sufficient. So far in repressed America, both "gays" and "straights" have yet to reach such human understandings.

8

The "Born That Way" Trap

Lindsy Van Gelder

When the Episcopal Diocese of Newark recently established a ministry to welcome gay people into the church, the bishop told the *New York Times*: "We are not ready to accept the prejudice and ignorance that homosexuality is a matter of choice or reflects moral depravity." And when *Child* magazine published a sympathetic article on how straight parents can learn to be supportive of their gay children, the lead quoted a gay man who recognized his sexual orientation when he was barely out of kindergarten. "Many people believe that a person chooses to be a homosexual, which is ludicrous," he explained to anxious parents.

I hear the same sentiment in liberal circles everywhere. Even Dear Ann and Dear Abby agree: being gay is something a person has no more control over than race or gender. Therefore, it's unfair to deprive us of our rights.

The people who say these things are all on my side. But they make me very, very nervous.

For starters, I personally don't think I was "born this way." (In fact, when I'm feeling hostile, I've been known to tell right-wingers that I'm a successfully "cured" hetero.) Until I was in my early thirties, I fell in love with men, took pleasure in sleeping with them, and even married one. But like most women, I experienced most of my closest emotional relationships with female friends. The only thing that made me different was that at some point I got curious about lesbian feminist claims that it was possible to combine that intense female intimacy with good sex. The good sex part turned out to be vastly easier than I anticipated. Even so, there was no immediate *biological* reason to stop having sex with men or to start living as a lesbian. Coming out was, for me, a conscious decision—every step of the way.

From *Ms.* magazine 1, no. 6 (May/June 1991). Copyright © by Lindsy Van Gelder. Reprinted by permission of the author.

Nor am I an aberration, at least among women. Virtually every self-identified gay man I've ever met has been convinced that his sexuality is a biological given, but lesbians are a mixed bag. My own wildly unscientific estimate is that it's a pretty even split between the born lesbians and the born agains. We talk about these differences within the lesbian community (and we bitch about the other side of the born-again syndrome—women who choose to stop being lesbians and go off with men). But out in the Big World, it's invisibility as usual. The gay party line reflects the universal male experience in this culture, not the complexities of the lesbian world.

Sexism? Probably. But the truth is that the "Born That Way" line has the public relations edge. At the root of a lot of homophobia is a fear that gayness is somehow contagious. If people really did fit into neat little either/or sexual pigeonholes from birth, no one would be able to say that gay teachers could possibly "recruit" their students. Parents of gays would be off the blame hook. Straights wouldn't have to feel threatened by passing queer attractions.

It seems like a quick-win strategy. But I suspect that it's shortsighted—and I'd say so even if it *didn't* ignore the experience of so many lesbians.

Remember when we got sucked into arguing not just about a woman's right to control her own body, but about whether the fetus was in fact a human being? We're making the same mistake here: letting the other side set the terms of this debate. The fundamentalists believe that being gay is definitely a matter of choice—specifically a matter of choosing to sin. . . . [W]e've essentially thrown up our hands and said, "But we can't *help* being this way."

Inherent in that response is the implication that if we *could* help it, we would. Even when that isn't what we mean, it's what a fair number of straight people hear, including some of our allies. It's easier for some of them to pity us as bearers of a genetic flaw than to respect us as sexual equals. Not challenging them might gain us some votes, but in the long run it means that we're subtly putting the word out that it's O.K. to regard us as sexually defective.

We're also staking our lives on scientific research that at the moment Is a crapshoot. I recently saw a debate on a computer bulletin board about whether gay men should be allowed to serve as Boy Scout leaders. The homophobes trotted out the usual . . . [argument] about child abuse; the liberals argued back that gay people are born, not made; the homophobes countered with testimonials from various ministries claiming to "cure homosexuality"; the liberals answered that most of these supposed rehabilitations don't last. But what if scientists *do* find a biological "cure" someday? How many of us would really want to swallow that vaccine? What if they could identify a gay fetus through amniocentesis? Amusing as it is to contemplate *our* side waving giant photos of tiny (limp?) fetal wrists outside fundamentalist clinics, it really isn't that funny—or that farfetched.

Or what if they discover that there's *no* biological basis to sexual orientation? Are we willing to promise that on that day, we'll give back any gay rights we've managed to win and march off to the psychic showers?

I'd rather see us acquire some new political underpinnings. As inspiring as the civil rights and feminist struggles have been to most of us, I think we have to stop trying to fit gay rights onto the same grid. Every time we talk about race, gender, and sexual orientation in the same breath, we merely invite more tedious debate on whether gays are a "real" minority group or just people with an elective "lifestyle."

Instead, I'd like us to start referring en masse to another bedrock American liberty: the right to worship in the faith of one's choice. Through much of history, people have been forced to change their religions or to practice them underground. The United States was founded upon a rejection of such "solutions," and they're recognized as oppressive worldwide. The principle here is *freedom of expression*. It doesn't matter if you're a Jew or Quaker because your parents were, or if you converted as an adult. You're still protected.

Most of all, I want us to get off the defensive. . . . The we-can't-help-it argument is a cop-out. It pretends that sex is something that white rats in a maze do because their hormones tell them to—not something humans do for fun. If there's anything we as feminists ought to be supporting, it's a frank, unapologetic celebration of sexual *choice*.

I'm personally for the right of happy heterosexuals to "experiment" with same-sex love and perhaps find that they like it. I'm for the right of bisexuals to opt for gay relationships, even though they don't have the excuse that they have no other choice. And I'm for the right of gay people to choose to act on their sexuality, whether society approves of it or not.

9

Are Some People Born Gay?

Michael Bailey and Richard Pillard

Science is rapidly converging on the conclusion that sexual orientation is innate. It has found that homosexuals often act differently from heterosexuals in early childhood, before they have even heard of sex. A recent study by Simon LeVay, a neurobiologist at the Salk Institute, reported a difference in the hypothalamus, a part of the brain that develops at a young age, between homosexual and heterosexual men.

If true, a biological explanation is good news for homosexuals and their advocates.

Our own research has shown that male sexual orientation is substantially genetic. Over the last two years, we have studied the rates of homosexuality in identical and nonidentical twin brothers of gay men, as well as adoptive brothers of gay men. Fifty-two percent of the identical twin brothers were gay, as against 22 percent of nonidentical twins and 11 percent of the adoptive, genetically unrelated brothers.

In contrast, research on social factors has been fruitless. Despite many attempts, there has been no clear demonstration that parental behavior, even a parent's homosexuality, affects children's sexual orientation. Cultures tolerant of homosexuals do not appear to raise more of them than do less permissive societies.

Homophobes sometimes justify their prejudice against homosexuals by alleging that homosexuality is contagious—that young homosexuals become that way because of older homosexuals and that homosexuality is a social corruption. Such beliefs form the core of the organized anti-homosexual movement. If homosexuality is largely innate, this would prove that these claims are groundless.

Given these implications, it may seem surprising that the biological studies disturb many gay and lesbian advocates. Misunderstanding them, the advocates often suggest that the search for a biological cause is motivated by an assumption that homosexuality is an illness. Behavioral scientists, however, have long searched for biological underpinnings of traits such as extroversion and intelligence, which no one considers negative. Furthermore, a biological explanation of homosexuality simultaneously explains heterosexuality.

The advocates worry that biological findings may be misused to try to alter or prevent homosexuality. But no scientific theory or finding by itself can lead to a proper attitude or policy toward homosexuality. Here, moral values must be primary.

This leads to a more pertinent fear of gays and lesbians, that people will assume that answers to moral questions hinge on the results of scientific study. Should a benevolent view of homosexuality depend on the assumption that it is innate? Are gays and lesbians to be tolerated only if they are "born that way"?

Regardless of what causes sexual orientation, there is no plausible justification for oppressing homosexuals. Reasons that have long been offered—that homosexuals disproportionately molest children, convert heterosexuals to homosexuality, are mentally ill, betray their country—have been shown to be false.

But homophobia remains the one form of bigotry that respectable people can express in public. If the long-overdue national debate on homosexuality took place, the poverty of the anti-homosexual case would become readily apparent.

If scientific study of the origins of sexual orientation would not directly resolve the public issue, why do it?

First, it can inform public debate. But, equally important, is the value of discovery, particularly self-discovery. A gay man with a heterosexual identical twin, both of whom we studied, put it this way: "I accepted being gay years ago, so that's not why I want to know. But sexual orientation is such an important part of my life—anyone's life—that I'm still curious why I turned out gay and my brother straight." How could anyone not be curious?

10

What Is Normal?

Steven Goldberg

In recent weeks the media have given wide exposure to the work of Michael Bailey and Richard Pillard. This coverage was justified. Bailey and Pillard provide powerful evidence for an hereditary component to homosexuality. While such a component has long been suspected, this work is the strongest argument for its existence.

However, the reports have almost universally misunderstood the meaning of Bailey and Pillard's conclusions as they relate to the question of psychological normality or abnormality. The reports have interpreted the conclusions as effectively demonstrating the normality of homosexual behavior. This is incorrect.

In essence, Bailey and Pillard conclude that, to the extent that homosexuality is innate, it should be considered a psychologically normal variation. This is certainly reasonable; it would be an exercise in pointless cruelty to assess as "abnormal" a behavior that, unlike hereditary blindness or an uncontrollable impulse to violence, is not inherently damaging to oneself, others, or society.

However, there is a crucial distinction that Bailey and Pillard did not make, a distinction between a predispositional and a *determinative* physiological factor. The latter would be a factor that generated basic sexual orientation *regardless of the environment in which the individual grew.*

Such a factor *would* render indefensible and cruel any assessment of homosexuality as psychologically abnormal. It would do so in the same way that such a factor renders discrimination on the basis of basic skin color indefensible and cruel. This is an analogy often used by spokesmen for the homosexual community; but the spokesmen invariably *assert* that which must be demonstrated—that homosexuality is, like basic skin color, the result of a physiologically *determinative* factor. Bailey and Pillard's own evidence argues against there being such a factor that causes much homosexuality.

Bailey and Pillard report that in half the cases of male identical twins of whom one is homosexual, the other is homosexual as well, while in only a fifth of the cases of male *non*identical twins of whom one is homosexual is the other homosexual. (A tenth of the male population—and of pairs of male identical twins—is homosexual.) This certainly does indicate the importance of heredity, but it just as strongly indicates the importance of environment: in half the cases of male identical twins of whom one was homosexual, the other was *not*; since identical twins have identical genetic makeup, this homosexuality *must* be the result of environmental factors. (Whether this environmental element is a fetal accident, a family of the sort described by the Freudians, or something different is beside the point.) It is only when *both* twins are homosexual that it *could* be the case that the homosexuality is caused by an hereditary *determinative* factor (i.e., a factor that is sufficient to cause homosexuality no matter what the environment).

Now, the fact that (*a*) when one identical twin is homosexual, the other is homosexual in 50 percent of the cases, but (*b*) when one nonidentical twin is homosexual the other is homosexual in only 20 percent of the cases, strongly suggests a physiological element—perhaps a physiological necessary condition. But this does *not* imply (and Bailey and Pillard do not claim that it implies) that it is ever the case that heredity alone is capable of generating homosexuality whatever the environment. The reason is that identical twins share a much more nearly identical familial environment than do nonidentical twins; nonidentical twin brothers are virtually as different physically and mentally as are nontwin brothers, and, as a result, their interactions with their parents are as different as are those of nontwin brothers. Thus, the 50 versus 20 percent could well be, at least in part, a function of the difference in familial environment of identical and nonidentical twins.

Indeed, one could argue, though I would not, that this leaves open the possibility that heredity plays *no* role. This view would argue that environment *alone* accounts for the homosexuality of the twin with the nonhomosexual identical twin brother and also the homosexuality of the twins who are both homosexual (and who shared an environment as nearly identical as was their shared heredity). Finally, this view would account for the 50–20 differential entirely in terms of the fact that identical twins have far more similar environments than do nonidentical twins.

Having raised this possibility, I would quickly add that I do so for logic's sake and that I find it much more plausible that the differential is usually owing to one nonidentical twin's meeting the physiological necessary condition and the other's failing to have this physiological factor.

The important point here is that Bailey and Pillard's work—which is of the utmost importance in its suggestion that there is an hereditary psychological *facilitator* for homosexuality—does not demonstrate, and the authors do not claim that it demonstrates, that homosexuality is ever caused by heredity *alone*. Their work does strongly indicate, however, that heredity does play a role and that the stronger the hereditary factor, the less "environmental push" is required.

Much of the complexity we have discussed falls away if we think of the hereditary element as quantitative, not qualitative—as rendering homosexuality more or less likely in a given environment. This is what Bailey and Pillard do, and it is only for questions of assessing normality that the issue of an hereditary *determinative* factor becomes important. The work of Bailey and Pillard tells us that heredity is very important and that some males are likely to become homosexual with only a slight "environmental push," while others are not likely to become homosexual even in a strongly "homosexuality-producing environment" (whatever that should turn out to be). It may or may not be the case that some individuals will not become homosexual *no matter what* their environments. The work of Bailey and Pillard does not tell us this.

Incidentally, there is a question whose answer is not clear: Why are 20 percent of the nonidentical twins of homosexuals homosexual when only 10 percent of the general population is homosexual? Is it that their parents presented a "more than average homosexuality-producing environment," one that is facilitated by the hereditary tendency of the other twin? Is the 20 percent simply a coincidence that would not occur if larger numbers of subjects had been used? Since only the expected percentage of adopted brothers in these families were homosexual, the 20 percent figure would not seem to be a statistical artifact or one of those surprising, but expected, results inherent in the notoriously tricky world of probability.

THE QUESTION OF NORMALITY

Thus, the work of Bailey and Pillard does not alter the logic by which homosexuality would be judged to be psychologically normal or abnormal; the assessment must be based on the normality or abnormality of the environmental factors in the causation of the individual's homosexuality.

The Freudian explanation—which stresses the mother's (perhaps justified) contempt for an overly passive or overly aggressive father and the son's resulting refusal to accept the male role—is now often simply asserted away, not because it has been refuted, but for psychological and ideological reasons. What Bailey and Pillard do indicate is that the factors stressed by the Freudian are not often *sufficient* to cause homosexuality. Male A, low in the physiological predisposing factor, is highly unlikely to become a homosexual even if his parents are a Freudian nightmare. Male B, having a strong hereditary predisposition, will need only the slightest familial push to become a homosexual. Thus, the homosexuality of the son is not a clear measure of the environmental contribution of the parents, a fact that should reduce the guilt of even those parents who accept the questionable assumption that parental guilt is justified when there is a parental environmental contribution.

This does not, however, cast doubt on the Freudian explanation. The Freudians do not claim that those who encounter the Freudian environment will usually become homosexual, but rather that those who become homosexual will usually be found to have encountered the Freudian familial environment. (One who says that most nuclear physicists went to college is not saying that most people who went to college became nuclear physicists.) The Freudian is analogous to the allergist who determines that a patient's symptoms are the result of a bee sting; the allergist is not denying that most people—not being allergic to bees—will not suffer these symptoms; he is merely saying that those who suffer these symptoms would not have been likely to suffer them had they not been stung by bees.

WEIGHING THE FACTORS

To oversimplify slightly (by treating the physiological factor as a necessary condition rather than as a facilitator): Homosexuality can be conceived as a series of "go"/"no go" steps, with a "go" required at every step if homosexuality is to develop. A person who lacks the physiological necessary condition (if there is such a condition), will not become a homosexual no matter what his subsequent environment. Another person, who meets the physiological necessary condition, will not become a homosexual if he encounters one series of environments, but will if he encounters another. This is now the implicit view of virtually all researchers who offer causal explanations of homosexuality.

There are many attempts to describe the environmental component. Alone among these, the Freudian view is complete in that—assuming we take the parents as givens—it does not raise further questions. Explanations stressing a childhood aversion to rough-and-tumble play, first childhood or adolescent sexual experience, being "labeled" a homosexual, and the like—while possibly identifying contributory factors—fail to explain why there is the aversion to rough-and-tumble play, why the first experiences are disproportionately often *homo*sexual, or why the individual exhibits the behavior that makes labeling possible.

Completeness is, of course, worthless if a theory is incorrect. But virtually all alleged refutations of the Freudian explanation are based on studies using a less discriminating methodology than that supporting the Freudian. (It is worth noting that the studies I refer to as supporting the Freudian view are not therapeutic studies or others about which the non-Freudian is justifiably dubious; they are more discriminating studies of the type used by those who incorrectly claim to refute them.) A non-null finding is *not* refuted by a null finding of a study using a less discriminating methodology; the usually correct explanation for the disagreement is that the former study used a methodology capable of discriminating what it was looking for and the latter did not. E.g., if you measure men and women with a ruler capable of measuring to the nearest inch and I do the same with a ruler capable of measuring only to the nearest yard, you will correctly conclude that men are taller, while I will not.

There is one environmental factor that, as homosexual spokesmen have demonstrated beyond a shadow of a doubt, cannot explain an American's homosexuality: positive societal sanction. That is, even if it were true (which it is not) that some societies positively sanctioned general adult male homosexuality, this would not explain an American's homosexuality. There is nothing inherently abnormal about preferring peanuts to popcorn; but, if a society ostracized peanut eaters and rewarded popcorn eaters, one would ask what caused the peanut eater to risk ostracism.

Now: questions of psychological normality are always in part nonscientific. They are scientific questions in that their answers depend on an understanding of causes and functions of the behavior if an assessment of its normality is to be made. They are nonscientific questions in that such an assessment is being made.

Thus, one can invoke the nonscientific aspect to reject the very act of making an assessment of normality. But this encounters two fatal problems.

1. Such a denial forces one to deny *all* assessments of normality, not merely of homosexuality, but also of coprophilia, necrophilia, and a host of other behaviors not clearly harmful to oneself, others, or society. Obviously, this is not what the homosexual spokesman wants. He does not want an absurd, if logically defensible, denial of the validity of the very concept of normality, but an acknowledgment that homosexuality is normal, while the other behaviors are not. To do this, he must reject the opportunity to deny the validity of all assessments of normality and he must be able to demonstrate that the Freudian is incorrect in his explanation of homosexuality.

2. More important to the happiness of the homosexual is an answer to this question: Is the greater frequency in homosexuals of depression, general unhappiness, and other undeniably undesirable tendencies a function only of social ostracism or also, perhaps primarily, of factors inherent in the development of homosexuality? At one time, homosexual spokesmen denied that there was any difference between homosexuals and heterosexuals other than in choice of sexual partner. This argument was surrendered even before the evidence required because it ignored the fact that it is only the negative *effects* of social sanctions that would lead anyone to be bothered by such sanctions.

One major study attempted to answer the question by studying societies with varying attitudes toward homosexuality. It found that the degree of tolerance was unrelated to the rates of depression, unhappiness, and the like. Astonishingly, the authors of this study concluded that this demonstrates that tolerance is not enough; equal acceptance is required if the rates of pathology are to decline. This is logically possible, but as improbable as a logical conclusion can be. What this evidence far more plausibly seems to imply is that social ostracism has little to do with the correlated behavior (which is a function of the same processes—whatever they are—that generate the homosexuality). And if this is the case, discovery of the environmental causal mechanism might well render possible the alleviation of the pathological companions of the homosexuality.

Assuming that knowledge of a determinative *physiological* causal factor would also permit alleviation of the pathological companions of the homosexuality, I too wish that there were a physiologically *determinative* factor, one that would refute the Freudian explanation and all explanations in which environment plays a role. Such a finding would demolish all attempts to term homosexuality "abnormal." But wishing does not make it so, and evidence like that provided by Bailey and Pillard indicates that such a physiologically determinative factor will not be found.

11

The Hamer Study

William A. Henry III

What makes people gay? To conservative moralists, homosexuality is a sin, a willful choice of godless evil. To many orthodox behaviorists, homosexuality is a result of a misguided upbringing, a detour from a straight path to marital adulthood; indeed, until 1974 the American Psychiatric Association listed it as a mental disorder. To gays themselves, homosexuality is neither a choice nor a disease but an identity, deeply felt for as far back as their memory can reach. To them, it is not just behavior, not merely what they do in lovemaking, but who they are as people, pervading every moment of their perception, every aspect of their character.

The origins of homosexuality may never be fully understood, and the phenomenon is so complex and varied—as is every other kind of love—that no single neat explanation is likely to suffice to explain any one man or woman, let alone multitudes. But the search for understanding advanced considerably . . . with the release of new studies that make the most compelling case yet that homosexual orientation is at least partly genetic.

A team at the National Cancer Institute's [NCI] Laboratory of Biochemistry reported in the journal *Science* that families of seventy-six gay men included a much higher proportion of homosexual male relatives than found in the general population. Intriguingly, almost all the disproportion was on the mother's side of the family. That prompted the researchers to look at the chromosomes that determine gender, known as X and Y. Men get an X from their mother and a Y from their father; women get two X's, one from each parent. Inasmuch as the family trees suggested that male homosexuality may be inherited from mothers, the scientists zeroed in on the X chromosome.

Sure enough, a separate study of the DNA from forty pairs of homosexual brothers found that thirty-three pairs shared five different patches of genetic material grouped around a particular area on the X chromosome. Why is that unusual? Because the genes on a son's X chromosome are a highly variable combination of the genes on the mother's two X's, and thus the sequence of genes varies greatly from one brother to another. Statistically, so much overlap between brothers who also share a sexual orientation is unlikely to be just coincidence. The fact that thirty-three out of forty pairs of gay brothers were found to share the same sequences of DNA in a particular part of the chromosome suggests that at least one gene related to homosexuality is located in that region. Homosexuality was the only trait that all thirty-three pairs shared; the brothers didn't all share the same eye color or shoe size or any other obvious characteristic. Nor, according to the study's principal author, Dean Hamer, were they all identifiably effeminate or, for that matter, all macho. They were diverse except for sexual orientation. Says Hamer: "This is by far the strongest evidence to date that there is a genetic component to sexual orientation. We've identified a portion of the genome associated with it."

The link to mothers may help explain a conundrum: If homosexuality is hereditary, why doesn't the trait gradually disappear, as gays and lesbians are probably less likely than others to have children? The answer suggested by the new research is that genes for male homosexuality can be carried and passed to children by heterosexual women, and those genes do not cause the women to be homosexual. A similar study of lesbians by Hamer's team is taking longer to complete because the existence and chromosomal location of responsible genes is not as obvious as it is in men. But preliminary results from the lesbian study do suggest that female sexual orientation is genetically influenced.

In a related, unpublished study, Hamer added to growing evidence that male homosexuality may be rarer than was long thought—about 2 percent of the population, versus the 4 percent to 10 percent found by Kinsey and others. Hamer notes, however, that he defined homosexuality very narrowly. "People had to be exclusively or predominantly gay, and had to be out to family members and an outside investigator like me. If we had used a less stringent definition, we would probably have found more gay men."

Before the NCI research is accepted as definitive, it will have to be validated by repetition. Moreover, the tight focus on pairs of openly homosexual brothers, who are only a subset of the total gay population, leaves many questions about other categories of gay men, lesbians, and bisexuals. The NCI researchers concede that their discovery cannot account for all male homosexuality and may be just associated with gayness rather than be a direct cause. But authors of other studies indicating a biological basis for homosexuality saluted it as a major advance.

Simon LeVay, who won wide publicity for an analysis of differences in brain anatomies between straight and gay men, acknowledges that the brains he studied were of AIDS victims, and thus he cannot be sure that what he saw was genetic rather than the result of disease or some aspect of gay life. Says LeVay:

"This new work and the studies of twins are two lines of evidence pointing in the same direction. But the DNA evidence is much stronger than the twin studies." Dr. Richard Pillard, professor of psychiatry at Boston University School of Medicine and co-author of some twin studies—showing that identical twins of gay men have a 50 percent chance of being gay—is almost as laudatory. Says he: "If the new study holds up, it would be the first example of a higher-order behavior that has been found to be linked to a particular gene."

Whatever its ultimate scientific significance, however, the study's social and political impact is potentially even greater. If homosexuals are deemed to have a foreordained nature, many of the arguments now used to block equal rights would lose force. Opponents of such changes as ending the ban on gays in uniform argue that homosexuality is voluntary behavior, legitimately subject to regulation. Gays counter that they are acting as God or nature—in other words, their genes—intended. Says spokesman Gregory J. King of the Human Rights Campaign Fund, one of the largest gay-rights lobbying groups: "This is a landmark study that can be very helpful in increasing public support for civil rights for lesbian and gay Americans." Some legal scholars think that if gays can establish a genetic basis for sexual preference, like skin color or gender, they may persuade judges that discrimination is unconstitutional.

In addition, genetic evidence would probably affect many private relationships. Parents might be more relaxed about allowing children to have gay teachers, Boy Scout leaders, and other role models, on the assumption that the child's future is written in his or her genetic makeup. Those parents whose offspring do turn out gay might be less apt to condemn themselves. Says Cherie Garland of Ashland, Oregon, mother of a 41-year-old gay son: "The first thing any parent of a gay child goes through is guilt. If homosexuality is shown to be genetic, maybe parents and children can get on with learning to accept it." Catherine Tuerk, a nurse psychotherapist who is Washington chapter president of Parents and Friends of Lesbians and Gays, regrets sending her son Joshua into therapy from ages eight to twelve for an "aggression problem"—preference for games involving relationships instead of macho play with, say, toy trucks. Says she: "We were trying to cure him of something that doesn't need to be cured. There was nothing wrong with him." On the other hand, mothers who used to blame themselves for faulty upbringing may start blaming themselves for passing on the wrong genes.

Gay brothers surveyed for the study welcome its findings. Rick and Randy Gordon, twins from Orlando, Florida, never felt being gay was a matter of free will. Rick, who works in a law firm, says, "I don't honestly think I chose to be gay." Randy, a supervisor at a bed-and-breakfast, agrees: "I always believed that homosexuality was something I was born with. If homosexuality is genetic, there is nothing you can do about it. If there is more research like this in years to come, hopefully homosexuality will be accepted rather than treated as an abnormality."

Ralph White, thirty-six, an attorney with the General Accounting Office, says he was fired from a senatorial staff in 1982 after admitting he was gay. He foresees abiding significance in the study: "I don't expect people to suddenly change their minds. But the long-term impact will be profound. I can't imagine that rational people, presented with evidence that homosexuality is biological and not a choice, would continue to discriminate." His brother David, thirty-two, a public relations officer, wishes he had had a basis for believing in a genetic cause during his turbulent adolescence: "I was defiant, and to this day I'm probably still that way, because when you're gay in this society you almost have to be."

While many gay leaders welcomed the study, some are queasy. Its very existence, they fret, implies that homosexuality is wrong and defective. Says Donald Suggs of the New York chapter of the Gay & Lesbian Alliance Against Defamation: "Homosexuality is not something to justify and explain, but something that should be accepted. Until people accept us, all the scientific evidence in the world will not do anything to change homophobia." Moreover, gays are worried that precise identification of a "gayness gene" might prompt efforts to tinker with the genetic code of gay adults or to test during pregnancy and abort potentially gay fetuses. Says Thomas Stoddard, director of the Campaign for Military Service: "One can imagine the science of the future manipulating information of this kind to reduce the number of gay people being born."

Warns Eric Juengst of the National Center for Human Genome Research: "This is a two-edged sword. It can be used to benefit gays by allowing them to make the case that the trait for which they're being discriminated against is no worse than skin color. On the other hand, it could get interpreted to mean that different is pathological."

Anti-gay activists took up that cry immediately, saying that a genetic basis for homosexuality does not make it any more acceptable. They noted that genetic links are known or suspected for other traits that society judges "undesirable," such as mental and physical illness. Said the Rev. Louis Sheldonzx, chairman of the Traditional Values Coalition: "The fact that homosexuality may be genetically based will not make much difference for us from a public policy perspective." Reed Irvine, whose watchdog group, Accuracy in Media, increasingly criticizes favorable reportage about gays and gay rights, called for more coverage of studies that he claims show homosexuality can be "cured"— an assertion that both gays and health professionals widely dispute. Says Irvine: "It's a little more complicated than just saying you can prove there's a hereditary factor. The media have given zero attention to the many, many homosexuals who have gone straight. I think it's sending gays the wrong message to say you cannot change because it's something your genes have determined."

Even gays admit that Irvine is partly right. Homosexuality is not simply programmed but is a complex expression of values and personality. As researcher Hamer says, "Genes are part of the story, and this gene region is a part of the genetic story, but it's not all of the story." We may never know all of the story. But to have even part of it can bring light where of late there has been mostly a searing heat.

Part Three

Homosexuality
and the Criminal Law

12

*Bowers v. Hardwick**

Michael J. BOWERS, Attorney
General of Georgia, Petitioner
v.
Michael HARDWICK, and John
and Mary Doe.
Argued March 31, 1986.
Decided June 30, 1986.
Rehearing Denied September 11, 1986.

Justice [BYRON] WHITE delivered the opinion of the Court.

In August 1982, respondent Hardwick (hereafter respondent) was charged with violating the Georgia statute criminalizing sodomy by committing that act with another adult male in the bedroom of respondent's home. After a preliminary hearing, the District Attorney decided not to present the matter to the grand jury unless further evidence developed.

Respondent then brought suit in the Federal District Court, challenging the constitutionality of the statute insofar as it criminalized consensual sodomy. He asserted that he was a practicing homosexual, that the Georgia sodomy statute, as administered by the defendants, placed him in imminent danger of arrest, and that the statute for several reasons violates the Federal Constitution. The District Court granted the defendants' motion to dismiss for failure to state a claim. . . .

A divided panel of the Court of Appeals for the Eleventh Circuit reversed. . . . The Court [held] that the Georgia statute violated respondent's fundamental

*This is a significantly edited version of *Bowers* v. *Hardwick* that has omitted the footnotes. (Eds.)

Reprinted with permission from *Supreme Court Reporter.* Copyright © by West Publishing Company.

rights because his homosexual activity is a private and intimate association that is beyond the reach of state regulation by reason of the Ninth Amendment and the Due Process Clause of the Fourteenth Amendment. . . .

Because other Courts of Appeals have arrived at judgments contrary to that of the Eleventh Circuit in this case, we granted the Attorney General's petition for certiorari questioning the holding that the sodomy statute violates the fundamental rights of homosexuals. We agree with petitioner that the Court of Appeals erred, and hence reverse its judgment.

This case does not require a judgment on whether laws against sodomy between consenting adults in general, or between homosexuals in particular, are wise or desirable. It raises no question about the right or propriety of state legislative decisions to repeal their laws that criminalize homosexual sodomy, or of state-court decisions invalidating those laws on state constitutional grounds. The issue presented is whether the Federal Constitution confers a fundamental right upon homosexuals to engage in sodomy and hence invalidates the laws of the many States that still make such conduct illegal and have done so for a very long time. The case also calls for some judgment about the limits of the Court's role in carrying out its constitutional mandate.

We first register our disagreement with the Court of Appeals and with respondent that the Court's prior cases have construed the Constitution to confer a right of privacy that extends to homosexual sodomy and for all intents and purposes have decided this case. The reach of this line of cases was sketched in *Carey* v. *Population Services International,* and *Pierce* v. *Society of Sisters* and *Meyer* v. *Nebraska* were described as dealing with child rearing and education; *Prince* v. *Massachusetts,* with family relationships; *Skinner* v. *Oklahoma ex rel. Williamson,* with procreation; *Loving* v. *Virginia,* with marriage; *Griswold* v. *Connecticut* and *Eisenstadt* v. *Baird,* with contraception; and *Roe* v. *Wade,* with abortion. The latter three cases were interpreted as construing the Due Process Clause of the Fourteenth Amendment to confer a fundamental individual right to decide whether or not to beget or bear a child.

Accepting the decisions in these cases and the above description of them, we think it evident that none of the rights announced in those cases bears any resemblance to the claimed constitutional right of homosexuals to engage in acts of sodomy that is asserted in this case. No connection between family, marriage, or procreation on the one hand and homosexual activity on the other has been demonstrated, either by the Court of Appeals or by respondent. Moreover, any claim that these cases nevertheless stand for the proposition that any kind of private sexual conduct between consenting adults is constitutionally insulated from state proscription is unsupportable. Indeed, the Court's opinion in *Carey* twice asserted that the privacy right, which the *Griswold* line of cases found to be one of the protections provided by the Due Process Clause, did not reach so far.

Precedent aside, however, respondent would have us announce, as the Court of Appeals did, a fundamental right to engage in homosexual sodomy.

This we are quite unwilling to do. It is true that despite the language of the Due Process Clauses of the Fifth and Fourteenth Amendments, which appears to focus only on the processes by which life, liberty, or property is taken, the cases are legion in which those Clauses have been interpreted to have substantive content, subsuming rights that to a great extent are immune from federal or state regulation or proscription. Among such cases are those recognizing rights that have little or no textual support in the constitutional language. . . .

Striving to assure itself and the public that announcing rights not readily identifiable in the Constitution's text involves much more than the imposition of the Justices' own choice of values on the states and the federal government, the Court has sought to identify the nature of the rights qualifying for heightened judicial protection. In *Palko* v. *Connecticut,* it was said that this category includes those fundamental liberties that are "implicit in the concept of ordered liberty," such that "neither liberty nor justice would exist if [they] were sacrificed." A different description of fundamental liberties appeared in *Moore* v. *East Cleveland,* where they are characterized as those liberties that are "deeply rooted in this Nation's history and tradition."

It is obvious to us that neither of these formulations would extend a fundamental right to homosexuals to engage in acts of consensual sodomy. Proscriptions against that conduct have ancient roots. Sodomy was a criminal offense at common law and was forbidden by the laws of the original states when they ratified the Bill of Rights. In 1868, when the Fourteenth Amendment was ratified, all but five of the thirty-seven states in the Union had criminal sodomy laws. In fact, until 1961, all fifty states outlawed sodomy, and today, twenty-four states and the District of Columbia continue to provide criminal penalties for sodomy performed in private and between consenting adults. Against this background, to claim that a right to engage in such conduct is "deeply rooted in this nation's history and tradition" or "implicit in the concept of ordered liberty" is, at best, facetious.

Nor are we inclined to take a more expansive view of our authority to discover new fundamental rights imbedded in the Due Process Clause. The Court is most vulnerable and comes nearest to illegitimacy when it deals with judge-made constitutional law having little or no cognizable roots in the language or design of the Constitution. That this is so was painfully demonstrated by the face-off between the Executive and the Court in the 1930s, which resulted in the repudiation of much of the substantive gloss that the Court had placed on the Due Process Clauses of the Fifth and Fourteenth Amendments. There should be, therefore, great resistance to expand the substantive reach of those Clauses, particularly if it requires redefining the category of rights deemed to be fundamental. Otherwise, the judiciary necessarily takes to itself further authority to govern the country without express constitutional authority. The claimed right pressed on us today falls far short of overcoming this resistance.

Respondent, however, asserts that the result should be different where the homosexual conduct occurs in the privacy of the home. He relies on *Stanley* v.

Georgia, where the Court held that the First Amendment prevents conviction for possessing and reading obscene material in the privacy of one's home: "If the First Amendment means anything, it means that a state has no business telling a man, sitting alone in his house, what books he may read or what films he may watch."

Stanley did protect conduct that would not have been protected outside the home, and it partially prevented the enforcement of state obscenity laws; but the decision was firmly grounded in the First Amendment. The right pressed upon us here has no similar support in the text of the Constitution, and it does not qualify for recognition under the prevailing principles for construing the Fourteenth Amendment. Its limits are also difficult to discern. Plainly enough, otherwise illegal conduct is not always immunized whenever it occurs in the home. Victimless crimes, such as the Possession and use of illegal drugs, do not escape the law where they are committed at home. *Stanley* itself recognized that its holding offered no protection for the possession in the home of drugs, firearms, or stolen goods. And if respondent's submission is limited to the voluntary sexual conduct between consenting adults, it would be difficult, except by fiat, to limit the claimed right to homosexual conduct while leaving exposed to prosecution adultery, incest, and other sexual crimes even though they are committed in the home. We are unwilling to start down that road.

Even if the conduct at issue here is not a fundamental right, respondent asserts that there must be a rational basis for the law and that there is none in this case other than the presumed belief of a majority of the electorate in Georgia that homosexual sodomy is immoral and unacceptable. This is said to be an inadequate rationale to support the law. The law, however, is constantly based on notions of morality, and if all laws representing essentially moral choices are to be invalidated under the Due Process Clause, the courts will be very busy indeed. Even respondent makes no such claim, but insists that majority sentiments about the morality of homosexuality should be declared inadequate. We do not agree, and are unpersuaded that the sodomy laws of some twenty-five states should be invalidated on this basis.

Accordingly, the judgment of the Court of Appeals is
Reversed.

Justice [LEWIS] POWELL, concurring.

I join the opinion of the Court. I agree with the Court that there is no fundamental right—i.e., no substantive right under the Due Process Clause—such as that claimed by respondent Hardwick, and found to exist by the Court of Appeals. This is not to suggest, however, that respondent may not be protected by the Eighth Amendment of the Constitution.* The Georgia statute at issue in this case authorizes a court to imprison a person for up to twenty years for a single private, consensual act of sodomy. In my view, a prison sentence for such conduct—cer-

---

*The text of the Eighth Amendment reads as follows: "Excessive bail shall not be required, nor excessive fines imposed, nor cruel and unusual punishments inflicted." (Eds.)

tainly a sentence of long duration—would create a serious Eighth Amendment issue. Under the Georgia statute a single act of sodomy, even in the private setting of a home, is a felony comparable in terms of the possible sentence imposed to serious felonies such as aggravated battery, first-degree arson, and robbery.

In this case, however, respondent has not been tried, much less convicted and sentenced. Moreover, respondent has not raised the Eighth Amendment issue below. For these reasons this constitutional argument is not before us.

Justice [HARRY] BLACKMUN, with whom Justice [WILLIAM] BRENNAN, Justice [THURGOOD] MARSHALL, and Justice [JOHN PAUL] STEVENS join, dissenting.

This case is no more about "a fundamental right to engage in homosexual sodomy," as the Court purports to declare, than *Stanley* v. *Georgia* was about a fundamental right to watch obscene movies. . . . Rather, this case is about "the most comprehensive of rights and the right most valued by civilized men," namely, "the right to be let alone."

The statute at issue denies individuals the right to decide for themselves whether to engage in particular forms of private, consensual sexual activity. The Court concludes that Ga. Code Ann. § 16-6-2 (1984) is valid essentially because "the laws of . . . many states . . . still make such conduct illegal and have done so for a very long time." . . . Like Justice Holmes, I believe that "[i]t is revolting to have no better reason for a rule of law than that so it was laid down in the time of Henry IV. It is still more revolting if the grounds upon which it was laid down have vanished long since, and the rule simply persists from blind imitation of the past." I believe we must analyze Hardwick's claim in the light of the values that underlie the constitutional right to privacy. If that right means anything, it means that, before Georgia can prosecute its citizens for making choices about the most intimate aspects of their lives, it must do more than assert that the choice they have made is an " 'abominable crime not fit to be named among Christians.' " *Herring* v. *State,* 119 Ga. 709, 721, 46 S.E. 876, 882 (1904).

I

In its haste to reverse the Court of Appeals and hold that the Constitution does not "confe[r] a fundamental right upon homosexuals to engage in sodomy," the Court regulates the actual statute being challenged to a footnote and ignores the procedural posture of the case before it. A fair reading of the statute and of the complaint clearly reveals that the majority has distorted the question this case presents.

First, the Court's almost obsessive focus on homosexual activity is particularly hard to justify in light of the broad language Georgia has used. . . . Georgia has provided that "[a] person commits the offense of sodomy when he performs or submits to any sexual act involving the sex organs of one person and the mouth or anus of another." Ga. Code Ann. § 16-6-2(a) (1984). The sex or status of the persons who engage in the act is irrelevant as a matter of state law. In fact, to the extent I can discern a legislative purpose for Georgia's 1968 enactment of § 16-6-2, that purpose seems to have been to broaden the coverage of the law to reach heterosexual as well as homosexual activity. . . .

II

"Our cases long have recognized that the Constitution embodies a promise that a certain private sphere of individual liberty will be kept largely beyond the reach of government." *Thornburgh* v. *American College of Obstetricians & Gynecologists*. In construing the right to privacy, the Court has proceeded along two somewhat distinct, albeit complementary, lines. First, it has recognized a privacy interest with reference to certain *decisions* that are properly for the individual to make. Second, it has recognized a privacy interest with reference to certain *places* without regard for the particular activities in which the individuals who occupy them are engaged. The case before us implicates both the decisional and the spatial aspects of the right to privacy.

. . . Only the most willful blindness could obscure the fact that sexual intimacy is "a sensitive, key relationship of human existence, central to family life, community welfare, and the development of human personality." The fact that individuals define themselves in a significant way through their intimate sexual relationships with others suggests, in a Nation as diverse as ours, that there may be many "right" ways of conducting those relationships, and that much of the richness of a relationship will come from the freedom an individual has to *choose* the form and nature of these intensely personal bonds.

In a variety of circumstances we have recognized that a necessary corollary of giving individuals freedom to choose how to conduct their lives is acceptance of the fact that different individuals will make different choices. . . . The Court claims that its decision today merely refuses to recognize a fundamental right to engage in homosexual sodomy; what the Court really has refused to recognize is the fundamental interest all individuals have in controlling the nature of their intimate associations with others.

The behavior for which Hardwick faces prosecution occurred in his own home, a place to which the Fourth Amendment attaches special significance. The Court's treatment of this aspect of the case is symptomatic of its overall refusal to consider the broad principles that have informed our treatment of privacy in specific cases. Just as the right to privacy is more than the mere aggregation of a number of entitlements to engage in specific behavior, so too, protecting the physical integrity of the home is more than merely a means of protecting specific activities that often take place there. . . .

. . . Indeed, the right of an individual to conduct intimate relationships in the intimacy of his or her own home seems to me to be the heart of the Constitution's protection of privacy. . . .

13

Changing Times: Gay Rights

John C. Jeffries, Jr.

While [Justice Lewis F. Powell, Jr.'s,] response to the women's movement was straightforward and secure, his reaction to the claim of gay rights was tortured and unsure. Never before had Powell faced an issue for which he was by instinct and experience so uniquely unprepared.*

Agitation for a constitutional right of homosexual relations began early in Powell's tenure. In 1965 the Supreme Court had held that married persons had a constitutional right to use contraceptives. A few years later, the Court had extended that right to unmarried persons. These decisions gave constitutional protection to nonprocreative sex and set the stage for a far-reaching claim. If unmarried individuals had a right to engage in heterosexual intercourse, why not homosexual also? Were not homosexual acts done for the same purposes of gratification and intimacy as other nonprocreative sex? Were they not similarly far removed from harm to third parties? Were they not therefore equally entitled to constitutional recognition under the newly declared right of privacy?

This line of questions might have remained on the periphery of constitutional argument had it not been for *Roe* v. *Wade*. The abortion decision showed that the Supreme Court was serious about privacy. Not only were the Justices ready to strike down unenforced legislative oddities such as Connecticut's ban on contraceptives; they were also prepared to uproot history and override current practice in order to guarantee individual autonomy in the realm of sexuality and reproduction. If the Justices were willing to constitutionalize freedom of choice in childbearing, why not also in sexual preference? The analogy

---

*Jeffries points out in his biography of Justice Powell that Powell most often cast the deciding vote in Supreme Court cases, including *Bowers* v. *Hardwick*. (Eds.)

seemed nearly exact. *Roe* v. *Wade* created a vast new structure of personal autonomy, of which homosexual relations between consenting adults seemed a natural part.

Would the Supreme Court agree? Many lawyers and activists were eager to find out, but they could not find the right case. Though sodomy had been a crime for centuries and in most states still was, the laws were not enforced against private acts by consenting adults. Technically, the crime of sodomy—the name comes from the biblical city of evil practices—condemned all oral or anal sex, even between a married couple, but no one imagined that the law would be, or constitutionally could be, enforced in that context. The laws remained on the books, as in popular understanding, only as strictures against homosexuals. Even in that context, the statutes were largely dormant. Strategists actively searching for the vehicle to mount a constitutional challenge to the sodomy laws could never find the right facts. Actual prosecutions always involved some aggravating factor—the use of force, or sex in public, or with an underage youth. The prospect of going to jail for purely private conduct with a consenting adult seemed entirely hypothetical. . . .

. . . The case that finally forced the issue began almost by accident. On the morning of July 5, 1982, Michael Hardwick left the gay bar where he had worked all night. A police officer ticketed him for carrying an open bottle of beer. When Hardwick did not show up for his court date eight days later, the policeman got a warrant for his arrest. Three weeks later the officer showed up at Hardwick's apartment to serve the warrant. By this time, Hardwick had paid the fine for drinking in public, but the paperwork never caught up with the policeman. He arrived at the apartment at 8:30 in the morning and was told by a friend who had spent the night on Hardwick's couch that he could come in. He walked down the hall, saw a door ajar, and pushed it open to find Michael Hardwick engaged in sex with another man. Hardwick's arrest for that act finally provided the right facts for a constitutional challenge.

The local prosecutor abhorred "that type of conduct" but never used the sodomy statute for simply having sex. Since no public display was involved, the prosecutor dropped the charge, but by that time Hardwick had been contacted by lawyers from the ACLU and had agreed to serve as the plaintiff in a test case. "God bless the police officer," said an ACLU attorney. After looking for five years, the ACLU lawyers had finally found the right case—sex with a consenting adult in the privacy of one's own home. The fact that Hardwick had actually been arrested and taken to jail—indeed, that he was technically still subject to indictment—showed that the dispute was not purely hypothetical. Of course, from a tactical point of view it would have been better still if Hardwick had been tried and punished, but that had not happened and was not likely to. Hardwick's was as good a case as anyone was likely to see. It would be the vehicle for an all-out attack on the sodomy laws.

Hardwick's lawyers lost at trial but won on appeal. By a divided vote the appeals court ruled that private sexual activity with a consenting adult was an individual decision critical to personal autonomy and was therefore protected by the Constitution against government interference. At about the same time another appeals court reached exactly the opposite conclusion. The conflict between them demanded resolution by the Supreme Court.

Still, Powell did not want to hear the case. On October 11, 1985, he joined the majority of his colleagues ([Byron] White and [William] Rehnquist dissenting) in refusing to grant review. White then took the unusual step of drafting a public dissent from the denial of certiorari,* in which he argued that the conflict in the lower courts required Supreme Court review. This action turned the tide, and a week later the Justices reversed course. Ironically, the decisive votes came from [William] Brennan and [Thurgood] Marshall, who joined White and Rehnquist in granting review and thus set the stage for their own defeat. Perhaps they expected to win, or perhaps they thought the case should be heard no matter what the outcome. Whatever their reasons, on November 4, the Supreme Court announced that it would hear the case destined to raise the last major constitutional issue of Powell's tenure—the appeal by Michael Bowers, Attorney General of the State of Georgia, in defense of the constitutionality of the Georgia sodomy law challenged by Michael Hardwick.

From the beginning, Powell found the case deeply troubling. As the arguments mounted and the Justices took sides, Powell felt forced to an unwelcome choice between extremes. As he saw it, neither side was entirely right. While others vehemently asserted one position or the other, Powell shied away from both, instinctively searching for a middle course. But this time he did not find one. Neither his colleagues, nor his clerks, nor the lawyers in the case helped him out of the dilemma. Left to his own resources, Powell waited and waffled, accepting finally what he thought to be the lesser of two evils. He never really came to rest or resolved his inner conflict, which surfaced long after his retirement as lingering vacillation and doubt about the vote he had cast. Most important, Powell did not find the means to translate his moderate impulses into legal doctrine. He failed to craft and publish a clear statement of his own views. In this sense, *Bowers* v. *Hardwick* was Powell's greatest defeat.

On one side was the argument—ably pressed by Laurence Tribe—that the constitutional right of privacy encompassed a realm of sexual intimacy with which the government could not interfere. No one doubted that such a right existed within marriage. The controversial question was whether the Constitution protected sexual relations outside marriage and specifically between persons of the same sex. Tribe insisted that it did. His argument was grounded in the precedents on contraception and abortion and the zone of sexual privacy that they seemed to create, but he also emphasized cases restricting police intrusion into the home. The "sanctity of the home" was Tribe's candidate for

---

*A writ of certiorari is an application to the Supreme Court to review a lower court's decision. (Eds.)

a limiting principle to his claim of personal autonomy. After all, a constitutional right to do as one pleased had to stop somewhere, or organized society would simply collapse. Tribe's answer—or part of it—was limitation by place. Persons had a right to engage in the thrill of their choice but only, he said, in the privacy of their own homes.

It is an indication of Powell's inner turmoil that Tribe's innocuous argument set him off. "Home," Powell wrote, "is one of the most beautiful words in the English language. It usually connotes family, husband and wife, and children—although, of course, single persons, widows and widowers, and others also have genuine homes." But what exactly did "home" embrace? Would it include a hotel room or "a private room made available in a house of prostitution"? Would it include sex in an automobile or in the "'sanctity' of a toilet in a public restroom"? Here Powell was over the edge. Obviously, sexual relations of any sort could be prohibited in public. As Powell himself recognized, "home" was merely a rhetorically attractive way of describing any "truly private setting." Powell's querulousness did not reflect confusion on the point or even real disagreement. Mostly, it revealed an emotional recoil from an argument that seemed to place homosexual sodomy on a par with the sexual intimacy between man and wife.

Powell also questioned whether Tribe's argument meant that other criminal acts would have to be allowed in the "sanctity of the home." "[I]f sodomy is to be decriminalized on constitutional grounds," Powell asked, "what about incest, bigamy, and adultery?" Would they also be brought within the constitutional right of privacy? One answer was that these acts might be differentiated in terms of the strength of society's interest in forbidding them. That the government might have to tolerate homosexual relations between consenting adults did not necessarily mean that it would also have to accept bigamy and incest. Powell acknowledged as much when he later wrote in the margin of his own memorandum: "I realize [that] these examples are not fairly comparable."

The strongest objection to Tribe's argument concerned not its boundaries but its premises. Where exactly did a constitutional right to homosexual sodomy come from? The Constitution did not mention privacy, much less sex, and there could be little doubt what the Framers would have thought of Hardwick's claim. On what basis, other than their personal predilections, could the Justices of the Supreme Court legitimately decide what the people of Georgia could and could not forbid?

An answer was made by the state of Georgia and from within Powell's chambers by the clerk assigned to this case. Mike Mosman was a Mormon by faith, a moralist by disposition, and a hard-nosed opponent of judicial innovation. His bench memo, given to Powell two days before oral argument, argued powerfully for limiting the constitutional right of privacy to those interests firmly rooted in the history and traditions of the people.

"The focus on history and tradition," Mosman explained, "results from the fact that the right of privacy is not intended to be the vanguard of changes in social values. It is intended to protect those values that are imbedded in the fabric of our society," not to add new ones. In this view, "homosexual sodomy [did] not fit within the right of privacy." Even Larry Tribe could not deny that such acts had long been condemned. Instead, Tribe tried to reshape the issue by bringing homosexual sodomy within the long-standing societal regard for other forms of sexual intimacy. Mosman countered by pointing out that [the] Supreme Court had "never recognized a broad-based right of sexual freedom. Instead, it has extended protection to those sexual relationships that have traditionally been protected and recognized in our society—those that relate to marriage and other family relationships. Up through the present time, every one of the Court's right of privacy cases can be explained in terms of a concern for the fundamental right of marital and family privacy."

According to Mosman, even abortion could be explained on that ground. Laws against abortion "have the effect of *forcing* a woman to bring a family into existence. For unmarried women, the abortion decision is not a decision about her commitment to her sexual partner; it is a decision about long-term commitments to her potential offspring." In Mosman's view, therefore, the abortion cases did not protect a woman's "sexual freedom," but rather her interest in "her potential relationship and commitment to a child she does not want to bear—her interest in not having the state require her to become a mother." So interpreted, the abortion and contraception cases extended the right of privacy no further than indicated by the "fundamental values of family and procreation."

"More importantly," Mosman concluded, "I think the fact that the right of privacy cases are limited to marriage, family, and procreation accurately reflects the traditions of our people. Personal sexual freedom is a newcomer among our national values, and may well be . . . a temporary national mood that fades. This may be reflected in the fact that in the 1970s twenty states decriminalized homosexual sodomy, while in the 1980s only two states have done so. . . . The right of privacy calls for the greatest judicial restraint, invalidating only those laws that impinge on those values that are basic to our country. I do not think this case involves any such value."

While this analysis put a plausible conservative gloss on most of the privacy cases, it could not explain abortion. *Roe* v. *Wade* did not recognize a right already deeply imbedded in the history and tradition of the nation. On the contrary, it uprooted existing law to make way for an entirely new right. Contrary to Mosman's memo, *Roe* put the right of privacy in the vanguard of social change. His argument therefore boiled down to this: Whatever had been done in *Roe,* the constitutional concept of privacy should not again be expanded to create a wholly new right. The bold experiment in Judicial innovation should not be repeated. The Court should return to a respect for history and tradition, which did not embrace a right to homosexual sodomy.

In this argument, Mosman had powerful allies. First, there was the ghost of John Harlan, who in *Griswold* v. *Connecticut* had endorsed the right of married couples to use contraceptives but had specifically rejected a right to homosexual sex. Fundamental rights, said Harlan, did not come from the personal whims of the Justices but reflected "the balance which our nation, built upon postulates of respect for the liberty of the individual, has struck between that liberty and the demands of organized society." The content of the right of privacy was therefore fixed by the traditions of the people, which clearly did not accept homosexual sex. Harlan concluded: "I would not suggest that adultery, homosexuality, fornication, and incest are immune from criminal inquiry, however privately practiced."

Second, Mosman could quote Powell's prior decisions—abortion excepted—in support of his historically grounded view of the right to privacy. In *Moore* v. *City of East Cleveland,* Powell struck down a single-family housing ordinance that defined single family so narrowly that even some close relatives could not live together in one dwelling. This ordinance, Powell argued, intruded into a "private realm of family life which the state cannot enter." When Justice White objected that no such right appeared in the text of the Constitution, Powell answered in the best Harlan tradition. "There *are* risks," he admitted, in recognizing unwritten rights, but the safeguard lay in "respect for the teachings of history [and] solid recognition of the basic values that underlie our society." Here, he said, "the Constitution protects the sanctity of the family precisely because the institution of the family is so deeply rooted in this Nation's history and tradition." The same could not be said for homosexual sex.

Most important, Mosman could appeal to Powell's emotions. However radical *Roe* v. *Wade* had been as a matter of constitutional law, it did not require that Powell transcend his private sensibilities. He did not find abortion personally offensive. Sodomy was different. Powell said that if he were in the legislature, he would vote to decriminalize sodomy, but that had to do chiefly with the practicalities of the situation. Even where the practice was prevalent, the laws were not enforced. "Moreover, police have more important responsibilities than snooping around trying to catch people in the act of sodomy." But Powell's intellectual commitment to toleration masked emotional misgiving. Abortion had seemed to him unfortunate but not wrong, while homosexuality struck him as profoundly unnatural. "At a very deep level," thought one clerk, "he found homosexual sodomy abhorrent."

These concerns converged at a point of practical importance. Powell wished, above all else, to avoid a broad declaration of a privacy right that would have consequences outside the field of criminal prosecution. Despite Tribe's effort to circumnavigate these issues, Powell feared that accepting Tribe's argument against criminal punishment for homosexual sodomy would entangle the Court in a continuing campaign to validate the gay "lifestyle" in a variety of other contexts. After all, if homosexuals had a constitutional right to engage in sex, would they not also have the right to object to any form of regulation or restriction disadvantaging them for having done so? Would gays then have a constitutional right to serve in the military or the intelligence agencies? Would they have a right to teach in public school or work in day care centers? Would there be a constitutional requirement that the law allow homosexual adoption or same-sex marriage?

This was not a revolution Powell was ready to lead. The eventualities down the road appalled him, but he could not see how they could be avoided if the Court were to declare a new fundamental right to engage in homosexual sodomy. Against the background of these concerns, Powell found his clerk's hard-hitting memo persuasive. Mosman's caution reinforced his own, and the narrow reading of the privacy cases helped Powell draw a line where his emotions indicated. He would not create a new constitutional right of consensual sodomy. He would not attempt another *Roe* v. *Wade* on behalf of homosexuals. To that extent Powell sided with the Court's conservatives and against the claim of Michael Hardwick.

But Powell was only partly persuaded by Mosman's memo; he was also pulled the other way. Unlike White and Rehnquist, who consistently opposed privacy claims, Powell had generally been in favor of them. He had never backed off from his support for abortion, so for him the analogy to *Roe* v. *Wade* was far from fatal. On questions of this sort, Powell voted with the liberals, and if he was not willing to go with them all the way to a new constitutional right, he at least respected what they had to say.

And on one crucial point he thought them entirely correct. Just as creating a new fundamental right went too far in one direction, flatly rejecting that claim went too far in the other. If, as the conservatives contended, consensual sodomy was not constitutionally protected, then presumably the states could regulate such acts as they pleased, including by criminal prosecution and punishment. Powell found this prospect barbaric. Whatever his private sensibilities, he was quite unwilling to see the Michael Hardwicks of the world imprisoned for acting on their sexual desires. It seemed to him senseless and cruel that persons afflicted—that was how he thought of it—with homosexuality should be condemned as criminals. Where there was no public display, no use of force, and [no] involvement with minors, the conduct was essentially harmless. Society did not have to approve such behavior, but it could not constitutionally prosecute and imprison those who engaged in it.

Powell therefore sought a middle course. He hoped to split the difference between sodomy as a major crime and sodomy as a fundamental right. He wanted to avoid approving homosexuality in the name of the Constitution but at the same time to protect homosexuals from criminal prosecution. He wanted to prevent oppression without requiring social revolution. As in *Bakke*,* he hoped to blur the edges of the controversy in a compromise that would allow the nation to muddle its way toward a better future.

But this inclination was more an instinct than an argument. Powell needed

---

**Regents of the University of California* v. *Bakke*, the racial quotas case decided in 1978. (Eds.)

to translate his intuition into law. He needed some doctrine or reasoning that would differentiate criminal punishment from other kinds of restrictions on homosexuals. He needed a legal theory.

Finding no better candidates, his clerks proposed the Eighth Amendment guarantee against "cruel and unusual punishments." Its attraction lay in the fact that it applied specifically and exclusively to the criminal law and therefore might plausibly be used to erect a doctrinal wall between criminal punishment and any other legal disadvantage imposed on homosexuals. Its weakness lay in the traditional understanding of what constituted "cruel and unusual punishments." The phrase obviously covered torture or confinement in inhuman conditions. Additionally, it had been held to forbid some uses of the death penalty, as in the long line of cases restricting capital punishment for murder and forbidding it altogether for rape. But none of these things had been done to Michael Hardwick. He had not been punished at all, much less threatened with torture or execution.

The clerks therefore invoked a different aspect of Eighth Amendment law, the 1962 decision in *Robinson* v. *California*. So obscure that a generation of legal scholars had debated its meaning, *Robinson* seemed to say that, while individuals could be held criminally responsible for their *acts*, no one could be punished criminally for a mere *status*. The "status" at issue in *Robinson* was being addicted to narcotics, which the Court said could not be made a crime. This ruling would have been precisely applicable if Georgia had punished the status of being homosexual, but that the state had not tried to do. Rather, Georgia condemned the *act* of homosexual sodomy, which, like the act of using narcotics, could be proscribed. Nevertheless, the clerks felt that the *act* of sodomy was so closely linked to the status of homosexuality that perhaps *Robinson* could be stretched to protect both from criminal prosecution.

That, at any rate, was the theory. It was a debatable use of an isolated precedent that did not fit the situation, but it was the best the clerks could come up with. Nor were these flaws the only problem. Perhaps more important, no Eighth Amendment issue had been raised in the courts below. The failure to litigate the claim in the trial court created a procedural obstacle to considering that issue in the Supreme Court. That problem was perhaps not insuperable, but it did further burden an already weak idea. Small wonder that others thought the *Robinson* argument simply "crazy."

Powell, however, was desperate to find some way out of his dilemma. In the days before the Conference,* he increasingly clutched the fragile thesis of the Eighth Amendment and its interpretation in *Robinson* v. *California* as the means of escape.

* * *

---

*The Conference is a meeting at which only Justices are present. During the Conference, cases that have been argued are discussed and preliminary votes taken. (Eds.)

Powell's search for a legal theory paralleled a search for personal under-standing. Sexual activity between men was something he did not comprehend. Unable to say exactly what he wished to learn, he nonetheless realized that he needed to know more.

Unknown to Powell, one of his clerks was gay. Powell merely identified the young man as the most liberal of the four clerks and so sought out his views as a counterbalance to the conservative Mike Mosman. Powell came into the clerk's office and casually asked him to review the arguments in this difficult case. When told that (as the clerk believed) 10 percent of the population was gay, Pow-ell was incredulous. "I don't believe I've ever met a homosexual," he told his astonished clerk. "Certainly you have," came back the reply, "but you just don't know that they are." In North Africa, Powell said, "not a single episode of homo-sexuality was reported" despite several months away from women, but the clerk insisted that the behavior would have occurred without Powell's knowledge.

The discussion edged toward Powell's true mission when he tried to find out from his startled clerk just what it meant to be gay:

> "Are gay men not attracted to women at all?"
> "They are attracted to women, but there is no sexual excitement."
> "None at all?"
> "Justice Powell, a gay man could not get an erection to have sex with a woman.

The answer left Powell even more confused. "Don't you have to have an erection to perform sodomy?" he asked.

"Yes," he was told, "but that's because of the sexual excitement."

What Powell found so difficult to grasp was that homosexuality was not an act of desperation, not the last resort of men deprived of women, but a log-ical expression of the desire and affection that gay men felt for other men.

A few days later he made another run at the same topic. Again the clerk tried to explain that gay men "love other men like straight men love women." Powell still found it hard to follow. In the words of the clerk: "He had no con-cept of it at all. He couldn't understand the idea of sexual attraction between two men. It just had no content for him."

A third conversation took place just before oral argument. Uncharacteris-tically, Powell had still not decided how he would vote. In great distress, the clerk debated whether to tell Powell of his sexual orientation. Perhaps if Pow-ell could put a familiar face to these incomprehensible urges, they would seem less bizarre and threatening. He came to the edge of an outright decla-ration but ultimately drew back, settling for a "very emotional" speech urging Powell to support sexual freedom as a fundamental right. "The right to love the person of my choice," he argued, "would be far more important to me than the right to vote in elections." "That may be," Powell answered, "but that doesn't mean it's in the Constitution."

In the end, Powell remained unsure. The issue was also difficult for his clerks, who, disagreeing among themselves and acutely aware of the high emotions on both sides, walked on eggshells to avoid an open breach. From them Powell received little real help. The middle course they suggested to him had not been well thought out, nor was it supported by any substantial writing. Though Powell had an instinct for where he wanted to end up, he had no sure idea of how to get there. In this unusual state of indecision, he went to the Conference on Wednesday, April 2, and shook hands with each of his colleagues as they prepared to decide the case of *Bowers* v. *Hardwick.*

[Warren] Burger led off with a tirade. Homosexual sodomy had been a crime for centuries. If sodomy were declared a fundamental right, incest, prostitution, and the like would surely follow. Quoting Harlan and Powell on the importance of history and tradition and the sanctity of the family, Burger voted to uphold the law.

Brennan followed with a defense of the right of privacy. He answered the objection to the far-reaching implications of a new fundamental right by emphasizing, as Tribe had, the sanctity of the home. For Brennan, the case involved the question of "sexual privacy in the home" and not any broader questions of the state's interest in regulating such acts as incest and adultery.

The other Justices then took sides. White, Rehnquist, and [Sandra Day] O'Connor lined up with the Chief. Marshall, [Harry] Blackmun, and [John Paul] Stevens (with misgivings) agreed with Brennan.

The four-four split gave Powell the controlling vote, which in a sense was also equally divided. On the one hand, he was not persuaded that Hardwick had any fundamental constitutional right to engage in homosexual sodomy. On the other hand, Powell thought it would violate the Eighth Amendment "to punish him criminally (*imprisonment*) for conduct based on a natural sexual urge, privately and with a consenting partner." Powell's views were finely balanced, but the case had to be decided one way or the other. Since his Eighth Amendment theory barred criminal punishment, he voted against the Georgia law.

Powell's speech made no one happy. The liberals thought his theory bizarre and the result distressingly narrow. It did no more than preclude criminal prosecution, a possibility that had never been realistic. That was at best a minor victory. The conservatives, on the other hand, were confused and disappointed. The Eighth Amendment issue had not even been raised in the courts below. Why did Powell raise it now? And if Powell agreed with them that sodomy was not a constitutional right, how could a law against it be unconstitutional?

If others were baffled, the Chief was outraged. On the day after the Conference, he sent Powell a private letter. The missive began cogently. First, Powell's theory had not been raised by the litigants. Indeed, Tribe's brief for Michael Hardwick did not even cite *Robinson,* on which Powell now tried to rely, or so much as mention the Eighth Amendment. Moreover, Powell's theory did not fit the case. "Georgia here criminalizes only the *act* of sodomy," Burger noted. "If the act of sodomy is a 'status,' then what about the acts of incest, exhibitionism, rape, and drug possession?" Of course, Powell did not dispute that sodomy was an act. He claimed rather that the act was so closely linked to the involuntary status of being homosexual that it could not constitutionally be punished as a crime. But this theory, Burger argued, "would swallow up centuries of criminal law," since anyone with a "psychological dependency" would be entitled to "carry out (at least in private or with a consenting partner) whatever is necessary to satisfy his cravings."

Burger then warmed to the theme. "[S]urely homosexuals are not 'sex crazed' automatons who are 'compelled' by their 'status' to gratify their sexual appetites only by committing sodomy. . . . It is extremely unlikely that what Western civilization has for centuries viewed as a volitional, reprehensible act is, in reality, merely a conditioned response to which moral blame may not attach."

In reality, Burger insisted, the case did not involve punishment of a status or of any involuntary act compelled by that status. Rather, "Hardwick merely wishes to seek his own form of sexual gratification." Others "seek gratification through incest, drug use, gambling, exhibitionism, prostitution, [and] rape." That persons were gratified by such activities did not make them constitutionally protected. "As Justice Holmes put it, 'pretty much all law consists in forbidding men to do some things that they want to do. . . .' "

Burger closed with a personal aside: "April 13, an unlucky day, will mark my thirtieth year on the Bench. This case presents for me the most far-reaching issue of those thirty years. I hope you will excuse the energy with which I have stated my views, and I hope you will give them earnest consideration."

Word of Burger's intervention soon leaked out, and it afterward became an article of faith in some quarters that the Chief had somehow "gotten to" Powell. In fact, the rumor captured only the least part of truth. Burger's devastating attack on the *Robinson* theory did make Powell uneasy, but the Chief's excesses put Powell off. That Burger could regard this as the most far-reaching issue of his thirty years as a judge seemed to Powell incredible. His reaction was summarized when he wrote on the top of Burger's statement: "There is both sense and nonsense in this letter—mostly the latter."

A more influential intervention came from Michael Mosman. A few days after the Conference, Mosman weighed in with a memo urging Powell to change his vote. Even if Powell's Eighth Amendment theory was right, Mosman argued, it did not apply to this case. The only question squarely before the Court was whether homosexual sodomy was a fundamental right. Powell agreed with the conservatives that it was not, and his vote should reflect that view. There was simply no reason on these facts to rush into the difficult question of what restrictions, if any, the Eighth Amendment placed on criminal penalties for consensual sodomy, especially since the issue had not been raised below. There would be time enough to consider the question of cruel and unusual punishments if and when someone actually went to jail. In the meantime, Powell should decide the case before him and leave other questions for another day.

On reflection, Powell agreed. On April 8, he wrote his colleagues: "At Conference last week, I expressed the view that in some cases it would violate the Eighth Amendment to imprison a person for a private act of homosexual sodomy." Powell adhered to that view, but "upon further study as to exactly what is before us," concluded that his "bottom line" should be to uphold Georgia's law. Accordingly, he changed his vote.

Powell's switch was variously greeted with jubilation and dismay. The conservatives would now control the outcome, if not the reasoning, and liberal resentment was bitter and deep. Amid all the recriminations then and later about why Powell changed his vote, the most insightful reaction came from Justice Stevens, who wrote Powell that his change of heart reminded Stevens of a curious case from the 1930s in which the Court, with all nine Justices participating, refused to resolve an issue on the ground that it was "equally divided." The vote, as Powell noted in the margin, must have been "4½ to 4½." A split vote was technically impossible, but it precisely reflected Powell's view.

That Powell had reversed himself quickly became known. Two weeks after the end of the term, Al Kamen published a remarkably complete and accurate account of the switch in the *Washington Post*. Unnoticed and unremarked was a decision of almost equal significance that occurred some weeks later.

With Powell now voting to uphold the law, the Chief Justice found himself in the majority. He assigned the case to White, who took barely a week to circulate a draft as abrupt in tone as it was quick in origin. In an opinion that struck many observers as "superficial, peremptory and insensitive," White dismissed the claim that sexual freedom was a fundamental right as "at best, facetious." Even more disturbing was White's "failure to acknowledge in any way the human dimension of this issue. Not a single sentence expresses any understanding of the fact that this case involves human beings who have needs for intimacy, love, and sexual expression like the rest of us. Not a single sentence acknowledges the human anguish that anti-homosexual statutes can create. . . ." Instead, White dispatched the issue and those affected by it with the same sympathy that he would have shown an opposing tackler in his football days. It was the intellectual equivalent of brute force.

Although Powell now planned to vote with White, his initial instinct was not to join this opinion. On April 22, he told White that he would write separately. Yet a month later, he changed his mind and joined White. This decision made White's opinion authoritative. If Powell had refused to join, White would have spoken for only four justices, and his views would have been exactly balanced and offset by the four Justices on the other side. If Powell had carried through his intention to speak for himself, his would have been the decisive voice, and though he could not have bridged the gulf between the two positions, he at least would have tried to seek out some middle ground. Lawyers and journalists would have focused on his position, which would have given neither side a clear-cut victory and imposed on neither a total defeat. He would neither have encouraged gays to think that all legal disadvantages could be attacked as unconstitutional nor invited their opponents to seek stricter enforcement of the laws against homosexuals. Instead, he would have attempted to refocus the constitutional debate by distinguishing criminal punishment from all other forms of legal regulation.

But this he did not do. He not only joined White's short-tempered outburst but abandoned his plan for a full-scale opinion of his own and issued instead a two-paragraph concurrence that was justly ignored. Why he did so is perhaps the greatest mystery of Powell's career. On other occasions, he knew well enough the uses of ambivalence. In *Bakke,* for example, he crafted a compromise that neither categorically condemned racial preferences nor unqualifiedly approved racial quotas. That opinion may have been an intellectual muddle, but it was a political masterpiece. And it was also successful in a personal sense, as it exactly reflected his heartfelt view of the case and the issue. In *Bakke,* Powell found a way to translate his conviction into a legal judgment and in so doing to dominate the decision of a divided Court. But in *Bowers* he did just the opposite, joining an ugly opinion with which he only partly agreed and muffling his own quite different views in a throwaway concurrence.

No single factor accounts for this default. Initially, Powell made an effort to learn what he did not know, to maintain his open-mindedness, and to bring to this emotional issue the dispassion that he thought judging required, but he did not follow through. In the end, he gave up on himself and his own perspective. Age and health played their part, as Powell was now seventy-eight years old and still recuperating from a major illness the year before. Infirmity made it more difficult to summon the sustained mental energy required to translate Powell's uncertain views into law. The unusual situation with his clerks may have mattered as well. Paralyzed by divisions that all of them describe as painful, the clerks were unable to coalesce in support of the Justice's instincts. Their conflict made Powell even more keenly aware of the difficulty of the question before him and forced him to fall back on his own resources.

Another factor—one easily overlooked by those who think the Supreme Court's work entirely political—was the shaky intellectual support for Powell's intuition. Powell went to the Conference of April 2 with an argument based on *Robinson* v. *California* and its teaching that a mere status could not be made a crime. Eventually, he had to recognize that the theory did not fit the case. Under effective attack from the Chief Justice and from Mosman, this approach was abandoned. Instead, Powell turned to another Eighth Amendment theory based on the idea that criminal punishment is "cruel and unusual" whenever it is grossly disproportionate to the crime committed. On this ground the Court had forbidden execution for the crime of rape and rejected life sentences for minor crimes. The lesson of these cases was that criminal punishment was unconstitutional if grossly excessive—that is, wildly out of proportion to any wrong done.

This last point perhaps could be adapted to this situation. Even if Michael Hardwick did not have a fundamental right to engage in homosexual sodomy, he did at least have an Eighth Amendment right not to be punished excessively for having done so. The Georgia statute at least raised the possibility of extravagant severity, as it authorized imprisonment for up to twenty years. Powell was prepared to rule that a lengthy prison sentence—indeed, any prison sentence—would be grossly excessive for private sexual activity between consenting adults. Of course, on these facts imprisonment was not an issue, as Michael Hardwick had not been prosecuted, much less imprisoned. Nevertheless, this reasoning allowed Powell—at least in his own mind—to forbid criminal punishment for homosexual sodomy without getting into the more difficult issues (such as same-sex marriage and gays in the military) that he did not want to face.

Unfortunately, Powell kept this conclusion mostly to himself. His position was not well advertised by his vote in favor of the Georgia law. His concurrence said merely that imprisonment for consensual sodomy would create a serious Eighth Amendment issue, which he would not get into as it had not been raised below. The point seemed almost an aside. It did not convey the strength of Powell's commitment to the Eighth Amendment theory or suggest how far he was prepared to go. It did not reveal the gulf that separated him from Burger and White. It said nothing about the doubts and concerns that had led Powell first to vote against the Georgia sodomy statute and only later to change his mind. It gave no hint that anyone in the Court's majority was the least concerned about the "human dimensions" of laws against homosexuals.

In short, Powell failed. He failed to capture the Court and make himself decisive, as he had in *Bakke*. More fundamentally, he failed to act on his own best judgment. He took a position he only partly believed in and submerged his disagreement in an elliptical concurrence. He failed, not because he contradicted someone else's expectations of what the law should be but because he did not bring his own wisdom and reflection to bear on the problem. In one of the most crucial constitutional issues of his time on the Court, Powell's voice was muffled, his position obscure, and the essential humanity of his own reactions hidden from public view.

At bottom, Powell suffered from lack of confidence. In *Bakke*, he knew where he wanted to go and, more to the point, knew how important it was that he get there. He was prepared to hold his ground, whatever the cost. In *Bowers*, Powell's every step was beset by doubt. He was unsure of his legal theory and of the underlying social reality, uncertain how to reach his desired result, and sufficiently unsettled in his own convictions that he did not force the issue to a successful conclusion.

Emblematic of Powell's difficulty with this case, and the most puzzling element in its history, was the remark that he had never known a homosexual. He said it at least twice, once to his clerk and once at the Conference of April 2. Blackmun later told his clerks that he thought of saying, "Of course you have. You've even had gay clerks." Instead, Blackmun said, "But surely, Lewis, you were approached as a boy?" There is no record of a response.

Was Powell being honest? He had in fact employed gay clerks and had also encountered homosexuals working elsewhere in the Court, as he must have encountered them in school, in private practice, in the army, and elsewhere. Of course Powell knew homosexuals. The question was whether he acknowledged anyone he knew as a homosexual. The answer is that he did not, largely because he did not want to. In his upbringing, homosexuality was at least a failing, if not a sin. He later came to think of it as an abnormality, an affliction for which its bearers perhaps should not be blamed but which was nevertheless vaguely scandalous. He would not make assumptions. He would not infer such misfortune without direct knowledge. Powell would not have known someone was homosexual unless that person told him so. . . .

Bowers v. *Hardwick* was announced on June 30, 1986. Both White and Blackmun read at length from their opinions in open display of the bitterness within the Court. Powell said nothing, and the amelioration at which he aimed remained buried in his brief concurrence. That evening he enjoyed the distraction of a dinner at the Phillips Museum, where he sat next to Helen Hayes.

The next morning brought harsh reactions to the decision of the day before. The *Boston Globe* called it "the most preposterous and contradictory ruling to be handed down in a long time." The *New York Times* inveighed against "a gratuitous and petty ruling, an offense to American society's maturing standards of individual dignity." Various protests occurred, including one by Alan Dershowitz, who attended and then walked out of Chief Justice Burger's speech to the American Bar Association so that he could announce that Burger would be "remembered in infamy" for his part in the decision.

Powell got a small taste of the same treatment in 1989 when he was awarded an honorary degree from Yale. President Benno Schmidt praised him for helping "to fashion justice, to bring us stability, and to accommodate change. It is with pride that Yale awards you a Doctor of Laws." After these kind words at the university graduation, Powell went to the smaller law school ceremony, where he was asked by Dean Guido Calabresi to make a few impromptu remarks. Though most of the audience applauded respectfully, at least one student rose, turned his back, and remain[ed] standing throughout the speech. Powell heard puzzling boos and hisses. As one graduate later explained, "it was important that he should have to bear some cost for his decision." . . .

But the most telling reaction to *Bowers* came from Powell himself. On October 18, 1990, Powell gave the annual James Madison lecture at New York University Law School and afterward answered students' questions. One asked how Powell could reconcile his vote in *Bowers* v. *Hardwick* with his support for *Roe* v. *Wade.* "I think I probably made a mistake in that one," Powell said of *Bowers.* When a reporter called to confirm the remark, Powell repeated the recantation: "I do think it was inconsistent in a general way with *Roe.* When I had the opportunity to reread the opinions a few months later, I thought the dissent had the better of the arguments."

One man who might have been embittered by this revelation reacted graciously. "I think it's an admirable thing," said Laurence Tribe. "All of us make mistakes, and not all of us are willing to admit them." Tribe also wrote Powell a personal letter recalling his oral argument, which he thought "one of my best," and praising Powell's "courage and candor" in acknowledging error. Tribe then ventured a sly request for something in writing: "Should you be willing to reply to this letter, my wife and I would count your response among our most cherished mementos." Unfortunately for Tribe, Powell's reply was not suitable for framing. "I had forgotten that you argued *Bowers,*" Powell wrote. "I did think the case was frivolous as the Georgia statute had not been enforced since 1935. The Court should not have granted certiorari."*

This was scarcely the ringing endorsement Tribe had in mind, but it truly reflected Powell's view. As startling as his change of heart may have seemed, it was really no more than his continuing unease at choosing between sodomy as a crime and sodomy as a fundamental right. He had never come to rest on that question—not when he voted at the Conference of April 2, 1986, or when he changed his vote on April 8, or some weeks later when he decided to join Byron White. Neither was he really at rest four years later when he came to think he should have stuck by his original inclination. On this issue, Powell never found the middle ground.

---

*Anthony Lewis made the same point in a column berating the Justices for rushing "to pass judgment on a criminal law that was not pressed against Mr. Hardwick and has not been used against anyone for decades." The result of this "unnecessary" decision, Lewis argued, would be to "legitimate atavistic attitudes in our society."

14

Gay Rights:
What the Courts Should (and Shouldn't) Do

Stuart Taylor, Jr.

The controversies over homosexuals in the military and gay rights in general provide an occasion for mulling over the capacity of the courts in the current era to help lead us toward a more progressive and tolerant society.

On the positive side, there is now some hope for the emergence of a Supreme Court majority willing to vindicate the most fundamental of homosexual rights, by overturning the Court's 1986 decision in *Bowers* v. *Hardwick,* which upheld laws criminalizing private homosexual acts between consenting adults. The retirement of *Hardwick*'s author, Justice Byron White, just might pave the way for getting rid of his most benighted ruling.

But the pending legal challenges to the military's exclusion of avowed homosexuals from its ranks offer less promise. The gay rights movement, and the country, would be better off if those lawsuits (which are probably losers anyway) were mooted by the kind of political compromise that President Bill Clinton is seeking, one that would end the gay ban without cutting off democratic debate or riding roughshod over the concerns of military leaders and personnel about morale and discipline.*

The heroic era of American constitutional jurisprudence—which began with *Brown* v. *Board of Education* and which saw courts stretching their powers to the breaking point by decreeing massive, sudden, messy changes in society and its major institutions—is over. That era served the uniquely important historical purpose of breaking the back of pervasive discrimination against black people. No entrenched evil of comparable magnitude exists now to justify a bold and disruptive move like clamping a gay rights injunction on the Pentagon.

---

*This essay was published before President Clinton's final "don't ask, don't tell" policy was announced. (Eds.)

Stuart Taylor, Jr., is a Senior Writer for *The American Lawyer.* This article is reprinted with permission from the June 1993 issue of *The American Lawyer.* © 1993 *The American Lawyer.*

But the Court should not shrink from considering—or, rather, reconsidering—a fundamental question of constitutional principle like whether homosexuals can be exposed to criminal penalties for engaging in what is, for them, the most intimate of associations, and the ultimate expression of love.

"A REALM OF PERSONAL LIBERTY"

The majority got it profoundly wrong in *Hardwick*. And although prosecutions for private homosexual relations between consenting adults are exceedingly rare, laws criminalizing such activity remain on the books in almost half the states and in the Uniform Code of Military Justice. Those laws threaten and stigmatize millions of citizens at the core of their being, while providing the military and others with pretexts for discrimination.

Sodomy laws cannot be reconciled with the evolving notion of constitutionally protected liberty into which five justices breathed new life last year [1992] when they reaffirmed that the Constitution protects a woman's right to choose abortion, in *Planned Parenthood* v. *Casey*.

The pivotal joint opinion of Justices Sandra Day O'Connor, Anthony Kennedy, and David Souter embraced without reservation the doctrine that the Constitution creates "a realm of personal liberty which the government may not enter," and that "our law affords constitutional protection to personal decisions relating to marriage, procreation, contraception, family relationships, child rearing, and education."

The reasons the three justices gave for protecting such personal decisions are equally applicable to *all* intimate associations between consenting adults: "These matters, involving the most intimate and personal choices a person may make in a lifetime, choices central to personal dignity and autonomy, are central to the liberty protected by the Fourteenth Amendment."

Of course, *Casey* also rested in considerable part on the need to respect *Roe* v. *Wade* as precedent, despite the doubts of the triumvirate about whether the Constitution's protection of liberty encompassed abortion. But overruling *Hardwick* would by no means shake the foundations of the Court's legitimacy in the way that the triumvirate feared overruling *Roe* might do. No body of law has grown up around *Hardwick*, nor has any group of citizens come to rely on its status as law, nor have the states even bothered to enforce their sodomy laws.

Hardwick seems an anomaly, out of tune with the line of privacy precedents dating back to 1923. It was even closer than most 5-to-4 decisions: The original vote in conference was 5 to 4 to strike down the Georgia sodomy law. Then Justice Lewis Powell, Jr., changed his mind, giving the majority to White. But Powell was still so torn that he added a concurrence suggesting that a prison sentence for private homosexual sodomy might be cruel and unusual punishment. And since his 1987 retirement, Powell has said he "probably made a mistake" and should have struck the law down.

MORAL DISAPPROVAL IS NO JUSTIFICATION

While sodomy laws have "ancient roots," as Justice White stressed in *Hardwick,* evolving standards of decency cannot countenance punishing people for intimate human associations that do no harm to others. As Justice Harry Blackmun said in his compelling dissent, mere moral disapproval cannot "justify invading the houses, hearts, and minds of citizens who choose to live their lives differently."

Indeed, the constitutional arguments for protecting homosexuals' rights of intimate association are arguably *stronger* than those for abortion rights. Both involve liberty and privacy interests of the highest order. But in the abortion context the woman's claim collides with the state's undoubtedly substantial countervailing interest in protecting potential human life. No state interest of comparable weight undergirds the laws penalizing gay sex.

The prospect of overruling *Hardwick* anytime soon depends on at least two members of the *Casey* triumvirate demonstrating the courage of their convictions about protecting "the most intimate and personal choices." O'Connor is not the best bet; she joined White's majority opinion in *Hardwick.* (So did Chief Justice William Rehnquist, and Justices Antonin Scalia and Clarence Thomas would almost surely support it now.)

If Blackmun and John Paul Stevens, who dissented in *Hardwick* (along with retired Justice William Brennan and the late Thurgood Marshall), were joined by President Clinton's choice to fill White's seat,* the fourth and fifth votes to overrule *Hardwick* would probably have to come from Kennedy and Souter. Those two, new to the Court since *Hardwick,* must realize that their handiwork in *Casey* will be exposed to damaging doctrinal erosion unless they adhere to the generous conception of liberty that animates their joint opinion. In the long run, the rights to choose abortion and to intimate association (homosexual and otherwise) are likely to stand or fall together.

THE COURT SHOULDN'T TRY TO RUN THE ARMY

A decision protecting gay sex would greatly improve the climate for unraveling other forms of discrimination against gays. This is not to suggest, however, that the Court should do the unraveling, or should abruptly declare a constitutional right for gays to enlist in the military on an equal basis.

A Supreme Court case on the constitutionality of the military's gay ban could have only two possible outcomes, both bad. The more likely one by far would be a decision deferring to the military and upholding the gay ban's constitutionality; such a judicial imprimatur would deal a heavy blow to President Clinton's efforts to end the gay ban through the democratic process.

---

*White's seat was ultimately filled by Judge (now Justice) Ruth Bader Ginsburg. (Eds.)

Even a (highly improbable) Court decision striking down the military gay ban could prove a Pyrrhic victory. It would be widely perceived as a judicial usurpation of power. And it might well spur a massive, sustained backlash, like the ones that made a quagmire of court-ordered busing and that put supporters of abortion rights on the political defensive for so many years after *Roe*.

The Court should not try to run the army. But as Judge Ruth Bader Ginsburg of the U.S. Court of Appeals for the D.C. Circuit has said in another context: "Without taking giant strides and thereby risking a backlash too forceful to contain, the Court, through constitutional adjudication, can reinforce or signal a green light for social change."

15

Gay Rights: What the Courts *Shouldn't* Do

Letter by George M. Weaver
and a Response by Stuart Taylor, Jr.

GEORGE WEAVER'S LETTER

This letter responds to Stuart Taylor's recent article [see chapter 14] regarding Justice White's retirement and prospects for overturning *Bowers* v. *Hardwick*, which upheld criminal laws against homosexual sodomy. His article is a morass of contradictions and pseudoanalysis.

Despite its unpopularity among self-appointed opinion makers, Justice White's majority opinion in *Hardwick* is eminently correct. The due process principle upon which *Roe* v. *Wade* and *Planned Parenthood* v. *Casey* expressly depend is that government may not invade the realm of personal liberty surrounding activities and decisions related to "marriage, procreation, contraception, family relationships, child rearing, and education" because they have in our society historically and traditionally been considered beyond the proper scope of government regulation. *Roe* and its progeny clearly hold that only that set of activities and decisions are protected by this constitutional right of privacy. Justice Harry Blackmun's dissenting opinion in *Hardwick* is astonishingly dishonest because it rejects the historical component implicit in the right of privacy as he defined it in *Roe*.

Certainly, strong policy arguments can be made for decriminalizing homosexual conduct. However, the constitutional right of privacy is not an appropriate vehicle. Rather, due to the absence of constitutional mandate, decriminalization and removal of other forms of discrimination are policy decisions belonging to the political branches.

One lesson we should have learned from *Roe* is that when courts are per-

From the September 1993 issue of *The American Lawyer.* Reprinted by permission of the authors.

ceived as reaching beyond the language and intent of the Constitution they supplant and destabilize democracy. Because pro-lifers believe that *Roe,* which is not amenable to legislative or executive change, is illegitimate, they have taken their frustrations to the streets. Prior to *Roe,* when abortion policy was in the process of state-by-state legislative change, there were no such protests because the views of those opposed to abortion were heard and considered by the political branches.

It is preposterous that Mr. Taylor proposes to legalize and mandate acceptance of homosexual sodomy without regard to popular opinion as expressed through the political branches. Overturning *Hardwick* would, as explained above, be utterly without any semblance of constitutional justification. Moreover, Mr. Taylor's proposal for determining the scope of the right to privacy— i.e., those "matters, involving the most intimate and personal choices a person may make in a lifetime, choices central to personal dignity and autonomy"— would also legalize polygamy, homosexual marriage, consensual incest, necrophilia, private use and possession of many controlled substances, bestiality, prostitution, and perhaps consensual pedophilia. There is no stable or enduring analysis that would distinguish decisions and activities regarding these matters from homosexual sodomy. By contrast, change imposed by the political branches, which would of course reflect public opinion, does not require or imply successive legalization of other arguably related decisions and activities.

The most glaring contradiction of Mr. Taylor's article remains. He lipserves that the "heroic era of American constitutional jurisprudence . . . which . . . saw courts stretching their powers to the breaking point by decreeing massive, sudden messy changes in society . . . is over." But he invites the Court and Justice White's successor now to legalize without responsible constitutional basis all activities and decisions "central to personal dignity and autonomy" even though this society has historically regulated some of them. Society has its own constitutional right to conclude, based on shared values and the lessons of history, that certain activities and decisions, even though consensual and "central to personal dignity and autonomy," should be discouraged as destructive and inconsistent with social obligations.

STUART TAYLOR, JR., RESPONDS

Contrary to his letter's apparent implication, Mr. Weaver's quarrel is not only with me but with five members of the Supreme Court.

The language that Mr. Weaver quotes and identifies as "Mr. Taylor's proposal for determining the scope of the right of privacy" was not coined by me. I took it (as my [article] indicated) from the June 29, 1992, plurality opinion of Justices Sandra Day O'Connor, Anthony Kennedy, and David Souter in *Planned Parenthood* v. *Casey.* After referring to various right-to-privacy precedents, they said: "These matters, involving the most intimate and personal choices a person may make in a lifetime, choices central to personal dignity and autonomy, are central to the liberty protected by the Fourteenth Amendment." Justice Harry Blackmun and Justice John Paul Stevens, who joined Blackmun's dissent in the *Hardwick* case, also made clear in *Casey* their agreement with the plurality's opinion on this point.

I also note Judge Ruth Bader Ginsburg's emphasis, in her remarks at the time of her June 14 nomination to replace Justice Byron White, on "principled commitment to defense of individual autonomy even in the face of majority action."

Mr. Weaver's argument that the language I took from the *Casey* plurality "would also legalize polygamy, homosexual marriage, consensual incest, necrophilia," etc., though overstated, makes the legitimate point that what we have here is a slippery slope. But I am confident that the aforementioned Justices will find a stopping point somewhere this side of "consensual pedophilia."

16

Commonwealth v. *Wasson*[*]

COMMONWEALTH of Kentucky,
Appellant,
v.
Jeffrey WASSON, et al., Appellees.
Supreme Court of Kentucky.
September 24, 1992.
Rehearing Denied January 21, 1993.

Defendant was charged with soliciting deviate sexual intercourse. The Fayette Circuit Court . . . affirmed [the] district court's findings that [Kentucky's] homosexual sodomy statute was unconstitutional, and the Commonwealth appealed. On transfer from the Court of Appeals, the Supreme Court, Leibson, J., held that [the] criminal statute proscribing consensual homosexual sodomy violates privacy and equal protection guarantees of [the] Kentucky Constitution.

Affirmed. . . .

[CHARLES M.] LEIBSON, Justice.

Appellee, Jeffrey Wasson, is charged with having solicited an undercover Lexington policeman to engage in deviate sexual intercourse. KRS [Kentucky State Statute] 510.100 punishes "deviate sexual intercourse with another person of the same sex" as a criminal offense, and specifies "consent of the other person shall not be a defense." Nor does it matter that the act is private and

---

*This is an edited version that has omitted all footnotes. (Eds.)

Reprinted with permission from *South Western Reporter.* Copyright © by West Publishing Company.

involves a caring relationship rather than a commercial one. It is classified as a Class A misdemeanor.

The appellee is actually charged under KRS 506.030, which covers "solicitation" to commit *any* criminal offense. If the offense solicited is a Class A misdemeanor, solicitation of the offense is punished as a Class B misdemeanor. The issue here is whether KRS 510.100 which defines the underlying criminal offense, is constitutional.

The charges were brought in the Fayette District Court where appellee moved to dismiss the charge on grounds that a statute criminalizing deviate sexual intercourse between consenting adults of the same sex, even if the act is committed in the privacy of a home, violates the Kentucky Constitution as: (1) an invasion of a constitutionally protected right of privacy; and (2) invidious discrimination in violation of constitutionally protected rights to equal treatment.

The Fayette District Judge held the statute violated appellee's right of privacy, and dismissed the charge. The Commonwealth appealed to Fayette Circuit Court which affirmed, and further held this statute infringed upon equal protection guarantees found in the Kentucky Constitution. Once more the Commonwealth appealed, and, because of the constitutional issues involved, this Court granted transfer.

Both courts below decided the issues solely on state constitutional law grounds, and our decision today, affirming the judgments of the lower courts, is likewise so limited. Federal constitutional protection under the Equal Protection Clause was not an issue reached in the lower courts and we need not address it. *Bowers* v. *Hardwick* (1986) held federal constitutional protection of the right of privacy was not implicated in laws penalizing homosexual sodomy. We discuss *Bowers* in particular, and federal cases in general, not in the process of construing the United States Constitution or federal law, but only where their reasoning is relevant to discussing questions of state law. . . .

The brief statement of facts upon which the District Court rendered judgment is as follows:

Lexington police were conducting a downtown undercover operation. Their modus operandi was to drive to a certain parking area, in plain clothes with microphones on their persons, and try to engage in conversation with persons passing by to see whether they would be solicited for sexual contact. The taped conversation between the undercover officer and Wasson covered approximately 20–25 minutes, toward the end of which Wasson invited the officer to "come home" to his residence. The officer then prodded Wasson for details, and Wasson suggested sexual activities which violated KRS 510.100. There was no suggestion that sexual activity would occur anyplace other than in the privacy of Wasson's home. The sexual activity was intended to have been between consenting adults. No money was offered or solicited.

Seven expert witnesses testified in support of Wasson's case: (1) a cultural anthropologist testified about the presence of homosexuals in every recorded human culture, including societies where they were rejected and those where they have been tolerated or even welcomed; (2) a Presbyterian minister discussed biblical references, providing a modern interpretation that these references were not an indictment of homosexuals as such, but rather statements against aggression, inhospitality, and uncaring relationships; (3) a social historian testified about the presence of homosexuals throughout the history of the United States, despite what was at times exceptionally strict punishment for homosexual acts; (4) a sociologist and sex researcher (a co-author of the Kinsey Report on homosexual behavior) testified that studies indicated "'homosexuality' is just as deep-rooted as 'heterosexuality,' " that it is not a choice and there is no "cure" for it, and that sexual acts prohibited to homosexuals by KRS 510.100, oral and anal sex, are practiced widely by heterosexuals; (5) a psychologist testified that homosexuality is no longer classified as a personality disorder by either the American Psychological Association or the American Psychiatric Association, and further, rather than being in and of themselves either harmful or pathological, the sexual acts outlawed by KRS 510.100 are a necessary adjunct to their sex life; (6) a therapist from a comprehensive care treatment center in Lexington, with fourteen years' experience counseling homosexual clients, testified that the statute criminalizing their sexual activities has an adverse impact on homosexuals and interferes with efforts to provide therapy to those who may need it; and (7) the Professor of Medicine at the University of Louisville, Chief of the Infectious Diseases section, testified at length about the origins and spread of AIDS, expressing the opinion that the statute in question offers no benefit in preventing the spread of the disease and can be a barrier to getting accurate medical histories, thus having an adverse effect on public health efforts.

The testimony from Wasson's expert witnesses is further substantiated by extensive citations to medical and social science literature and treatises supplied in Amicus Curiae Briefs filed by national and state associations of psychologists and clinical social workers, various national and state public health associations, and organizations covering a broad spectrum of religious denominations.

The Commonwealth, on the other hand, presented no witnesses and offers no scientific evidence or social science data. Succinctly stated, its position is that the majority, speaking through the General Assembly, has the right to criminalize sexual activity it deems immoral, without regard to whether the activity is conducted in private between consenting adults and is not, in and of itself, harmful to the participants or to others; that, if not in all instances, at least where there is a biblical and historical tradition supporting it, there are no limitations in the Kentucky Constitution on the power of the General Assembly to criminalize sexual activity these elected representatives deem immoral.

The Commonwealth maintains that the United States Supreme Court's decision in *Bowers* v. *Hardwick* is dispositive of the right to privacy issue; that the "Kentucky Constitution did not intend to confer any greater right to privacy than was afforded by the U.S. Constitution." Turning to the equal protection argument raised by a statute which criminalizes oral or anal intercourse between persons of the same sex, but not between persons of different sexes, which was not addressed in the *Bowers* case, the Commonwealth argues there is "a rational basis for making such a distinction." To support this argument the Commonwealth takes bits and pieces from the testimony of Wasson's expert witnesses out of context and disregards their overwhelming evidence to the contrary. The thrust of the argument advanced by the Commonwealth as a rational basis for criminalizing consensual intercourse between persons of the same sex, when the same acts between persons of the opposite sex are not punished, is that the level of moral indignation felt by the majority of society against the sexual preference of homosexuals justifies having their legislative representatives criminalize these sexual activities. The Commonwealth believes that homosexual intercourse is immoral, and that what is beyond the pale of majoritarian morality is beyond the limits of constitutional protection. . . .

The grounds stated by the District Court for striking down the statute as unconstitutional are:

> KRS 510.100 clearly seeks to regulate the most profoundly private conduct and in so doing impermissibly invades the privacy of the citizens of this state. Having so found, the Court need not address the other issues raised by the parties.

The Order expressing the judgment of the Fayette Circuit Court "agree[d] with that conclusion," and further held the statute "unjustifiably discriminates, and thus is unconstitutional under Section 2 and 3 of our Kentucky Constitution." These Sections are:

> §2. Absolute and arbitrary power over the lives, liberty and property of freemen exists nowhere in a republic, not even in the largest majority.
> §3. All men, when they form a social compact, are equal. . . .

These Sections, together with Sections 59 and 60 of our Kentucky Constitution which prohibit "local or special" legislation, express the guarantee of equal treatment provided by the law in our Kentucky Constitution. The lower courts' judgments limit their finding of unconstitutionality to *state* constitutional grounds. *Bowers* v. *Hardwick* speaks neither to rights of privacy under the state constitution nor to equal protection rights under either federal or state constitutions. *Bowers* addressed the constitutionality of a Georgia statute prohibiting acts of consensual sodomy between persons of the same sex *or* the opposite sex. Because the Georgia statute embraced both heterosexual and homosexual conduct, the *Bowers* opinion did not involve the Equal Protection Clause of the Fourteenth Amendment.

For reasons that follow, we hold the guarantees of individual liberty provided in our 1891 Kentucky Constitution offer greater protection of the right of privacy than provided by the Federal Constitution as interpreted by the United States Supreme Court, and that the statute in question is a violation of such rights; and further, we hold that the statute in question violates rights of equal protection as guaranteed by our Kentucky Constitution.

I. RIGHTS OF PRIVACY

No language specifying "rights of privacy," *as such,* appears in either the Federal or State Constitution. The Commonwealth recognizes such rights exist, but takes the position that, since they are implicit rather than explicit, our Court should march in lock step with the United States Supreme Court in declaring when such rights exist. Such is not the formulation of federalism. On the contrary, under our system of dual sovereignty, it is our responsibility to interpret and apply our state constitution independently. We are not bound by decisions of the United States Supreme Court when deciding whether a state statute impermissibly infringes upon individual rights guaranteed in the State Constitution so long as state constitutional protection does not fall below the federal *floor,* meaning the minimum guarantee of individual rights under the United States Constitution as interpreted by the United States Supreme Court. *Oregon* v. *Hass* (1975). The holding in *Oregon* v. *Hass* is:

> [A] State is free *as a matter of its own law* to impose greater restrictions on police activity than those this [United States Supreme] Court holds to be necessary upon federal constitutional standards. (Emphasis in original)

Contrary to popular belief, the Bill of Rights in the United States Constitution represents neither the primary source nor the maximum guarantee of state constitutional liberty. Our own constitutional guarantees against the intrusive power of the state do not derive from the Federal Constitution. The adoption of the Federal Constitution in 1791 was preceded by state constitutions developed over the preceding fifteen years, and, while there is, of course, overlap between state and federal constitutional guarantees of individual rights, they are by no means identical. State constitutional law documents and the writings on liberty were more the source of federal law than the child of federal law. . . .

. . . Thus while we respect the decisions of the United States Supreme Court on protection of individual liberty, and on occasion we have deferred to its reasoning, certainly we are not bound to do so, and we should not do so when valid reasons lead to a different conclusion.

We are persuaded that we should not do so here for several significant reasons. First, there are both textual and structural differences between the United States Bill of Rights and our own, which suggest a different conclusion from that reached by the United States Supreme Court is more appropriate. More significantly, Kentucky has a rich and compelling tradition of recognizing and protecting individual rights from state intrusion in cases similar in nature, found in the Debates of the Kentucky Constitutional Convention of 1890 and cases from the same era when that Constitution was adopted. The judges recognizing that tradition in their opinions wrote with a direct, firsthand knowledge of the mind set of the constitutional fathers, upholding the right of privacy against the intrusive police power of the state. . . .

Kentucky cases recognized a legally protected right of privacy based on our own constitution and common law tradition long before the United States Supreme Court first took notice of whether there were any rights of privacy inherent in the Federal Bill of Rights. . . .

The list of individual rights guaranteed by the Federal Bill of Rights is patently incomplete; ergo the Ninth Amendment stating:

> The enumeration in the Constitution, of certain rights, shall not be construed to deny or disparage others retained by the people.

Federal constitutional analysis has proceeded from so-called emanations and penumbras of the First, Third, Fourth, and Fifth Amendments in the Bill of Rights. These amendments elaborate *some* of the "blessings of liberty" referred to in the Preamble to the United States Constitution, but by no means all of them. It is because the United States Supreme Court has recognized that the list is not exclusive, not even for purposes of federal constitutional protection, that it has undertaken, using the Due Process Clauses in the Fifth and Fourteenth Amendments, to create a so-called zone of privacy constitutionally beyond the reach of governmental intrusion. But the United States Supreme Court is extremely reticent in extending the reach of the Due Process Clauses in substantive matters, albeit this is the jurisprudence of this century and not before, following President Franklin D. Roosevelt's court-packing efforts in the 1930s.

Bowers v. *Hardwick* expresses this reticence. The United States Supreme Court, defining the reach of the zone of privacy in terms of federal due process analysis, limits rights of privacy to "liberties that are 'deeply rooted in this Nation's history and tradition.' " Sodomy is not one of them. *Bowers* v. *Hardwick* decides that rights protected by the Due Process Clauses in the Fifth and Fourteenth Amendments to the United States Constitution do not "extend a fundamental right to homosexuals to engage in acts of consensual sodomy."

Bowers decides nothing beyond this. But state constitutional jurisprudence in this area is not limited by the constraints inherent in federal due process analysis. Deviate sexual intercourse conducted in private by consenting adults is not beyond the protections of the guarantees of individual liberty in our Kentucky Constitution simply because "proscriptions against that conduct have ancient roots." Kentucky constitutional guarantees against government intrusion address substantive rights. The only reference to individual liberties in the Federal Constitution is to "secure the Blessings of Liberty to ourselves and our Posterity." Similarly, the Kentucky Constitution has a preamble:

> We, the people of the Commonwealth of Kentucky, grateful to Almighty God for
> the civil, political, and religious liberties we enjoy, and invoking the continuance
> of these blessings, do ordain and establish this Constitution.

But the Kentucky Constitution of 1891 does not limit the broadly stated guarantee of individual liberty to a statement in the Preamble. It amplifies the meaning of this statement of gratitude and purpose with a Bill of Rights in 26 sections, the first of which states:

> § 1. All men are, by nature, free and equal, and have certain inherent and
> inalienable rights, among which may be reckoned:
> First: The right of enjoying and defending their lives and liberties.
> . . . .
> Third: The right of seeking and pursuing their safety and happiness.
> . . . .
> § 2. Absolute and arbitrary power over the lives, liberty and property of
> freemen exists nowhere in a republic, not even in the largest majority.

While addressing *some* of the same considerations as those expressed in the Preamble to the Federal Constitution, none of this textual material appears in the Federal Constitution. . . .

The leading case on this subject is *Commonwealth* v. *Campbell.* At issue was an ordinance that criminalized possession of intoxicating liquor, even for "private use." Our Court held that the Bill of Rights in the 1891 Constitution prohibited state action thus intruding upon the "inalienable rights possessed by the citizens" of Kentucky.

Our Court interpreted the Kentucky Bill of Rights as defining a right of privacy, even though the constitution did not say so in that terminology:

> Man in his natural state has the right to do whatever he chooses and has the power
> to do. When he becomes a member of organized society, under governmental regulation, he surrenders, of necessity, all of his natural right the exercise of which
> is, or may be, injurious to his fellow citizens. This is the price that he pays for
> governmental protection, but it is not within the competency of a free government
> to invade the sanctity of the absolute rights of the citizen any further than the
> direct protection of society requires. . . . It is *not within the competency of government to invade the privacy of a citizen's life and to regulate his conduct in matters in which he alone is concerned,* or to prohibit him any liberty the exercise
> of which will not directly injure society. [Emphasis added by the Court]
> . . . .
> . . . let a man therefore be ever so abandoned in his principles, or vicious in his
> practice, provided he keeps his wickedness to himself, and does not offend
> against the rules of public decency, he is out of the reach of human laws.

The Court concludes,

The theory of our government is to allow the largest liberty to the individual commensurate with the public safety, or, as it has been otherwise expressed, that government is best which governs least. Under our institutions there is no room for that inquisitorial and protective spirit which seeks to regulate the conduct of men in matters in themselves indifferent, and to make them conform to a standard, not of their own choosing, but the choosing of the lawgiver. . . .

The right of privacy has been recognized as an integral part of the guarantee of liberty in our 1891 Kentucky Constitution since its inception. The *Campbell* case is overwhelming affirmation of this proposition:

[W]e are of the opinion that it never has been within the competency of the Legislature to so restrict the liberty of this citizen, and certainly not since the adoption of the present [1891] Constitution. The Bill of Rights, which declares that among the inalienable rights possessed by the citizens is that of seeking and pursuing their safety and happiness, and that the absolute and arbitrary power over the lives, liberty, and property of freeman exists nowhere in a republic, not even in the largest majority, would be but an empty sound if the Legislature could prohibit the citizen the right of owning or drinking liquor, when in so doing he did not offend the laws of decency by being intoxicated in public. . . .

At the time *Campbell* was decided, the use of alcohol was as much an incendiary moral issue as deviate sexual behavior in private between consenting adults is today. Prohibition was the great moral issue of its time. . . .

Notwithstanding their strong views that drinking was immoral, this same Court . . . in the *Campbell* case recognized that private possession and consumption of intoxicating liquor was a liberty interest beyond the reach of the state.

Nor is the *Campbell* case an aberration. Subsequent cases cited and followed *Campbell*. . . .

The clear implication is that immorality in private which does "not operate to the detriment of others," is placed beyond the reach of state action by the guarantees of liberty in the Kentucky Constitution. . . .

In the area of civil law, Kentucky has been in the forefront in recognizing the right of privacy. . . .

In the *Campbell* case our Court quoted at length from the "great work" *On Liberty* of the nineteenth-century English philosopher and economist John Stuart Mill. We repeat the quote in part:

The only part of the conduct of anyone, for which he is amenable to society, is that which concerns others. In the part which merely concerns himself, his independence is, of right, absolute. . . . The principle requires liberty of taste and pursuits; of framing the plan of our life to suit our own character; of doing as we like, subject to such consequences as may follow; without impediment from our fellow creatures, so long as what we do does not harm them, even though they should think our conduct foolish, perverse, or wrong.

Mill's premise is that "physical force in the form of legal penalties," i.e., criminals sanctions, should not be used as a means to improve the citizen. The majority has no moral right to dictate how everyone else should live. Public indignation, while given due weight, should be subject to the overriding test of rational and critical analysis, drawing the line at harmful consequences to others. Modern legal philosophers who follow Mill temper this test with an enlightened paternalism, permitting the law to intervene to stop self-inflicted harm such as the result of drug taking, or failure to use seat belts or crash helmets, not to enforce majoritarian or conventional morality, but because the victim of such self-inflicted harm becomes a burden on society.

Based on the *Campbell* opinion, and on the Comments of the 1891 Convention Delegates, there is little doubt but that the views of John Stuart Mill, which were then held in high esteem, provided the philosophical underpinnings for the reworking and broadening of protection of individual rights that occurs throughout the 1891 Constitution.

We have recognized protection of individual rights greater than the federal floor in a number of cases. . . .

We view the United States Supreme Court decision in *Bowers* v. *Hardwick* as as a misdirected application of the theory of original intent. To illustrate: as a theory of majoritarian morality, miscegenation was an offense with ancient roots. It is highly unlikely that protecting the rights of persons of different races to copulate was one of the considerations behind the Fourteenth Amendment. Nevertheless in *Loving* v. *Virginia* (1967), the United States Supreme Court recognized that a contemporary, enlightened interpretation of a liberty interest involved in the sexual act made its punishment constitutionally impermissible.

According to *Bowers* v. *Hardwick,* "until 1961, all fifty States outlawed sodomy and today, twenty-five States and District of Columbia continue to provide criminal penalties for sodomy performed in private and between consenting adults." In the space of three decades half the states decriminalized this conduct. . . .

Two states by court decisions hold homosexual sodomy statutes of this nature unconstitutional for reasons similar to those stated here. . . .

The *Bonadio** case from Pennsylvania is particularly noteworthy because of the common heritage shared by the Kentucky Bill of Rights of 1792 and the Pennsylvania Bill of Rights of 1790. Decisions of the Pennsylvania Supreme Court interpreting like clauses in the Pennsylvania Constitution are uniquely persuasive in interpreting our own. It is a singular coincidence that in 1980 the Pennsylvania Supreme Court reached to the same roots in interpreting its Constitution as our Court did in the *Campbell* case, quoting at length from the "great philosopher, John Stuart Mill, in his imminent and apposite work, *On Liberty* (1859)," and utilizing the *same* quotes. The Pennsylvania Court also provides this guidance:

Commonwealth v. *Bonadio* (1980). (Eds.)

With respect to regulation of morals, the policy power should properly be exercised to protect each individual's right to be free from interference in defining and pursuing his own morality but not to enforce a majority morality on persons whose conduct *does not harm others.* "No harm to the secular interest of the community is involved in atypical sex practice in private between consenting adult partners." [Quoting the Model Penal Code]

Many issues that are considered to be matters of morals are subject to debate, and no significant state interest justifies legislation of norms simply because a particular belief is followed by a number of people, or even a majority. . . . Enactment of the voluntary deviate sexual intercourse statute, despite that it provides punishment for what many believe to be abhorrent crimes against nature and perceived sins against God, is not proper in the realm of the temporal police power. . . .

II. EQUAL PROTECTION

As stated earlier, in *Bowers* v. *Hardwick* the Equal Protection Clause was not implicated because the Georgia statute criminalized both heterosexual and homosexual sodomy. Unlike the Due Process Clause analysis provided in *Bowers* v. *Hardwick,* equal protection analysis does *not* turn on whether the law (KRS 510.100) transgresses "liberties that are 'deeply rooted in this Nation's history and tradition.' "

In *Watkins* v. *U.S. Army* (9th Cir. 1989), involving the constitutionality of an Army regulation which made homosexuality a nonwaivable disqualification for reenlistment, Judge Norris, concurring in the judgment, explained the difference between Due Process Clause analysis and Equal Protection Clause analysis as follows:

The due process clause, as the Court recognized in *Hardwick,* protects practices which are "deeply rooted in this Nation's history and tradition." The Equal Protection Clause, in contrast, protects minorities from discriminatory treatment at the hands of the majority. Its purpose is not to protect traditional values and practices, but to *call into question* such values and practices when they operate to burden disadvantaged minorities. . . .

The Equal Protection Clause, by contrast protect[s] disadvantaged groups from discriminatory practices, however deeply ingrained and long-standing. (Emphasis in original)

Further explaining:

It is perfectly consistent to say that homosexual sodomy is not a practice so deeply rooted in our traditions as to merit due process protection, and at the same time to say, for example, that because homosexuals have historically been subject to invidious discrimination, laws which burden homosexuals as a class should be subjected to heightened scrutiny under the equal protection clause. Indeed, the two propositions may be complementary: In all probability, homosexuality is not considered a deeply rooted part of our traditions *precisely because* homosexuals have been subjected to invidious discrimination. In any case, homosexuals do not become "fair game" for discrimination simply because their sexual practices are not considered part of our mainstream traditions. (Emphasis in original)

. . . .

This principle of equal treatment, when imposed against majoritarian rule arises from the Constitution itself, not from judicial fiat. Moreover, equal protection doctrine does not prevent the majority from enacting laws based on its substantive value choices. Equal protection simply requires that the majority apply its values evenhandedly.

Certainly, the practice of deviate sexual intercourse violates traditional morality. But so does the same act between heterosexuals, which activity is decriminalized. Going one step further, *all* sexual activity between consenting adults outside of marriage violates our traditional morality. The issue here is not whether sexual activity traditionally viewed as immoral can be punished by society, but whether it can be punished solely on the basis of sexual preference.

The Commonwealth's argument against permitting sexual behavior preferred by homosexuals the protection of the Equal Protection Clause has centered solely on denying homosexuals status as a protected class, claiming society has a right to discriminate so long as such discrimination is not race related or gender related and this law punishes the act and not the preference of the actor. In *American Constitutional Law,* 2d ed., 1988, Laurence H. Tribe [Mineola, N.Y.: Foundation Press], p. 1616, the author answers the Commonwealth's claims:

Not only is the characteristic of homosexuality or heterosexuality central to the personal identities of those singled out by laws based on sexual orientation, but homosexuals in particular seem to satisfy all of the Court's implicit criteria of suspectness. As subjects of age-old discrimination and disapproval, homosexuals form virtually a discrete and insular minority. Their sexual orientation is in all likelihood "a characteristic determined by causes not within [their] control. . . ."

Professor Tribe's view is fully supported, not only by his own documentation, but by the testimony of record in this case and by the medical, scientific, and social science data provided in the briefs filed herein by Amici Curiae. The truth is, one's sexual partner is chosen usually, if not exclusively, based on sexual orientation. We cannot deny the evidence before us in analyzing how our state constitution should apply.

We do not speculate on how the United States Supreme Court as presently constituted will decide whether the sexual preference of homosexuals is entitled to protection under the Equal Protection Clause of the Federal constitution. We need not speculate as to whether male and/or female homosexuals will be allowed status as a protected class if and when the United States Supreme Court confronts this issue. They are a separate and identifiable class for Kentucky constitutional law analysis because no class of persons can be discriminated against under the Kentucky Constitution. All are entitled to equal treatment, unless there is a substantial governmental interest, a rational basis, for different treatment. The statute before us is in violation of Kentucky constitutional protection in Section Three that "all men (persons), when they form a social compact, are equal," and in Section Two that "absolute and arbitrary power over the lives, liberty, and property of free men (persons) exists nowhere in a republic, not even in the largest majority." We have concluded that it is "arbitrary" for the majority to criminalize sexual activity solely on the basis of majoritarian sexual preference, and that it denied "equal" treatment under the law when there is no rational basis, as this term is used and applied in our Kentucky cases. . . .

The Commonwealth has tried hard to demonstrate a legitimate governmental interest justifying a distinction [between the treatment of homosexual acts and heterosexual acts], but has failed. Many of the claimed justifications are simply outrageous: that "homosexuals are more promiscuous than heterosexuals, . . . that homosexuals enjoy the company of children, and that homosexuals are more prone to engage in sex acts in public." The only proffered justification with superficial validity is that "infectious diseases are more readily transmitted by anal sodomy than by other forms of sexual copulation." But this statute is not limited to anal copulation, and this reasoning would apply to male-female anal intercourse the same as it applies to male-male intercourse. The growing number of females to whom AIDS (Acquired Immune Deficiency Syndrome) has been transmitted is stark evidence that AIDS is not only a male homosexual disease. The only medical evidence in the record before us rules out any distinction between male-male and male-female anal intercourse as a method of preventing AIDS. The act of sexual contact is not implicated, per se, whether the contact is homosexual or heterosexual. In any event, this statute was enacted in 1974 before the AIDS nightmare was upon us. It was 1982 or 1983 before AIDS was a recognized diagnostic entity.

In the final analysis we can attribute no legislative purpose to this statute except to single out homosexuals for different treatment for indulging their sexual preference by engaging in the same activity heterosexuals are now at liberty to perform. By 1974 there had already been a sea change in societal values insofar as attaching criminal penalties to extramarital sex. The question is whether a society that no longer criminalizes adultery, fornication, or deviate sexual intercourse between heterosexuals, has a rational basis to single out homosexual acts for different treatment. Is there a rational basis for declaring this one type of sexual immorality so destructive of family values as to merit criminal punishment whereas other acts of sexual immorality which were likewise forbidden by the same religious and traditional heritage of Western civilization are now decriminalized? If there is a rational basis for different treatment it has yet to be demonstrated in this case. We need not sympathize, agree with, or even understand the sexual preference of homosexuals in order to recognize their right to equal treatment before the bar of criminal justice.

To be treated equally by the law is a broader constitutional value than due process of law as discussed in the *Bowers* case. We recognize it as such under the Kentucky Constitution, without regard to whether the United States Supreme Court continues to do so in federal constitutional jurisprudence. "Equal Justice Under Law," inscribed above the entrance to the United States Supreme Court, expresses the unique goal to which all humanity aspires. In Kentucky it is more than a mere aspiration. It is part of the "inherent and inalienable" rights protected by our Kentucky Constitution. Our protection against exercise of "arbitrary power over the . . . liberty . . . of freemen" by the General Assembly . . . and our guarantee that all persons are entitled to. "equal" treatment . . . forbid a special act punishing the sexual preference of homosexuals. It matters not that the same act committed by persons of the same sex is more offensive to the majority. . . ."

The purpose of the present statute is not to protect the marital relationship against sexual activity outside of marriage, but only to punish one aspect of it while other activities similarly destructive of the marital relationship, if not more so, go unpunished. Sexual preference, and not the act committed, determines criminality, and is being punished. Simply because the majority, speaking through the General Assembly, finds one type of extramarital intercourse more offensive than another, does not provide a rational basis for criminalizing the sexual preference of homosexuals.

For the reasons stated, we affirm the decision of the Fayette Circuit Court, and the judgment on appeal from the Fayette District Court.

LAMBERT, Justice, dissenting.

The issue here is not whether private homosexual conduct should be allowed or prohibited. The only question properly before this Court is whether the Constitution of Kentucky denies the legislative branch a right to prohibit such conduct. Nothing in the majority opinion demonstrates such a limitation on legislative prerogative.

To justify its view that private homosexual conduct is protected by the Constitution of Kentucky, the majority has found it necessary to disregard virtually all of recorded history, the teachings of the religions most influential on Western Civilization, the debates of the delegates to the Constitutional Convention, and the text of the Constitution itself. Rather than amounting to a decision based upon precedent as is suggested, this decision reflects the value judgment of the majority and its view that public law has no right to prohibit the conduct at issue here.

The majority concedes that "proscriptions against that conduct [sodomy] have ancient roots." It fails, however, to describe the depth of such roots as was done in *Bowers* v. *Hardwick*:

> Sodomy was a criminal offense at common law which was forbidden by the laws of the original thirteen States when they ratified the Bill of Rights.

In his concurring opinion in *Bowers,* Chief Justice Burger elaborated upon the historical condemnation of sodomy as follows:

> Decisions of individuals relating to homosexual conduct have been subject to state intervention throughout the history of Western civilization. Condemnation of those practices is firmly rooted in Judeao-Christian moral and ethical standards. Homosexual sodomy was a capital crime under Roman law. During the English Reformation, when powers of the ecclesiastical courts were transferred to the King's Courts, the first English statute criminalizing sodomy was passed. Blackstone described "the infamous crime against nature" as an offense of "deeper malignity" than rape, a heinous act "the very mention of which is a disgrace to human nature" and "a crime not fit to be named." . . . To hold that the act of homosexual sodomy is somehow protected as a fundamental right would be to cast aside millennia of moral teaching.

The history and traditions of this Commonwealth are fully in accord with the biblical, historical, and common law view. Since at least 1860, sodomy has been a criminal offense in Kentucky and this fact was well known to the delegates at the time of the 1890 Constitutional Convention.

Embracing "state constitutionalism," a practice in vogue among many state courts as a means of rejecting the leadership of the Supreme Court of the United States, the majority has declared its independence from even the influence of this nation's highest court. The majority cannot, however, escape the logic and scholarship of *Bowers* which reached the conclusion that nothing in the Due Process Clause of the United States Constitution prevented a state from punishing sodomy as a crime. While I do not advocate the view that state courts should march in lock step with the Supreme Court of the United States, on those occasions when state courts depart from that Court's reasoned interpretations, it should be for compelling reasons, usually text or tradition, and only in clearly distinguishable circumstances, none of which is present here.

. . . *[T]he debates of the Kentucky Constitutional Convention of 1890 contain no mention of a right of privacy or a right to engage in homosexual sodomy.* . . . [T]he debates contain only the most limited and inexplicit reference to any concept which could be translated into privacy.

Perhaps the greatest mischief to be found in the majority opinion is in its discovery of a constitutional right which lacks any textual support. . . . None of the sections cited or quoted contain an inkling of reference to rights of privacy or sexual freedom of any kind. *This is conceded by the majority as follows: "No language specifying 'rights of privacy,' as such, appears in either the Federal or State Constitution."* The majority opinion is a departure from the accepted methodology of constitutional analysis which requires that text be the beginning point. The majority reasons that differences between the text of the Kentucky Constitution and the United States Constitution free this Court from federal influence, but it fails to explain its discovery of the rights announced here in the absence of any textual basis. This is a dangerous practice. When judges free themselves of constitutional text, their values and notions of morality are given free rein and they, not the Constitution, become the supreme law. Justice White cautioned against this practice in *Bowers* v. *Hardwick* as follows:

> The Court is most vulnerable and comes nearest to illegitimacy when it deals with judge-made constitutional law having little or no cognizable roots in the language or design of the Constitution.

As has been demonstrated, a right of privacy protecting homosexual sodomy between or among consenting adults has no basis in the history and traditions of Western culture or in this nation or state. Likewise, the constitutional debates contain only the most oblique references to any right of privacy and Kentucky constitutional text is totally silent. As such, the majority must and does rest its entire case on a line of decisions rendered by this Court in the early twentieth century in which a right of privacy was held to exist with respect to the consumption of alcoholic beverages. . . . The leading decision of this genre is *Commonwealth* v. *Campbell,* in which a statute which criminalized the possession of intoxicating liquor for private use was held unconstitutional and which, with rhetorical flourish declared the broadest possible right of privacy.

As the majority relies entirely on the doctrine of *stare decisis,** brief comment on its use in the context of constitutional interpretation is appropriate. When courts construe statutes or principles of common law, error in such construction is subject to correction by the people through their elected representatives. With constitutional interpretation, however, such correction is not possible. As only the highest court of a jurisdiction possesses power to say finally what the constitution means (save the right of the people to amend it), courts have a duty to continually reexamine their prior constitutional interpretations to prevent perpetuation of error. Thus, the doctrine of *stare decisis* lacks the vigor in the arena of constitutional law that it possesses in other fields. A well known exponent of this view was Justice Brandeis, who said:

> The Court bows to the lessons of experience and the force of better reasoning, recognizing that the process of trial and error, so fruitful in the physical sciences, is appropriate also in the judicial function.

The fact that this Court broadly declared a right of privacy prior to World War I in cases which one suspects were influenced by local economic forces does not mean that such a doctrine should be applied in the extreme nearly a century later to a moral question not remotely considered by the *Campbell* court.

The major premise in the majority opinion is that the Constitution forbids any legal restriction upon the private conduct of adults unless it can be shown that such conduct is harmful to another. This view represents the essence of the

---

*A Latin term meaning to abide by, or adhere to, decided cases. (Eds.)

philosophy of John Stuart Mill in his essay *On Liberty.* While espousing such a view, however, Mill recognized the difficulty of distinguishing that part of a person's life which affected only himself from that which affected others. He recognized that one who by deleterious vices harmed himself indirectly harmed others and that society suffered indirect harm by the mere knowledge of immoral conduct. Nevertheless, Mill clung to his philosophy by insisting that society was without power to punish gambling or drunkenness. He made a ringing defense of the right of persons so disposed to practice polygamy.

While the philosophy of John Stuart Mill as adopted by this Court in *Campbell* v. *Commonwealth* exalts individuality in the extreme, it has, nevertheless, a superficial appeal. It rejects majoritarian morality as a basis for law and imposes legal limits on the conduct of man only insofar as it may harm others. Unfortunately for the purposes of the majority, the philosophy of Mill and the views contained in the *Campbell* case, if logically applied, would necessarily result in the eradication of numerous other criminal statutes. For example, if majoritarian morality is without a role in the formulation of criminal law and the only standard is harm to another, all laws proscribing the possession and use of dangerous or narcotic drugs would fall. Likewise, incest statutes which proscribe sexual intercourse between persons of close kinship regardless of age or consent would be rendered invalid. Laws prohibiting cruelty to animals, the abuse of dead human bodies, suicide, and polygamy would be held unconstitutional. Despite the majority's disingenuous departure from Mill based on "an enlightened paternalism" to prevent self-inflicted harm, many prevailing criminal statutes would nevertheless fail the "harm to another" test. While the majority of this Court manifestly sees the proposition otherwise, the Supreme Court of the United States has addressed the role of morality as a rationale to support criminal law and found no impediment.

> The law, however, is constantly based on notions of morality, and if all laws representing essentially moral choices are to be invalidated under the Due Process Clause, the courts will be very busy indeed. *Bowers* v. *Hardwick* .

The majority has characterized Kentucky's highest Court of the early twentieth century as being "in the forefront in recognizing the right of privacy." . . . It has created an impression that this Court of that era was filled with enlightened jurists who sought to elevate mankind. Unfortunately, there is a darker side to this Court's past as evidenced by a decision rendered just three years prior to the *Campbell* case. In *Berea College* v. *Commonwealth* (1906), Judge O'Rear, writing for this Court, enthusiastically upheld the constitutionality of a statute which prohibited "white and colored persons from attending the same school." The Court said:

> The natural separation of the races is therefore an undeniable fact, and all social organizations which lead to their amalgamation are repugnant to the law of

> nature. From social amalgamation it is but a step to illicit intercourse, and but another to intermarriage. . . . When, therefore, we declare a right to maintain separate relations, so far as is reasonably practicable, but in a spirit of kindness and charity, and with due regard to equality of rights, it is not prejudice, nor caste, nor injustice of any kind, but simply to suffer men to follow the law of races established by the Creator himself and not to compel them to intermix contrary to their instincts.

A cursory reading of *Berea College* v. *Commonwealth* will convincingly dispel any notion of social enlightenment on the part of this Court's justices during the first decade of the twentieth century. . . .

This dissenting opinion, as it relates to a "right of privacy" under the Constitution of Kentucky, could be concluded without further elaboration. As heretofore demonstrated, neither the text nor the Constitutional Debates nor the history and traditions of this Commonwealth provide any basis for concluding that there is a right of privacy so broadly defined as to protect homosexual conduct. Nevertheless, the majority has discovered such a right in this Court's prior decisions. An examination of the cases upon which it relies reveals that . . . [i]n each case, the conduct or interest protected on privacy grounds was deeply entrenched in this Commonwealth's history and traditions. I do not regard these decisions as aberrational, but merely overstated. It was hardly necessary to call upon the writings of John Stuart Mill to justify protection of the right of Kentuckians to drink liquor. . . .

From my study . . . I have concluded that the privacy right found in the Constitution of Kentucky does not apply to claimed rights not remotely envisioned by the delegates to the Constitutional Convention or reasonably emerging from our history and traditions. As such, the right to determine whether sodomy should be a criminal offense belongs to the people through their elected representatives. We should not deprive the people of that right. As the majority has observed, many states have already decriminalized consensual sodomy. Appellee should take his case to the Kentucky General Assembly and let that branch of government say whether the crime shall remain or be abolished.

To resolve the equal protection issue, one must first review the statute, KRS 510.100. This Act is not limited in its application to persons who consider themselves homosexual nor is it limited to the male or female gender. Any person who engages in deviate sexual intercourse with another person of the same sex is in violation. The statute prohibits conduct and says nothing of the sexual preference or gender of the violator. The United States Court of Appeals for the Fifth Circuit found this dispositive in upholding a Texas anti-sodomy statute.

> The statute is directed at certain conduct, not at a class of people. Though the conduct be the desire of the bisexually and homosexually inclined, there is no necessity that they engage in it. The statute affects only those who choose to act in the manner proscribed. *Baker* v. *Wade* (1986).

There is nothing in the statute by which persons are classified and certainly nothing which accords unequal treatment to persons comprising a recognizable class on factors such as race, gender, or ethnic origin.

The heart of the majority contention is that unequal treatment results when the same conduct is deemed criminal if committed by persons of the same sex, but not if the actors are of different sexes. It correctly observes that in former times all sexual contact between unmarried persons was viewed as immoral. From this the majority concludes the statute must be invalidated.

In *Plyler* v. *Doe* (1982), the Supreme Court addressed this contention:

> The Equal Protection Clause directs that "all persons similarly circumstanced shall be treated alike." But so too, "[t]he Constitution does not require things which are different in fact or opinion to be treated in law as though they were the same." The initial discretion to determine what is "different" and which is "the same" resides in the legislatures of the states. A legislature must have substantial latitude to establish classifications that roughly approximate the nature of the problem perceived, that accommodate competing concerns both public and private, and that account for limitations on the practical ability of the state to remedy every ill. In applying the Equal Protection Clause to most forms of state action, we thus seek only the assurance that the classification at issue bears some fair relationship to a legitimate public purpose. . . .

As persons who engage in homosexual sodomy have never been held to constitute a suspect classification, to be upheld, the statute at issue need only satisfy the lowest level of judicial scrutiny and demonstrate that it bears a rational relationship to a legitimate legislative objective. Protection of public "health, safety, and morality" was held to be such an objective in *Bosworth* v. *City of Lexington* (1930). This objective found new vitality with the emergence of the AIDS epidemic which indisputably originated in this country in the homosexual community. Moreover, *Bowers* v. *Hardwick* held forthrightly that the rational basis standard was satisfied by majority sentiments as to the immorality of homosexuality.

In final analysis, the question is whether a rational distinction may be drawn between acts of sodomy committed by heterosexuals and homosexuals. As cases such as *Griswold* v. *Connecticut, Eisenstadt* v. *Baird, Loving* v. *Virginia,* and *Roe* v. *Wade* demonstrate, there is a heightened protection of the right of persons with respect to conduct in the context of marriage, procreation, contraception, family relationships, and child rearing and education. As such considerations are without any application as to acts of homosexual sodomy, the distinction is manifest.

"We do not condone the immorality of such activity," says the majority. Despite this statement, it should not be doubted that this decision will be regarded as the imprimatur of Kentucky's highest court upon homosexual conduct. The moral opprobrium of the majority will be lost and the popular perception will be that if the Constitution protects such conduct, it must be okay. While this is not an accurate line of thought, it is a natural one. Those who wish to urge that homosexual conduct is immoral and those who oppose the portrayal of homosexuality as an acceptable alternative lifestyle will encounter the majority opinion as a powerful argument to the contrary.

I conclude with the view that this Court has strayed from its role of interpreting the Constitution and undertaken to make social policy. This decision is a vast extension of judicial power by which four Justices of this Court have overridden the will of the Legislative and Executive branches of Kentucky State Government and denied the people any say in this important social issue. No decision cited by the majority has ever gone so far and certainly none comes to mind. Where this slippery slope may lead is anybody's guess, but the ramifications of this decision will surely be profound.

For these reasons, I dissent.

17

Recent Case: Kentucky Supreme Court Finds that Criminalization of Homosexual Sodomy Violates State Constitutional Guarantees of Privacy and Equal Protection*

Harvard Law Review Case Note

Advocates of state constitutionalism call on state supreme courts to interpret their constitutions to extend greater protections and liberties than those embodied in the Federal Constitution. In *Commonwealth* v. *Wasson,* the Kentucky Supreme Court adopted this approach to expand homosexual rights and to strike down a state statute that criminalized homosexual sodomy, despite the United States Supreme Court's refusal to do so in *Bowers* v. *Hardwick.* For state constitutionalists and advocates of homosexual rights alike, *Wasson's* value will come in its ability to transcend the state of Kentucky and to inspire other states to follow. However, doctrinal ambiguity and the inherent weaknesses of state constitutional rights will likely diminish the inspirational power of this important opinion.

In *Wasson,* the state charged the defendant with solicitation to commit sodomy. The district court held that the sodomy law infringed upon the defendant's state constitutional right to privacy and dismissed the claim. On appeal, the circuit court affirmed and further held that the law denied the defendant equal protection under the state constitution.

The Supreme Court of Kentucky affirmed. In a 4–3 decision, the court held that the criminalization of homosexual sodomy violated the defendant's rights to privacy and to equal protection under Kentucky's constitution. Before addressing these substantive claims, the court disposed of the state's contention that Kentucky had to adhere to the Supreme Court's decision in *Bowers* v. *Hardwick* and declared that "[w]e are not bound by decisions of the United States Supreme Court when deciding whether a state statute impermissibly infringes upon individual rights guaranteed in the State Constitution so long as state constitutional protection does not fall below the federal floor."

---

*All footnotes omitted. (Eds.)

From the *Harvard Law Review* 106, no. 6 (April 1993). Copyright © 1993 by The Harvard Law Review Association.

Freed from *Bowers,* the court then considered the state right to privacy in light of the unique text of the Kentucky constitution and the common law at the time of the constitution's adoption. The court noted that, unlike the Federal Constitution, the Kentucky Constitution of 1891 made repeated references to positive liberty and imposed upon Kentucky an affirmative duty to protect individual liberties. The court also pointed to *Commonwealth* v. *Campbell,* a 1909 case that stated that "the theory of [Kentucky's] government is to allow the largest liberty to the individual commensurate with the public safety. . . . [T]here is no room for that inquisitorial and protective spirit which seeks to regulate the conduct of men in matters in themselves indifferent." The *Wasson* court thus concluded that "long before the United States Supreme Court first took notice of whether there were any rights of privacy inherent in the Federal Bill of Rights," Kentucky had recognized a right of privacy in the Kentucky Constitution—a right broad enough to encompass consensual homosexual sexual behavior.

Turning to the defendant's equal protection claims, the court stated that regardless of the status of homosexuals under federal equal protection law, homosexuals constituted "a separate and identifiable class for Kentucky constitutional law analysis because no class of persons can be discriminated against under the Kentucky Constitution." The state failed to meet its burden of demonstrating a "legitimate governmental interest justifying a distinction" based on sexual preference, and the court held that a belief by a majority of the public in the immorality of homosexual conduct "does not provide a rational basis for criminalizing the sexual preference of homosexuals."

The majority opinion met a vigorous dissent. Justice Lambert criticized the majority's refusal to adhere to *Bowers* and its embrace of " 'state constitutionalism,' a practice in vogue among many state courts as a means of rejecting the leadership of the Supreme Court of the United States." He argued that the majority opinion had failed to find "any textual support" for a right to privacy in the 1891 Constitution, and that its reading of the contemporaneous case law was flawed. . . . Justice Lambert argued that morality must and will remain a part of the criminal law, and that constitutional protection of all private conduct that is not "harmful to another" would result in the invalidation of many other criminal statutes.

Rejecting the majority's equal protection analysis, Justice Lambert asserted that homosexuals do not constitute a suspect class, and hence that the Kentucky sodomy statute "need only satisfy the lowest level of judicial scrutiny and demonstrate that it bears a rational relationship to a legitimate legislative objective."

With *Wasson,* the Kentucky Supreme Court became the highest state court to extend privacy protection to homosexual sodomy since *Bowers* v. *Hardwick.* More importantly, Wasson broke from the trend of other courts and recognized homosexuals as a "separate and identifiable class" for equal protection purposes. *Wasson's* equal protection holding, moreover, may provide a more far-reaching doctrinal base for the expansion of gay rights than does the right to privacy, because it protects homosexuality as status rather than as conduct. Equal protection may thus pave the way for greater protection against discrimination in many areas, including employment, housing, custody of children, and marriage.

The majority opinion, however, lacked the doctrinal clarity to provide a firm equal protection basis for the expansion of gay rights. For instance, although the court claimed to rely on Kentucky's unique constitution, it borrowed the language of federal equal protection doctrine for its analysis. The majority then applied that language carelessly, shifting between the language of strict scrutiny and heightened rational basis review. Thus, when the court found no "rational basis" for the statute in question, it left unresolved whether the statute was being struck down under strict or minimal scrutiny or a completely independent standard unique to Kentucky. Moreover, the court's bold assertion that "no class of persons can be discriminated against under the Kentucky Constitution" creates an unworkable situation for the state legislature if applied literally, and may unduly trample on the rights of the majority in many instances.

Although unlikely to establish a solid doctrinal basis for the expansion of homosexual rights, the majority opinion may provide another kind of support. As *Wasson* highlights, state constitutional rights take on heightened significance when the Supreme Court denies rights to certain individuals or groups under the Federal Constitution, as it did in *Bowers* v. *Hardwick*. For proponents of state constitutionalism who urge broad expansion of fundamental rights under state constitutions, *Wasson*'s significance will thus likely be measured by its ability to inspire other state courts. But the frail nature of state constitutional rights suggests that *Wasson* may merit only limited optimism on the part of advocates of expanded homosexual rights at the state level and of state constitutionalism more generally.

First, state constitutional rights suffer from fundamental weaknesses not shared by federal constitutional rights. Because Kentucky's judges may be voted out of office, because the state constitution may be amended more easily than the Federal Constitution, and because the geographical application of its mandate is limited, the Kentucky Constitution, like that of other states, may ultimately be "render[ed] a less distinctive and prestigious source of legal limits and also a less reliable check on majoritarian impulses." Indeed, state constitutions simply have no "claim as a 'civil religion' or as the perfect embodiment of justice."

Although *Wasson* represents an important victory for supporters of homosexual rights, gay rights advocates and other groups seeking expanded rights at the state level have good reason to receive *Wasson* cautiously. *Wasson*'s doctrinal ambiguity, when combined with the inherently weak nature of state constitutional rights, will likely diminish this opinion's ability to inspire other state courts to expand homosexual rights; *Wasson* may just represent one state's efforts to tap the potential for expanded rights that lurks within state constitutions.

Part Four

Homosexuality and the Military

18

Homosexuality in the
United States Armed Forces

Randy Shilts

The history of homosexuality in the United States armed forces has been a struggle between two intransigent facts—the persistent presence of gays within the military and the equally persistent hostility toward them. All the drama and controversy surrounding the demand for acceptance by lesbians and gay men in uniform represents the culmination of this conflict, one that dates back to the founding of the Republic.

Over the past twenty years, as the gay community has taken form in cities across the nation, a vast gay subculture has emerged within the military, in every branch of the service, among both officers and enlisted. Today, gay soldiers jump with the 101st Airborne, wear the Green Beret of the Special Forces, and perform top-level jobs in the "black world" of covert operations. Gay air force personnel have staffed missile silos in North Dakota, flown the nuclear-armed bombers of the Strategic Air Command, and navigated *Air Force One.* Gay sailors dive with the Navy SEALS, tend the nuclear reactors on submarines, and teach at the Naval War College. A gay admiral commanded the fleet assigned to one of the highest-profile military operations of the past generation. The homosexual presence on aircraft carriers is so pervasive that social life on the huge ships for the past fifteen years has included gay newsletters and clandestine gay discos. Gay marines guard the president in the White House honor guard and protect U.S. embassies around the world.

Gay military personnel are among the graduates of Annapolis, West Point, and the Air Force Academy in Colorado Springs. At least one gay man has served in the astronaut program. Recent gay general-staff officers have included one army four-star general, renowned in military circles, who served

From Randy Shilts, *Conduct Unbecoming: Lesbians and Gays in the U.S. Military, Vietnam to the Persian Gulf* (New York: St. Martin's Press, 1993). Copyright © 1993 by Randy Shilts. Reprinted by permission.

as head of one of the most crucial military missions of the 1980s. In the past decade, gay people have served as generals in every branch of the armed forces. The Marine Corps has also had at least one gay person at four-star rank since 1981, and at least one gay man has served on the Joint Chiefs of Staff in that time.

Never before have gay people served so extensively—and, in some cases, so openly—in the United States military. And rarely has the military moved so aggressively against homosexuality. The scope and sweep of gay dragnets in the past decade have been extraordinary. Their aim is to coerce service personnel into revealing names of other homosexuals. If investigators are successful, the probes turn into purges in which scores of people are drummed out within weeks. The pressure to cooperate is so fierce that lovers sometimes betray their partners and friends turn against one another.

Separation hearings and courts-martial follow the investigations. But finding witnesses for the defense can be a problem. In the recent purge of lesbians at the Parris Island Marine Corps Recruit Training Depot, two marines who stepped forward as character witnesses for an accused lesbian were reduced in pay, demoted, and received negative job evaluations. Their superiors openly admitted the marines' testimony was the reason for the poor ratings. The accused lesbian was quickly dispatched to prison, and lawyers for later defendants found it very difficult to solicit character witnesses. An administrative board in a related case recommended a less than honorable discharge for a marine captain because she had a civilian lesbian friend. In another case, a senior navy officer was consistently passed over for promotion after testifying on behalf of an accused gay ensign. Though the ensign was his own son, in the navy, fathers are expected to turn against their children if their children are accused of homosexuality.

The ruthlessness of the investigations and hearings serves a central purpose: to encourage lesbian and gay soldiers to resign from the military, to accept passively an administrative discharge or, if they are officers, to leave quietly under the vague rubric of "conduct unbecoming." Such quiet separations help conceal the numbers of lesbians and gay men the military turns out of the service, as many as two thousand a year during the past decade.

In the past decade, the cost of investigations and the dollars spent replacing gay personnel easily amount to hundreds of millions. The human costs are incalculable. Careers are destroyed; lives are ruined. Under the pressure of a purge, and in the swell of rumors that often precedes one, despairing men and women sometimes commit suicide.

The military's policies have had a sinister effect on the entire nation: Such policies make it known to everyone serving in the military that lesbians and gay men are dangerous to the well-being of other Americans; that they are undeserving of even the most basic civil rights. Such policies also create an ambience in which discrimination, harassment, and even violence against lesbians and gays is tolerated and to some degree encouraged. Especially for lesbians, the issues are far more complex than simple homophobia, because they also involve significant features of sex-based discrimination.

There are many men who never wanted women in *their* army or *their* navy in the first place, and the military regulations regarding homosexuality have been the way to keep them out for the past decade. Until proven otherwise, women in the military are often suspected of being lesbian. Why else, the logic goes, would they want to join a man's world? Many of these women take jobs that have traditionally been held by men. If they are successful, they are suspect for not being womanly enough; if they fall, they are harassed for not being man enough to do the job.

The way women can prove themselves to be nonlesbians is to have sex with men. Thus antigay regulations have encouraged sexual harassment of women. Those who will not acquiesce to a colleague's advances are routinely accused of being lesbian and are subject to discharge. Some women have allowed themselves to be raped by male officers, afraid that the alternative would be a charge of lesbianism. Those who do complain of sexual harassment often find themselves accused: Their commands are far more intrigued with investigating homosexuals than with investigating sexual harassment. Several investigations of suspected lesbians in the 1980s presaged waves of pregnancies on various installations, as women became pregnant in order to avoid suspicion that they were gay.

There is a saying among gay women in the military: One accusation means an investigation. Two accusations mean guilt. And when a woman mutters, "I'm under investigation," she rarely has to say what for. The branches of the service most resistant to allowing women in their ranks—the navy and marines—are the branches that drum out the most women for being gay. The navy releases twice as many women as men on grounds of homosexuality. In the Marine Corps, the figure is seven times higher for women than men.

Of course, sex discrimination in the military's enforcement of anti-homosexual regulations since 1981 mirrors deeper conflicts. We are a nation in transition when it comes to attitudes toward gender roles and sexuality in general, and homosexuality in particular. Military service was once considered a rite of male passage. This clearly was the case during the early years of the Vietnam conflict; and it remains so among those who were trained during that era of military history—the people who are at the top of the military's chain of command today. In different ways, the presence of women and gays in the ranks challenges the traditional concept of manhood in the military, just as the emergence of women and gays in other fields has done in society at large.

The profound victimization of lesbians in the military has less to do with homophobia than with sexual discrimination and harassment, the kind faced by women breaking into occupations once reserved for men. Meanwhile, the presence of gay men—especially so many who are thoroughly competent for military service—calls into question everything that manhood is supposed to mean. For both women and men, the story of gays in the military is a story about manhood. For generations, after all, the military has been an institution that has promised to do one thing, if nothing else, and that is to take a boy and make him a man. The military's gay policy crisis in the past decade reflects the turmoil of a nation thrust into conflict over our society's changing definition of manhood.

Strikingly, the new aggression against homosexuals in uniform during the 1980s came at a time when just about everyone in the military, from the secretary of defense on down, seemed aware that these policies would be abolished. During the Vietnam War, the military had slowed the enforcement of its gay regulations when it appeared that the proscriptions on gay soldiers might interfere with manpower needs. When the next major war broke out a generation later in the Persian Gulf, the armed forces once again curtailed enforcement of policies excluding gays, at least until the exigencies of war were behind them.

What is clear is that the military is far less concerned with having no homosexuals in the service than with having people think there are no homosexuals in the service. Time and again, if a military staffer is someone whom the service needs, his or her discharge is lost or delayed. The military always needs physicians, for example, so it has sometimes taken as long as two years for the gay-related discharge of a doctor, even though such paperwork is routinely completed in two weeks for less valued service members. More than one general and admiral in the armed forces' medical branches have commented privately that if they really went after all the gay doctors and medics, the military would have to close down its medical centers, because there aren't enough heterosexuals in the military medical fields to staff them all.

The candor with which government lawyers and top military men have privately admitted the policies' flaws have surprised civil liberties advocates. In 1982, lawyers took a deposition from a two-star general who made an impassioned defense of the gay exclusion for the court record in a gay-rights court case, but then, over lunch, unofficially admitted he expected that the regulations would fall within a few years. He added, while he would deny saying this in court, that the change would be fine with him, because he knew many fine gay soldiers. That general, Norman H. Schwarzkopf, led U.S. troops in the Persian Gulf and later reaffirmed his public opposition to allowing gays in the military. By then, however, a staff officer with the Joint Chiefs had already drafted the regulations to allow gays to serve in the armed forces. . . .

19

Policy on Homosexual Conduct in the Armed Forces

Les Aspin

DATE: July 19, 1993

SUBJECT: Policy on Homosexual Conduct in the Armed Forces

On January 29, 1993, the president directed me to review DoD [Department of Defense] policy on homosexuals in the military. The president further directed that the DoD be "practical, realistic, and consistent with the high standards of combat effectiveness and unit cohesion our armed forces must maintain."

An extensive review was conducted. I have paid careful attention to the hearings that have been held by both the House and Senate Armed Services Committees, conferred with the Joint Chiefs and acting secretaries of the military departments, and considered recommendations of a working group of senior officers in the Department of Defense and those of the Rand Corporation.

The Department of Defense has long held that, as a general rule, homosexuality is incompatible with military service because it interferes with the factors critical to combat effectiveness, including unit morale, unit cohesion, and individual privacy. Nevertheless, the Department of Defense also recognizes that individuals with a homosexual orientation have served with distinction in the armed services of the United States.

Therefore, it is the policy of the Department of Defense to judge the suitability of persons to serve in the armed forces on the basis of their conduct. Homosexual conduct will be grounds for separation from the military services. Sexual orientation is considered a personal and private matter, and homosexual orientation is not a bar to service entry or continued service unless manifested by homosexual conduct.

I direct the following:

Applicants for military service will not be asked or required to reveal their sexual orientation. Applicants will be informed of accession and separation policy.

Servicemembers will be separated for homosexual conduct.

Commanders and investigating agencies will not initiate inquiries or investigations solely to determine a member's sexual orientation. Servicemembers will not be asked or required to reveal their sexual orientation. However, commanders will continue to initiate inquiries or investigations, as appropriate, when there is credible information that a basis for discharge or disciplinary action exists. Authority to initiate inquiries and investigations involving homosexual conduct shall be limited to commanders. Commanders will consider, in allocating scarce investigative resources, that sexual orientation is a personal and private matter. They will investigate allegations of violations of the Uniform Code of Military Justice in an even-handed manner without regard to whether the conduct alleged is heterosexual or homosexual or whether it occurs on-base or off-base. Commanders remain responsible for ensuring that investigations are conducted properly and that any abuse of authority is addressed.

The constraints of military service require servicemembers to keep certain aspects of their personal lives private for the benefit of the group. Our personnel policies will be clearly stated and implemented in accordance with due process of law.

Commanders remain responsible for maintaining good order and discipline. Harassment or violence against other servicemembers will not be tolerated.

Homosexual conduct is a homosexual act, a statement by the servicemember that demonstrates a propensity or intent to engage in homosexual acts, or a homosexual marriage or attempted marriage.

A statement by a servicemember that he or she is homosexual or bisexual creates a rebuttable presumption that the servicemember is engaging in homosexual acts or has a propensity or intent to do so. The servicemember has the opportunity to present evidence that he does not engage in homosexual acts and does not have a propensity or intent to do so. The evidence will be assessed by the relevant separation authority.

A homosexual act includes any bodily contact, actively undertaken or passively permitted, between members of the same sex for the purpose of satisfying sexual desires or any bodily contact which a reasonable person would understand to demonstrate a propensity or intent to engage in homosexual acts. Sexual orientation is a sexual attraction to individuals of a particular sex.

The interim policy and administrative separation procedures that I established on February 3, 1993, will remain in effect until October 1, 1993. Secretaries of the military departments and responsible officials within the Office of the Secretary of Defense shall, by October 1, 1993, take such actions as may be necessary to carry out the purposes of this directive. Secretaries of the military departments will ensure that all members of the armed forces are aware of their specific responsibilities in carrying out this new policy. This memorandum creates no substantive or procedural rights. Any changes to existing policies shall be prospective only.

20

Summary Report of the Military Working Group on Recommended Department of Defense Homosexual Policy*

On 8 June [1993], we forwarded a recommended policy outline (reference) describing, in our judgment, the only option that complies with the president's direction to end discrimination while maintaining high standards of combat effectiveness and unit cohesion. The attachment provides a more indepth explanation of the policy detailing the process and explaining the findings and conclusions that led to our recommendation.

I. BACKGROUND

A. Guidance

1. On 29 January 1993, the president directed the secretary of defense to develop a policy "ending discrimination on the basis of sexual orientation in determining who may serve in the Armed Forces of the United States." The president further directed that the policy be implemented in a manner that is "practical, realistic, and consistent with the high standards of combat effectiveness and unit cohesion our armed forces must maintain."

2. On 5 April 1993, the secretary of defense directed that a Military Working Group (MWG) be formed to develop and assess alternative policy options to meet the president's requirements.

---

*John P. Otjen, Major General, U.S. Army; William B. Davitte, Major General, U.S. Air Force; Gerald L. Miller, Brigadier General, U.S. Marine Corps; John Scott Redd, Rear Admiral, U.S. Navy; and James M. Loy, Rear Admiral, United States Coast Guard.

B. Perspective in Formulating This Policy

Although the all-volunteer military is drawn from civilian society, and generally reflects society's norms, the military institution differs in several important ways. These differences were an essential part of MWG's perspective in formulating this policy.

1. *Military mission.* Ultimately, the military's mission is to fight and win the nation's wars.

   a. The "terms of employment" for an individual servicemember include the real possibility that he or she will be called upon to make the ultimate sacrifice in service to our country. For military leaders, the moral imperative is to accomplish the mission with the least loss of life possible. Accordingly, any change to the military institution must be weighed in light of this responsibility.

   b. Similarly, there is no "right to serve" in the armed forces. Military service is clearly a privilege afforded only to those who are qualified. There are many features that are disqualifying, such as height, weight, prior conduct record, membership in groups with certain objectives, or mental category. These disqualifying factors are directly related to combat effectiveness and apply whether the force is all-volunteer or conscript.

2. *Institutional values.* Values are important to any institution, but they are critical to the military of a democratic nation.

   a. The nation calls upon its military to be prepared to kill and destroy— acts which, in any other context, would be immoral. The shared moral values of the institution—the collective sense of right and wrong—provide the foundation which ensures that license will not be abused. This foundation is the essential difference between a professional armed force and a mercenary force. It also provides to individual servicemembers the moral basis for personal service, commitment, and sacrifice in a profession which is demanding in the extreme.

   b. As citizen soldiers, military members bring their values with them when they enter the service. Whether based on moral, religious, cultural, or ethical considerations, those values and beliefs are often strongly held and not amenable to change. While we indoctrinate and train recruits, leadership and discipline cannot—and generally should not — attempt to counter the basic values which. parents and society have taught. Indeed, efforts to do so will likely prove counterproductive.

3. *Military environment.* Military operations are team operations—units win wars, not individuals.

   a. The rights and needs of the group are emphasized while individual rights and needs are often set aside or sacrificed for military necessity. For example, if military members aren't satisfied with the conditions of their environment, they have no right to quit and, in fact, are subject to prosecution if they do. Similarly, members of the military often are not able to separate their private lives from their working environment. They may be required to work, eat, recreate, sleep, and bathe in cramped spaces for prolonged periods of time, sometimes in the most remote parts of the world. Indeed, separation of the sexes is often the only concession to privacy.

b. In the short term, the military is facing a number of issues—budget reductions, early retirements, reorganizations, health care worries, base closures, reductions in force—that have had a severe negative impact on morale. Any change in policy which would further exacerbate this "misery squeeze" must be carefully weighed.

II. PROCESS

A. Composition and Organization

The MWG, composed of a general or flag officer from each service and a support staff of approximately fifty officers, enlisted personnel, and civilian employees convened on 6 April 1993. To facilitate examination of various options, the staff was organized into four functional panels: military operations, service life, personnel policy, and legal.

B. Policy Boundaries

The MWG worked within specific limitations which were confirmed with the Office of the Secretary of Defense. Returning to the pre-29 January 1993 policy of "asking the question" was not an option; nor was changing the Uniform Code of Military Justice. These limitations defined the boundaries within which the MWG developed its recommended options.

C. Deliberations

Fairness and objectivity were major aims of the MWG's process. In pursuit of those aims, the MWG met with individuals and groups holding a broad spectrum of views on the subject. This included meetings with uniformed and civilian experts from inside and outside the Department of Defense (DoD), including the soldiers, sailors, airmen, marines, and Coast Guardsmen who would be most affected by the policy. To broaden understanding of the issue, the MWG also compared experiences of the militaries of other countries, researched available literature, and performed statistical analyses of military separation data obtained from the services.

D. Results

Several policy options were developed and assessed. After extensive review and consultation, the MWG ultimately focused on a single policy recommendation and a plan to implement that policy. This policy, discussed in detail below, meets the president's guidance, maintains combat effectiveness, and is sustainable for the foreseeable future.

E. Definitions

The public debate over homosexuals in the military has often been further confused by a lack of a common usage of terms. For clarity, the MWG used the following definitions:

1. *Bisexual.* A person who engages in, desires to engage in, or intends to engage in both homosexual and heterosexual acts.

2. *Homosexual.* A person, regardless of sex, who engages in, desires to engage in, or intends to engage in homosexual acts

3. *Homosexual act.* Bodily contact, actively undertaken or passively permitted, between members of the same sex for the purpose of satisfying sexual desires. (This includes sodomy and acts other than sodomy, such as kissing and dancing between members of the same sex for the purpose of satisfying sexual desires.)

4. *Homosexual conduct.* Evidenced by homosexual acts and attempts or solicitations to engage in such acts, statements by a member that he or she is homosexual or bisexual, or homosexual marriage or attempted homosexual marriage.

5. *Homosexual marriage.* When a member has married, or attempted to marry, a person he or she knows to be of the same biological sex (as evidenced by external anatomy).

6. *Homosexual statement.* The member has stated that he or she is homosexual or bisexual.

7. *Homosexuality.* The quality, condition, or fact of being a homosexual.

8. *Sexual orientation.* A sexual attraction to individuals of a particular gender.

III. FINDINGS

Following extensive review, the MWG made the following findings:

A. Combat Effectiveness

The Armed Forces of the United States serve an important role in our society by furthering our national interests abroad, defending our borders, and protecting the American way of life. To accomplish this unique mission, the military must be fully combat effective. Combat effectiveness is the *sine qua non* of any armed force and any prospective change must be assessed first and foremost in light of its effect on the military's ability to fight. High combat effectiveness embodies a synergistic mix that can be best expressed as the product of unit cohesion and readiness.

1. *Unit cohesion.* Unit cohesion encompasses a number of factors which, although often intangible, are fundamental to combat effectiveness. These include:

a. **Bonding.** The essence of unit cohesion is the bonding between members of a unit which holds them together, sustains their will to support each other, and enables them to fight together under the stress and chaos of war. The MWG found that the presence of open homosexuals in a unit would, in general, polarize and fragment the unit and destroy the bonding and singleness of purpose required for effective military operations. This phenomenon occurs whether or not homosexual acts are involved. By simply stating that he or she is a homosexual, the individual becomes isolated from the group and combat effectiveness suffers.

b. **Leadership.** In addition to tactical and technical competency, effective leadership depends on mutual respect, fairness, and concern for the well-being of subordinates. If the values and lifestyle of a leader are perceived as contrary to those of the unit, the leader will be, at best, ineffective. That ineffectiveness would be further undermined by perceptions of unfairness or fraternization. The MWG found it would be extremely difficult for an open homosexual to exercise authority or serve effectively as a leader in the Armed Forces of the United States.

c. **Good order and discipline.** Good order and discipline refers to behavior based on respect for authority, other servicemembers, established laws, and regulations and is critical for the effectiveness of leadership and the ability of the unit to carry out its mission. Information presented to the MWG clearly indicated that the introduction of individuals identified as homosexuals into the military would severely undermine good order and discipline. Moral and ethical beliefs of individuals would be brought into open conflict. Leadership priorities would, of necessity, be reoriented from training for combat to preventing internal discord. Additionally, the military would be perceived as "turning a blind eye" to conduct proscribed by the Uniform Code of Military Justice and regulations, thereby undermining the very basis for good order and discipline.

d. **Privacy.** Sexual orientation alone is, and should remain, a personal and private matter. However, once an individual's homosexual orientation becomes known, privacy becomes a significant issue. Military members give up many rights—including the right to free association—upon joining the military. When deployed on ships or overseas, members often work, eat, relax, bathe, and sleep together in close proximity twenty-four hours a day. Further, the space individuals can call their own—their personal sanctuary—may be only slightly larger than a coffin. For many members, the presence of openly homosexual individuals in that environment constitutes a major and unacceptable invasion of what little privacy remains.

e. **Morale.** Lifting the ban on homosexuals serving in the military would be perceived by many servicemembers as the imposition of a political agenda by a small group—an agenda which is seen as having no military necessity and as being, in fact, destructive to the finest fighting force in the world. Morale would suffer accordingly.

f. **Core values.** The core values of the military profession would be seen by many to have changed fundamentally if homosexuals were allowed to serve. This would undermine institutional loyalty and the moral basis for service, sacrifice, and commitment for those members.

2. *Readiness.* Readiness includes traditional hardware areas such as technology, equipment, and spare parts as well as the training, education, and fitness of quality personnel. The presence of homosexuals in the military would impact readiness in several ways.

a. **Medical.** The readiness of the military to deploy and perform its combat mission is directly linked to the medical well-being of the force. The homosexual lifestyle has been clearly documented as being unhealthy. Due to their sexual practices, active male homosexuals in the military could be expected to bring an increased incidence of sexually transmitted diseases and other diseases spread by close personal contact. Additionally, the association of the homosexual lifestyle as a high-risk behavior in contracting AIDS could create the perception of an "enemy within" which has the potential to harm not only other servicemembers, but family members as well.

b. **Recruiting.** Open homosexuality in the military would likely reduce the propensity of many young men and women to enlist due to parental concerns, peer pressure, and a military image that would be tarnished in the eyes of much of the population from which we recruit.

c. **Retention.** Discharges for homosexual conduct account for only about one-third of one percent of all United States military discharges. Conversely, recent surveys indicate a significant number of servicemembers say they would not reenlist if open homosexuals were allowed to serve. These views were supported by military personnel who appeared before the MWG. Of note, the members most likely to leave the service would be those with the best options for employment elsewhere—i.e., the most skilled—and those with strong moral beliefs.

3. *All homosexuality is incompatible with military service.* The effect on combat effectiveness is not limited to known homosexuals.

    a. Even if officially unknown, individuals who engage in homosexual conduct can undermine combat effectiveness through, for example, high-risk behavior and the formation of "subcultures" outside the chain of command. Further, they may not remain unknown over the course of several years of an enlistment or for a full military career. For example, an "unknown" homosexual can become "known" overnight as a result of a police blotter entry or any other incident by which his or her homosexuality becomes officially known. The resultant effect on readiness can thus manifest itself quickly and without warning.

    b. Currently unknown and nonpracticing homosexuals are also cause for concern. Homosexual activist groups argue that the productivity of individual homosexuals is reduced by virtue of having to hide their true orientation. While the immediate impact on combat effectiveness for those individuals is limited, it nonetheless exists. Further, by definition, even nonpracticing homosexuals either intend to engage in homosexual acts or desire to engage in homosexual acts. Some may remain celibate for a time, but it is reasonable to presume that, over a period of years, many will engage in homosexual conduct.

    c. The salient point is that what the military doesn't know can—and over time will—negatively impact combat effectiveness. While the immediate effect on combat readiness varies depending on whether a homosexual is known or unknown, and whether or not the servicemember engages in homosexual conduct, it is nonetheless true that *all* homosexuality is incompatible with military service and has some measure of negative impact.

B. Practical Considerations

In addition to the direct effects on combat effectiveness described above, a number of practical considerations were examined in assessing policy options.

1. *Longevity of the policy.* One of the tests for an effective policy is that it withstand the test of time.

    a. A key element is the likelihood of surviving challenge in the courts. A central finding of the MWG is that statements that one is a homosexual are inextricably linked to homosexual acts. To suggest otherwise is contrary to logic, MWG research, and the publicly expressed view of homosexual advocates. Authorities on military law expressed concern that drawing an artificial distinction between homosexual statements and homosexual acts would undercut the legal precedent upholding the military's homosexual policy. Conversely, a policy which correctly includes as its underlying premise the linkage between homosexual statements and homosexual acts can draw from established precedent and is therefore likely to endure.

b. Any policy that condones homosexual conduct would require congressional action to change the Uniform Code of Military Justice. Failure to do so would establish an untenable situation, creating a perceived conflict between stated policy and military law. This would, in turn, create leadership and legal problems and ultimately would have to be resolved.

2. *Personnel policies.* Military personnel policies are designed by necessity to manage large groups or categories of people, as opposed to individuals, for the purpose of achieving maximum combat effectiveness. During its deliberations, the MWG found that current DoD policy, directives, and regulations regarding homosexuality generally are not well understood.

a. **Accessions.** The questions formerly asked during the accession process regarding an applicant's sexual orientation appear to have been ineffective either in deterring homosexuals from entering the military or in articulating DoD policy on homosexuality.

b. **Assignments.** The issue of assignment restrictions poses a particular dilemma. On the one hand, there are significant problems with overall combat effectiveness associated with assigning open homosexuals to units that require higher degrees of cohesion (e.g., combat units, special forces) or close quarters berthing. On the other hand, restricting their assignments would cause resentment among those who must serve in their place while tending to concentrate open homosexuals into a narrow selection of skill fields. Since assignment to combat skills and combatant vessels is career enhancing, excluding homosexuals from these duties would inhibit their promotion and advancement opportunities and bring a new set of problems.

c. **Berthing/billeting.** The presence of known homosexuals in a unit will create tension which may require them to be berthed/billeted and segregated from the remainder of the unit in order to maintain good order and discipline. This would entail additional and unbudgeted costs. On the other hand, segregating certain members of the group will isolate those individuals, possibly highlighting them as a special class, and further degrade unit cohesion. Additionally, there are situations where separate berthing/billeting—such as aboard ships—is not practical at any cost.

3. *Investigations*

a. DoD has no written, uniform policy guidelines for investigating cases involving allegations of homosexuality. This lack of policy may have contributed to a misperception that the military's investigative agencies conduct "witch hunts" to weed out suspected homosexuals.

b. Commanders must have the discretion to inquire and investigate when there is credible information of misconduct or basis for discharge. However, a balance must be struck. While servicemembers set aside certain individual rights while they serve, they still retain freedom from unwarranted intrusion into their private lives.

4. *Military family issues.* Service life is all encompassing. While spouses and children obviously do not serve in the armed forces, military policies and personnel touch every aspect of family life. Servicemembers, both single and married, are often involved as leaders in military youth activities—for example, scouting, little league, church youth groups, and social clubs. Indeed, most morale, welfare, and recreation programs rely almost exclusively on these volunteers. Many military families would object to the participation of open homosexuals in these programs—programs to which they entrust their children. Additionally, family members are worried about the same issues that concern their military sponsors—such as encumbered privacy during deployments, medical risks, and the breakdown of the unit—because they are perceived as a threat to their loved ones.

5. *Common misperceptions concerning homosexuals and the military*

   a. **Foreign militaries**

      (1) The policy and practice of foreign militaries regarding homosexuals actively serving do not always match. In countries where policies are "accepting," practice typically involves exclusion of homosexuals for medical/psychological reasons. Even where policy and law allow homosexuals to serve, few servicemembers openly declare their homosexuality due to fears of baiting, bashing, and negative effects to their careers.

      (2) Extended deployments and berthing/billeting privacy are not significant issues for most foreign militaries. Additionally, no country has as high a proportion of its servicemembers billeted/berthed together on military installations and deployed aboard ships or overseas at any given time as does the United States. Most importantly, no other country has the global responsibilities, operational tempo, or worldwide deployment commitments of the Armed Forces of the United States.

   b. **Police/Fire departments.** Parallels cannot be accurately drawn between the experiences of police and fire departments and the armed forces. While there are some organizational similarities, there are also some very fundamental differences in the areas of mission and related training, deployments, work environment, authority of the commander over subordinates, living conditions, and personal privacy.

   c. **Discharge and discipline of homosexuals in the armed forces.** Incorrect perceptions exist that the military discharges large numbers of personnel for homosexuality and that most of those discharges are for reasons of homosexual "status" only—i.e., statements alone that one is a homosexual, with *no* homosexual acts involved. Additionally, some believe the military prosecutes homosexual sodomy cases but does not prosecute heterosexual sodomy cases.

(1) Analysis of armed forces separations over the four-year period of fiscal years 1989 through 1992 reveals:

(a) Only one-third of one percent (0.3 percent) of all separations were for homosexuality.

(b) Of those discharged for administrative or punitive reasons, only 1.5 percent were for homosexuality.

(c) Drug and alcohol abuse discharges were nine times greater than those for homosexuality. Overweight discharges were five times greater.

(d) Of all discharges for homosexuality, at least 79 percent clearly involved homosexual conduct. There was insufficient documentation to determine whether conduct was involved in the remaining 21 percent.

(2) Similarly, a review of 1,141 military courts-martial involving Article 125 (sodomy) indicated that heterosexual sodomy cases outnumbered homosexual sodomy cases by a 4-to-1 ratio.

IV. CONCLUSIONS

After extensive research and prolonged deliberations, the MWG concluded the following:

A. Since it is impossible to determine an individual's sexual orientation unless he or she reveals it, sexual orientation alone is a personal and private matter.

B. Homosexuality is incompatible with military service. The presence in the military of individuals identified as homosexuals would have a significantly adverse effect on both unit cohesion and the readiness of the force—the key ingredients of combat effectiveness. If identified homosexuals are allowed to serve, they will compromise the high standards of combat effectiveness which must be maintained, impacting on the ability of the armed forces to perform its mission.

C. For practical reasons, servicemembers should be discharged only when their homosexuality is manifested by objective criteria—homosexual acts, homosexual statements, or homosexual marriages.

D. Applicants for military service should be clearly advised of the military's policy regarding homosexuals prior to their entering active duty. Specifically applicants should be briefed and acknowledge in writing that they understand: (1) homosexuality is incompatible with military service; (2) they may be denied enlistment or separated if they have engaged in homosexual conduct (acts, statements, or marriage); or (3) they are not required to reveal their sexual orientation, even if asked, but if they do, it is of their own free will and can be used as a basis for separation from the armed forces.

E. A single, clear investigative policy should be adopted to provide uniform guidance to the services for conducting inquiries and investigations into allegations of homosexual conduct.

F. All serving members should be educated on the military's policy on homosexuals. This education should be factual in nature and should not include sensitivity training or attempt to change deeply held moral, ethical, religious values.

V. THE RECOMMENDED POLICY

A. Overview

After extensive research and assessment of several options, the MWG submitted the following policy for consideration by the secretary of defense on 8 June 1993. In the judgment of the MWG, the policy represented the only option which complied with the president's guidance to end discrimination while maintaining high standards of combat effectiveness and unit cohesion.

B. Key Policy Features

1. Sexual orientation will be considered a personal and private matter. The armed forces won't ask and servicemembers will not be required to reveal their sexual orientation.

2. The presence in the armed forces of persons who engage in homosexual acts, who state they are homosexual or bisexual, or marry or who attempt to marry persons of the same gender remains inconsistent with the requirement to maintain high standards of combat effectiveness and unit cohesion.

3. Sexual orientation alone is not a bar to service entry or continued service unless manifested by homosexual acts, statements, or marriages.

4. Neither commander's inquiries (normally for minor offenses) nor military criminal law enforcement investigations (normally for criminal violations) will be conducted absent credible information. Commanders will continue to initiate inquiries or investigations, as deemed necessary, when credible information that a basis for discharge or disciplinary action exists.

5. Servicemembers will be discharged if they are found to have engaged in homosexual conduct.

6. An education plan will be developed to inform servicemembers, commanders, and military investigators about this policy so as to reinforce the princi-

ple that all servicemembers can serve without fear of unwarranted intrusion into their personal lives.

C. Discussion of the Policy

1. Military personnel policies are designed by necessity to manage large groups or categories of people for the purpose of achieving maximum combat effectiveness . The basis for our personnel policy regarding homosexuals has been and remains that homosexuality is incompatible with service in the armed forces.

2. For practical reasons, we implement that policy by discharging service-members only when their homosexuality is manifested by objective criteria—homosexual acts, statements, or marriage. As a practical result of the implementation of this policy, homosexuals who keep their sexual orientation private have served and will continue to serve.

3. While maintaining the de jure basis of the previous policy, this policy acknowledges the de facto situation that some homosexuals have served, and presumably will continue to serve, in the armed forces under the unique constraints of military life. These constraints require members of the armed forces to keep certain aspects of their personal life private for the benefit of the group.

D. Implementation

1. *Accessions policy.* Applicants for service in the armed forces will not be required to declare their sexual orientation or answer questions about their orientation. They will be briefed on departmental policies governing conduct proscribed for members of the armed forces. All applicants will sign a statement acknowledging they understand these policies. Additionally, homosexual behavior will no longer be listed as a mental disorder in the DoD Physical Standards directive.

2. *Investigative policy.* Commanders may initiate investigations or inquiries into homosexual conduct as defined by DoD policy. However, no investigations or inquiries will be conducted solely to establish an individual's sexual orientation, nor will servicemembers be required to answer questions concerning their sexual orientation. This provision does not create a protected class. Acknowledgment by a member that he or she is a homosexual—even in reply to a question asked in error—continues to be basis for separation. No investigations or inquiries will be conducted absent credible information of the commission of a crime or basis for discharge or disciplinary action. Military investigative agencies, at the direction of a commander, may investigate misconduct and violations of the Uniform Code of Military Justice. Investigations

will not go beyond establishing the elements of the offense or basis for discharge. There will be no stake-outs, testing operations, or roundups absent specific allegations of proscribed conduct.

3. *Discharge policy.* Homosexual conduct is inconsistent with the high standards of combat effectiveness and unit cohesion our armed forces must maintain. Servicemembers will be discharged if they engage In homosexual conduct. Homosexual conduct is evidenced by any act involving bodily contact, actively undertaken or passively permitted, between members of the same sex for the purpose of sexual gratification, and attempts or solicitations to engage in such acts; a statement by the member that he or she is a homosexual or bisexual; or homosexual marriage or attempted homosexual marriage. Normally, administrative separations involving homosexual conduct will be under honorable conditions, unless there are aggravating circumstances—such as acts with a minor.

4. *Education policy.* Each service will provide training to their personnel, at every level, to explain the new policy regarding homosexuals. The DoD will provide an education plan for the services to use as a guideline in their separate training programs. The education package will focus on the changes to the DoD policy and will not be an attempt to change any deeply held religious and ethical beliefs; that is, sensitivity training.

21

Small Comfort for Gay Soldiers

New York Times Editorial

The Pentagon's new rules on homosexuals are a sad reminder of the shellacking President Clinton and the gay soldiers whose cause he once championed suffered at the hands of the Joint Chiefs of Staff and Congress. The rules, which institute a policy announced July 19 [1993], were described by Defense Secretary Les Aspin as "a greatly improved policy" and "the right solution" to "an enormously divisive and emotional issue."

In truth they are but a modest advance that does away with the worst abuses of the old system while entrenching the archaic and homophobic ban on gay soldiers more firmly than ever.

This was a triumph of politics over principle. Mr. Aspin gave the game away when he boasted that "the important thing is that an acrimonious fight in Congress was avoided . . . and the White House was permitted to preserve its political capital for other fights." Rather than seek a principled compromise, the administration sacrificed gay soldiers to expediency.

True, there are some gains toward more humane treatment of homosexuals under the new "don't ask, don't tell, don't pursue" policy. Recruits will no longer be asked point blank about their sexual preferences or activity. Instead they will be told that those who commit or are likely to commit homosexual acts are subject to discharge. Homosexuals no longer have to lie to get into the military; they just have to keep quiet.

The witch hunts that terrorized thousands of gay service members over the years will be curbed. If a commander receives a credible allegation that two soldiers have engaged in a homosexual act, for example, he is supposed to investigate only that situation and not browbeat them into naming other sex partners, who could be discharged as well.

But one supposed advance toward fairness may be less than it seems. Pentagon officials stress that the new rules are based on conduct, not sexual orientation; gay men and lesbians cannot be drummed out simply because they are homosexual but only if they commit or are likely to commit homosexual acts. Finding the difference with past policy, though, requires hair-splitting distinctions.

Under the old rules, a soldier who let slip that he or she was homosexual could be discharged unless there was a further finding that that soldier did not desire or intend to engage in homosexual acts. Under the new rules, a soldier who acknowledges homosexuality can be discharged unless the military can be persuaded that he or she does not have a propensity or intention to engage in homosexual acts, including hand-holding and kissing. If that's an advance, it's modest.

The ending of past abuses is more than offset by the codification of discrimination as official policy. Any sane policy would hold that what consenting adults do in private is nobody else's business. The new rules acknowledge as much by suggesting that criminal investigations should not ordinarily be squandered on such activity. But it remains grotesquely unfair that talented, dedicated homosexuals can serve only if they stay hidden in the closet or are perpetually, provably celibate.

This fundamental unfairness is now locked into regulations. Although in the long run social attitudes are apt to change, even in the military, Mr. Aspin said the new policy was now fixed "for the foreseeable future."

So now the battle is moving to the courts, where the administration's cave-in will make the fight for fairness all the harder. The old policy, whose constitutionality is under attack in several pending cases, was essentially a Pentagon creation. But the new policy will be on firmer legal footing, Mr. Aspin suggested, because it has been developed and endorsed by the executive branch, the military, and Congress, giving it very wide backing.

"We fully expect that there will be lawsuits on this," he said. "But we would like to fight them out on the new policy rather than the old policy."

So the administration that took office pledging to end discrimination now takes pride in strengthening the legal ground for retaining the discrimination. The blame for this debacle rests not only on the obstructionists in Congress and the military but also on President Clinton, who missed his chance to issue an immediate executive order ending all discrimination against gay soldiers.

Mr. Aspin says the administration needed the support of the Joint Chiefs to win over Congress and to effect the new rules. But given the administration's ultimate capitulation, it is hard to see how Mr. Clinton could have done much worse by ordering the Joint Chiefs to obey and daring Congress to overrule him. His loss of nerve has simply allowed the bigots to tighten their grip.

22

Admission of Gays to the Military: A Singularly Intolerant Act

R. D. Adair and Joseph C. Myers

The United States armed forces are in the process of drawing down. There appears to be a national consensus in support of this drawdown, a broad realization that it is one of the tough choices needing to be made if we are to get at our difficult domestic challenges. It appears likely, however, that the American military and, indeed, all American citizens are on the verge of embroilment in what may ultimately prove to be an even more difficult challenge than that of force reduction. It will question our nation's values, beliefs, and societal norms. It will challenge us as a people and define us as an organized society. In fact, it threatens to divide the nation. This challenge is the integration of avowed homosexuals into the force.

The broad domestic conflict of which the homosexual issue is only a part is often described as a cultural war, and sometimes even a cultural civil war. It is being fought now, as it has been fought over the past generation, on a number of fronts. The Equal Rights Amendment, abortion, multiculturalism, publicly funded art, affirmative action, and the content of public school curricula have been just a few of the issues vigorously debated over the past decade.

James Carville, the media consultant for President Clinton, said that the 1992 election was about "the economy, stupid!" And indeed, according to a number of exit polls, the economy may have been the deciding factor. It would be a mistake, however, to conclude that economic issues are always paramount. In the United States, politics often divides Americans along cultural lines too—along lines of region, race, ethnicity, religion, and personal values.[1] The military services, never immune to the spillover effects of society's cultural divisions, may now confront the intractable problem of homosexual integration. In the present article, we shall argue against such a policy.

From *Parameters: US Army War College Quarterly* 23, no. 1 (Spring 1993). Reprinted by permission of the authors.

This question is at once moral, philosophical, and political. For while the state of the economy may ebb and flow with the fluctuations of the business cycle, the ideas by which we define our culture endure. Ideas have consequences. As intellectual historian Christopher Dawson put it: "It is clear that a common way of life involves a common view of life, common standards of behavior, and common standards of value."[2] What Dawson says applies doubly to military life, where mission accomplishment depends to a great extent on the molding to common purpose of millions of individual soldiers. The idea of homosexual integration, so divisive in its implications, thus presents profound questions and practical considerations for the institution.

We believe there exists a cultural divide in our society, an ideological chasm between competing views of morality. In many instances this is a conflict between a traditional view of morality on one side and an opposing view which holds that there exist *no* objective standards of morality. However one chooses to view morality, it is safe to say that it is a unique aspect of our human nature, one which separates man from the animal world. And whether it has been workers' safety regulations, the repeal of slavery, or modern-day civil rights legislation, our laws have found their basis in moral judgments—this despite what may have seemed like sound economic or rational arguments against their enactment.[3] As Judge Robert Bork pointed out in his book *The Tempting of America,* it is a "common yet wholly fallacious" cliché to say that "you can't legislate morality."[4] On the contrary, that is precisely what we do legislate—otherwise we would be free to rob, steal, swindle, and kill without fear of legal sanction. It is clear that most people understand and accept the concepts of good and bad, right and wrong, and live by such creeds, morals, and laws on a daily basis. Some may argue theoretically that morals are relative and subjective, but they rarely live that way. A civilized community cannot long bear the anarchy inherent in such a view. If the statement that one man's moral judgment is as good as another's were taken seriously, it would be impossible for law on any subject to exist. After all, one man's larceny would become another's just redistribution of goods.[5]

In our democracy we handle our moral differences through mutual toleration. We can tolerate a range of undesirable practices or beliefs while recognizing the bad or falsehood in them. In recognizing our human failing, the vices within us all, toleration precludes the resort to the totalitarian impulse of imposing a single virtue over society.[6] Ill-fated attempts to create a "new man," an inherent goal in all manifestations of totalitarianism[7]—from the mass slaughters of Stalinism to the carnage of Pol Pot—testify to the difficulties of that approach.

It must be recognized, however, that toleration, by definition, is inherently judgmental, permitting some morally questionable practices of fellow human beings while simultaneously recognizing that those practices constitute a deviation from the established norm. It respects and recognizes the rights, opinions, and practices of others, while still allowing us to discriminate between right and wrong in establishing desirable norms of conduct and behavior.[8]

The "new morality" of the last thirty years, however, goes much further; it demands *neutrality* (as opposed to toleration) toward competing views of moral life.[9] It does not accept judicious discrimination. In fact the very word "discrimination" now carries with it a negative connotation, regardless of the purpose or goal involved. Surprisingly few people understand that the notion of discrimination is in fact central to the function of government—especially with regard to the legislative role. That is to say, Congress discriminates on a daily basis, setting up standards of discrimination to determine eligibility for benefits, services, jobs, etc. It is, after all, discrimination to decree that Social Security payments are only for people over sixty-two, just as it is, say, to decree that those citizens who are only seventeen years old cannot vote, or to decide that families earning over $50,000 per year cannot receive food stamps. What we seek to avoid in trying to create a more just society is *irrational* discrimination. Toward that end we have eliminated legally sanctioned discrimination based on certain demographic classifications such as race, ethnicity, religion, color, national origin, and so forth.

Historical analysis suggests that homosexuals have not been characterized as a group until relatively recently—and even that has been a result of their own organized lobbying to be recognized as such. For, unlike demographic groups, they have been distinguished not by physical characteristics, place of birth, or creed, but by individual behavior. But the banding together of individuals, united by shared behavior or lifestyles, to seek redress does not make it incumbent on government to acquiesce in legally sanctioning their particular behavior. Otherwise there would be no preventing other people from forming associations based on other shared behaviors—no matter how far removed from societal norms—and obtaining "rights" based solely on discrimination against them.

Lobbyists for "neutrality," however, demand that the government not discriminate against one view of life—one "valid lifestyle" as it were—over another.[10] By this approach, the "gay" lifestyle becomes just as valid a manifestation of human existence, and presumably just as vital to the continuation of family and of mankind, as heterosexuality. However, without the ability to distinguish, to discriminate, or to recognize differences, then the concept of equality of treatment before the existing law is debased to mean, in effect, that all individuals—regardless of their behavior—are "the same." But this idea of equality is a radical one, egalitarian in design. It turns on its head the notion of individual equality before the law to one where law that makes moral distinctions itself becomes invalid before equal individuals. This tactic results in "the legal disestablishment of morality."[11]

POWER, SOCIAL MORALITY, AND PERSONAL VALUES

Some researchers have sought to find a genetic or physiological root to homosexuality to lessen or remove moral judgments about it. But the jury is still out on the degree to which prenatal (as opposed to postnatal) determinants affect sexual orientation.[12] On the other hand, some homosexuals maintain that homosexuality is a behavior of choice, "a political statement"—or as PBS's "Tongues Untied" described it, "the revolutionary act." This dynamism, then, this energy and force that characterize the homosexual movement in America, places the question of the avowed homosexual's integration into the armed forces in a new light: the issue is about power, political power, and revolutionary change. As columnist Samuel Francis writes, it is about who determines "the norms by which we live, and by which we define and govern ourselves."[13]

Who decides these questions for the military services? Tradition? Religion? Congress? The president? Ultimately, service mores are a reflection of values held by the civil society from which service members are drawn. Roger H. Nye explains: "Military courses in ethics and professionalism teach a lengthy process of reasoning one's way through moral dilemmas. But the decisions of junior commanders reflect less of what they have been taught as soldiers and more of the moral characteristics they brought with them into the army from their teachers, parents, and childhood environments."[14] Our leadership must understand that simply declaring a new morality by executive or legislative fiat does not automatically imbue soldiers and officers with a new professional ethic concerning issues of right and wrong, particularly if it is seen as an overtly political act.[15]

What about rights? Excessive talk about rights tends to polarize debate between absolutes and does not allow for political consensus-building. Does anyone have an unconditional right to be in the army (or in any of the services)? The historical answer is clearly no. The army routinely discriminates when recruiting soldiers, enrolling ROTC [Reserve Officers Training Corps] cadets, or considering appointments to West Point. The army must consider not only skill requirements and the educational level of applicants, but such factors as personal histories, past criminal behavior, and overall mental and physical aptitudes. It is simply a fact that some of these discriminators are based in part on the negative impact some people would have on the ability of the army to "preserve good order and discipline" and accomplish its missions. Some will say that these same arguments were made against the integration of minorities and women, but the fact is that race and gender are not behavior. Sexual conduct is. We all have choices to make in life about who we want to be. By these choices we define and limit ourselves from being other things. A homosexual can no more claim an absolute right to admission to the army than can anyone else who fails to meet the standards that the army and society deem optimum for building the force.

The argument is sometimes heard that the proposed policy would embrace the notion of demonstrated behavior only. That is, homosexuals would be incorporated into the force, but only on the condition that they never engage in homosexual activities. In other words, their army lives would be celibate, or, more properly, chaste. This notion appears to be a remarkably hopeful one, for it contemplates a degree of sexual discipline imposed on one set of young men and women that is but a forlorn hope in the secular community at large. It denies that which is perhaps the most powerful of human drives. Thus, to argue with a straight face for chastity as a condition for service membership by homosexuals is either fatally naive or cynically disingenuous.

But there are more serious objections. If this policy is to be strictly behavior-based, then we would, in effect, be adopting a policy of partial legitimization. If those supporting homosexual integration are sincere in their behavior-based policy proposals, then the signal that we contemplate sending is essentially this: homosexual soldiers, as a matter of legal right, may now serve, but they must understand that that right is limited. Yes, they can serve, but they cannot have a spouse or act out the very lifestyle which is the basis of their newfound rights in the first place. All of this begs an obvious question: Is the lifestyle or sexual orientation (or whatever term might be used in an executive order or act of Congress) legitimate or not? If it is, then why delimit anyone's rights that flow from that lifestyle? It seems difficult to imagine our leadership sending a mixed message of this kind to any group, at least for very long. One may understand the suspicions of those opposed that "behavior" is being used only to sell a policy, and that once implemented behavioral restrictions will inevitably erode.

CONSEQUENCES OF INTEGRATION

What would be the practical consequences for the army if given the order to integrate homosexuals? The Uniform Code of Military Justice [UCMJ], which now proscribes sodomy (Art. 125), codifies the institutional service morality. In addition to Article 125's specific prohibition against sodomy, Article 133 proscribes "conduct unbecoming an officer and gentleman," and Article 134 proscribes all forms of conduct that "prejudice good order and discipline" or "bring discredit upon the armed forces."[16] What if these limitations were removed or reinterpreted, and the term "alternative lifestyle" were made the standard by which we judge behavior? There would be little to restrain any kind of alternative lifestyle which a consenting adult may wish to assert as his or her right. Concern for off-duty behavior may have to become a thing of the past.

Would polygamy or consensual open marriage then constitute an alternative lifestyle? Would adultery, now punishable under the UCMJ (and not infrequently punished), still be grounds for punishment? Before quickly answering "no" to the first question, and "yes" to the second, one must review the standard by which those conclusions are reached and compare it with those standards that would be used to give legal sanction to the homosexual lifestyle. Acceptance of the neutrality principle of the new morality loosens the underpinnings not only of societal norms, but of many of our legal concepts. Once we slip the shackles of "antiquated legal and moral notions," we find ourselves suddenly in the broken field of moral relativism. The oft-repeated cliché "I'm okay, you're okay" can then come to be applied to all the standards that govern the manner in which citizens of a civilized society conduct themselves.

If avowed homosexuals are allowed in the armed forces, would homosexual marriage be recognized for the purpose of conferring survivor pay and benefits? Homosexual "spouses," officially or informally, would inevitably be a part of army life. Would we recognize a homosexual couple as parents? Would they be assigned government quarters on military installations? How would army service community organizations be affected? Would officers' and noncommissioned officers' spouses' clubs open themselves to the significant other of homosexual members? This new "civil right" could hardly be limited to lower-ranking soldiers—OCS [Officer Candidate School], ROTC, and the service academies would all be affected as well.

If integration occurs, would the "privacy" of behavior then be the new standard for judging conduct, or, going further, would the privatization of morals lead to their disappearance altogether? Would the army protect the privacy of heterosexuals vis-à-vis homosexuals in the same way it now protects the privacy of gender, with separate sleeping quarters, showers, and latrines? Or would this simply be a one-way street, with homosexuality emerging as a newly recognized, constitutionally protected right which overrides privacy concerns by heterosexuals both male and female? Before saying no, the reader must consider that the advocates of these new policies seek the same rights and privileges which accrue on the basis of race, color, and creed.

The implications are endless. How, for example, is the army to defend itself against charges of imputed bias in the case of promotion passovers, SERBS [Selective Early Retirement Boards], RIFs [Reduction in Forces], nonselection for coveted schools, undesirable assignments, etc., that occur with avowedly homosexual personnel? We all know the story: disproportionately low minority representation among select groups is often construed as prima facie evidence of discrimination. Within a very short period after the new policy's implementation, we could well see tacit floors, quotas, and other affirmative action devices to assure that homosexual personnel receive their "fair share" of benefits. These and similar results represent the logical extension of an integration order on the army, which, like other political policies, may have unintended or unanticipated second- and third-order effects.

What would be the impact on readiness, deployability of units, and the army health care system? Study of this issue would be incomplete without a realistic risk assessment with regard to AIDS. According to Alfred Kinsey, whose figures remain remarkably current based on later assessments, the average homosexual has 1,000 sex partners in a lifetime. *Village Voice* put the figure at 1,600.[17] No one debates the linkage between male homosexual behavior and this the most serious disease of the generation. It is generally conceded that homosexuals account for 65 to 70 percent of all AIDS cases in the United States. When intravenous drug-users, hemophiliacs, and Haitians are deducted from the population figures (a valid adjustment because of the reduced likelihood of these groups serving in the armed forces), homosexuals account for between 90 and 95 percent of cases.[18] An article appearing in the *Journal of the American Medical Association*[19] reported the average direct medical cost of the earliest group of AIDS cases to be $147,000 per patient. Using Consumer Price Index [CPI] averages, that cost will grow to some $386,000 per patient by the year 2000, and almost $639,000 by 2008. . . .[20]

Assuming the frequently heard claim that homosexuals represent 10 percent of the American population is true, and that policy changes currently under consideration are made, an active duty military force with some 140,000 to 150,00 gays within the next ten to fifteen years can reasonably be posited.[21] What would be the effect on the military medical system if there were, say, 10,000 (about 3 percent of the expected male homosexual accessions)[22] new full-blown AIDS cases among active duty personnel through the first several years of the next century? This is a conservative assumption considering that some 5.8 percent of male homosexuals in the United States have already tested positive for HIV.[23] Can the Department of Defense afford outlays of nearly $6.5 billion ($639,000 times 10,000 cases) just for AIDS-related costs by 2008? Can the Department of Veterans Affairs? What effect would such additional costs have on care for other active duty personnel? On family members? On retirees? On the CHAMPUS [Civilian Health and Medical Program for the Uniformed Services] system? What would be the cost of replacing the military occupational specialties lost by AIDS casualties?

But that is not the whole story. Over 50 percent of syphilis cases in the United States occur in homosexual men.[24] Fifty to 75 percent of gay men have or have had hepatitis B (a highly contagious disease, potentially devastating to a military unit),[25] while 90 percent demonstrate chronic or recurrent viral infections with herpesvirus, cytomeglavoris, and the same hepatitis B.[26] The implications for the army blood supply, particularly in combat situations, are obvious. War is a bloody business, and the adverse impact on individual morale and unit cohesiveness of encountering potentially AIDS-infected blood while handling or treating war-wounded comrades should not be lightly brushed aside.

THE ROLE OF LEADERSHIP

Soldiers must depend on and have confidence in the decisions of their leaders. There exists a vital link between trust and morale. Good staff work, sober study and reflection, and common sense are prerequisites to command decision. In the heat of crisis, of course, arms and equipment may be placed in service without being thoroughly tested. But that is a calculated risk soldiers understand. They intuitively accept the state's right to impose risk. But trust presumes that such risk is firmly related to, and bears directly on, operational necessity.

With regard to new social policy in the armed forces, however, no such risk is justified. A rush to judgment on this issue may take its toll in the confidence that soldiers feel toward their leadership. Our leadership must not sacrifice that trust by appearing to act quickly and politically. Too much is at stake. A drastic change in the social fabric of the army such as that now being considered must be closely analyzed in terms of its effects on cohesion, teamwork, and, yes, trust and confidence. Our leadership should seek answers to the quite natural questions being raised. Failing satisfactory answers, it is the duty of our leadership to urge restraint.

Such a course will take courage, a different kind of courage from that required on the battlefield. For we live in an age of increasing intolerance in American politics. It is an age of rhetorical excess, which recalls the totalitarian penchant for linguistic polarization[27] which some have likened to verbal terrorism. In the issue at hand, opposition to recognition of homosexuality as a constitutionally protected classification is automatically termed "homophobia." This is a favorite media shibboleth, though etymologically inaccurate. A phobia is "an abnormal or illogical fear of a specific thing or situation." To attack someone's mental state as "phobic" simply because he has a moral reservation or opposing view is not unlike the approach used in the old Soviet Union where dissidents were diagnosed as requiring psychological treatment and placed in "mental hospitals." The two approaches are closely related: one who disagrees with proposed policy changes is ridiculed as having a mental disorder.

Philosophically construed, one of the main purposes of the present essay is to urge that the majority deserves toleration as well as the minority. Societal norms now in effect are indeed those of toleration. All but a tiny minority, the likes of which infect every society, are willing to live and let live. With few exceptions the American people show no inclination to interfere in the private lives of homosexuals, transsexuals, transvestites, and others regarded as deviant. It is quite another thing, however, to say that because of the lifestyle a minority chooses to adopt, it can demand legal reform that impinges adversely on the lives and security of the majority.

The army as an institution, imperfect as it is, should aspire to our highest values. The most tolerant approach would be to recognize the practical and moral consequences of this proposed change on the army and its members. As currently constituted, the integrity and cohesion of the army as an institution are intact. It can continue to defend the nation, defending a common way of life that can tolerate the uncommon. But to impose a neutral legal standard and a new moral view of homosexuality on the army would be a singularly intolerant act, striking at the heart of cohesion and institutional morality. It would be a remarkably divisive decision.

The decision to integrate, should it occur, should be taken only as the logical result of a "positive" finding: a determination that the integration of homosexuals would in fact strengthen the force and lay the groundwork for the superb military team the challenges of the twenty-first century will require.

Columnist George Will has written, "The alternative to waging the cultural war is acquiescence in the atrophy of democratic processes."[28] The pressures on the army leadership to acquiesce in the "politically correct" position on the homosexual issue (as well as others) are enormous. But since the final decision does not rest with the services, our leaders' legacies will be determined not by the final decision itself, but rather by the quality of their advice, their representation of the army's and services' interests, and their stewardship with regard to future readiness. Thus if our leadership merely fulfills its responsibilities for ascertaining the facts and making a considered policy recommendation, then it will have done its duty.

While serving as president of the Naval War College, Admiral James Stockdale lamented the ethical decline in the military during the Vietnam era. He said this:

> Society as a whole has adopted the judicial process as its moral yardstick and forfeited common sense and personal responsibility. . . . Too many have become relativists without any defined moral orientation. Too many are content to align their value systems with fads and buzzwords, and mindlessly try to obey what amounts to a hodgepodge mixture of inconsistent slogans. . . . However, if anything has power to sustain an individual in peace or war, regardless of occupation, it is one's conviction and commitment to defined standards of right and wrong. . . . Each man must bring himself to some stage of ethical resolution.[29]

Surely, as we approach a decision on the vexed issue of admitting avowed homosexuals into the force, adherence to Admiral Stockdale's appeal to principle represents the ultimate tolerant act.

NOTES

1. Michael Barone, *Our Country* (New York: The Free Press, 1990) p. xi.

2. Christopher Dawson, quoted in William J. Bennett, *The Devaluing of America: The Fight for Our Culture and Our Children* (New York: Summit Books, 1992), p. 25.

3. Robert Bork, *The Tempting of America* (New York: The Free Press, 1990), pp. 115–26.

4. Ibid., p. 246.

5. Ibid., p. 249.

6. John Gray, *The Loss of Virtue* (New York: National Review Books, 1995).

7. Carl J. Friedrich and Zbigniew Brzezinski, *Totalitarian Dictatorship and Autocracy* (New York: Praeger), pp. 15–27, 183–202.

8. Gray, *The Loss of Virtue.*

9. Ibid.

10. Ibid. For an excellent brief debunking of propaganda asserting the moral equivalence of the homosexual and heterosexual lifestyles, see George Will, "Respect OK, Not Indifference," *The Sentinel* (Carlisle, Pa.), 7 December 1992, p. B3.

11. Ibid.

12. E. L. Pattullo, "Straight Talk about Gays," *Commentary* 94 (December 1992): 21–24.

13. Samuel Francis, cited in Patrick Buchanan, "Yes, Governor Cuomo There Is a Cultural War," *Conservative Chronicle* 23 (September 1992).

14. Roger H. Nye, *The Challenge of Command* (Wayne, N.J.: Avery Publishing Group, 1986), p. 94.

15. Enrique T. Rueda, *The Homosexual Network: Private Lives and Public Policy* (Old Greenwich, Conn.: The Devin Adair Company, 1982), p. 139.

16. *Manual for Courts-Martial, United States,* 1951, pp. 447, 449.

17. As cited in R. Emmett Tyrrell, Jr., ed., *Orthodoxy* (New York: Harper & Row, 1987), p. 170.

18. S. L. Sivak and G. P. Wormer, "How Common Is HTLV-III Infection in the United States?" *New England Journal of Medicine* 313 (1985): 1352–53, as cited in Gene Antonio, *The Aids Cover-up? The Real and Alarming Facts about AIDS* (San Francisco: Ignatius Press, 1986), p. 132.

19. Hardy et al., "The Economic Impact of the First 10,000 Cases of Acquired Immuno-deficiency Syndrome in the United States," *Journal of the American Medical Association* (1986): 209–11. Cited in Antonio, *The Aids Cover-up?* p. 132.

20. *The World Almanac and Book of Facts 1991* (New York: Pharos Books, 1990), p. 113. The 1985 cost of $147,000, compounded annually using the CPI medical cost inflation rate through 1989, and assuming a 6.5 percent rise in each year thereafter. (6.5 percent is the lowest annual rise for the medical cost component of the CPI between 1985 and 1989.)

21. The plan currently in place calls for an FY95 DoD [Department of Defense] end strength of 1,644,000. Then President-elect Clinton indicated he would go "some 200,000 beyond that." An eventual DoD end strength of between 1.4 and 1.5 million appears to be a reasonable planning figure.

22. According to the *Defense 92* "Almanac" (September/October 1992), accessions have averaged approximately 14.3 percent of the average annual DoD end strength. While this percentage has fallen since 1989, we assume that over the next fifteen years the ratio of accessions to end strength will reflect historical levels. Based on the lowest planning figures, total accessions between 1993 and 2008 would be approximately 3,468,000. Assuming a constant rate of 10.96 percent female (the current figure), 3,088,000 men will be recruited or commissioned over the next fifteen years. According to Gay Rights organizations, approximately 308,800 are likely to be gay.

23. Michael Fumento ("Do You Believe in Magic?" *American Spectator* 25 [February 1992]: 16–21) cites statistics from the Center for Disease Control indicating that approximately one million Americans have contracted HIV (100,000 have died). According to Fumento, some 700,000 of these are homosexual males. Again, assuming that 10 percent of the male population are gay (12 million), this would mean that approximately 5.8 percent have already been infected with HIV. Since approximately 26 percent of males are under eighteen, the adult homosexual infection rate would be approximately 8 percent.

24. Pearl Ma and Donald Armstrong, *The Acquired Immune Deficiency Syndrome and Infections of Homosexual Men* (New York: Yorke Medical Books, 1984), p. 6, as cited in Antonio, *The Aids Cover-up?* p. 54.

25. Jeanne Kessler, *Gay Men's Health: A Guide to the AID Syndrome and Other Sexually Transmitted Diseases* (New York: Harper and Row, 1983), p. 38, as cited in Antonio, *The Aids Cover-up?* p. 45.

26. David G. Ostrow, Terri A. Sandholzer, and Yehudi M. Felman, *Sexually Transmitted Diseases in Homosexual Men* (New York: Plenum Medical Book Co., 1983), p. 204, as cited in Antonio, *The Aids Cover-up?* p. 45.

27. Robert Jay Lifton, "Death and History: Ideological Totalism, Victimization, and Violence," in *Totalitarianism Reconsidered,* ed. Ernest A. Menze (Port Washington, N.Y.: Kennikat Press, 1981), p. 227.

28. George F. Will, *Suddenly: The American Idea at Home and Abroad* (New York: Free Press, 1990), p. 358.

29. James B. Stockdale, "Taking Stock," *Naval War College Review* 31 (Fall 1978): 1–2.

23

The Gay Ban: Just Plain Un-American

Barry Goldwater

After more than fifty years in the military and politics, I am still amazed to see how upset people can get over nothing. Lifting the ban on gays in the military isn't exactly nothing, but it's pretty damned close.

Everyone knows that gays have served honorably in the military since at least the time of Julius Caesar. They'll still be serving long after we're all dead and buried. That should not surprise anyone.

But most Americans should be shocked to know that while the country's economy is going down the tubes, the military has wasted a half-billion dollars over the past decade chasing down gays and running them out of the armed services.

It's no great secret that military studies have proven again and again that there's no valid reason for keeping the ban on gays. Some thought gays were crazy, but then found that wasn't true. Then they decided gays were a security risk, but again the Department of Defense decided that wasn't so—in fact, one study by the navy in 1956 that has never been made public found gays to be good security risks. Even Larry Korb, President Reagan's man in charge of implementing the Pentagon ban on gays, now admits it was a dumb idea. No wonder my friend Dick Cheney, secretary of defense under President Bush, called it "a bit of an old chestnut."

When the facts lead to one conclusion, I say it's time to act, not to hide. The country and the military know that eventually the ban will be lifted. The only remaining questions are how much muck we will all be dragged through, and how many brave Americans like Tom Paniccia and Col. Margarethe Cammermeyer will have their lives and careers destroyed in a senseless attempt to stall the inevitable.

---

*From the *Washington Post,* June 10, 1993. © The Washington Post. Reprinted by permission.

Some in Congress think I'm wrong. They say we absolutely must continue to discriminate or all hell will break loose. Who knows, they say, perhaps our soldiers may even take up arms against each other.

Well, that's just stupid.

Years ago I was a lieutenant in charge of an all-black unit. Military leaders at the time believed that blacks lacked leadership potential—period. That seems ridiculous now, as it should. Now, each and every man and woman who serves this nation takes orders from a black man—our own Gen. Colin Powell.*

Nobody thought blacks or women could ever be integrated into the military. Many thought an all-volunteer force could never protect our national interest. Well, it has—and despite those who feared the worst, I among them, we are still the best and will continue to be.

The point is that decisions are always a lot easier to make in hindsight, but we seldom have that luxury. That's why the future of our country depends on leadership, and that's what we need now.

I served in the armed forces. I have flown more than 150 of the best fighter planes and bombers this country manufactured. I founded the Arizona National Guard. I chaired the Senate Armed Services Committee. And I think it's high time to pull the curtains on this charade of policy.

We have the strongest military in the world because our service people respect the chain of command and know how to follow orders. The military didn't want blacks in integrated units, or women, and now it doesn't want gays. Well, a soldier may not like every order, or every member of his or her unit, but a good soldier will always follow orders—and, in time, respect those who get the job done.

What would undermine our readiness would be a compromise like "Don't ask, don't tell." That compromise doesn't deal with the issues—it tries to hide it.

We have wasted enough precious time, money, and talent trying to persecute and pretend. It's time to stop burying our heads in the sand and denying reality for the sake of politics. It's time to deal with this straight on and be done with it. It's time to get on with more important business.

The conservative movement, to which I subscribe, has as one of its basic tenets the belief that government should stay out of people's private lives. Government governs best when it governs least—and stays out of the impossible task of legislating morality. But legislating someone's version of morality is exactly what we do by perpetuating discrimination against gays.

We can take polls. We can visit submarines to get opinions on who are the best citizens. But that is not the role of a democratic government in a free society. Under our Constitution, everyone is guaranteed the right to do as he pleases as long as it does not harm someone else. You don't need to be "straight" to fight and die for your country. You just need to shoot straight.

---

*Colin Powell retired as head of the Joint Chiefs of Staff in September 1993. He was replaced by General John Shalikashvili. (Eds.)

With all the good this country has accomplished and stood for, I know that we can rise to the challenge, do the right thing and lift the ban on gays in the military. Countries with far less leadership and discipline have traveled this way, and successfully.

When you get down to it, no American able to serve should be allowed, much less given an excuse, not to serve his or her country. We need all our talent.

If I were in the Senate today, I would rise on the Senate floor in support of our commander in chief. He may be a Democrat, but he happens to be right on this question.

When the government sets policy, it has a responsibility to acknowledge facts, tell the truth, and lead the country forward, not backward. Congress would best serve our national interest by finding the courage to rally the troops in support of ending this un-American discrimination.

24

Uncle Sam Doesn't Want You!

Robert Stone

1

In 1956 I was eighteen years old and a Seaman First Class in the United States Navy. I had joined during the summer of 1955 at seventeen and been sent to the Navy's Radio School at Norfolk. Later that year I was assigned to the class of ship known as an AKA or attack transport. In those grainy old wire photos of the Normandy invasion or Okinawa, AKAs are always visible offshore. They have the classic single stack and superstructure outline of cargo ships but with large A-frames fore and aft. Amphibious landing craft are stacked and secured over their cargo hatches. The ship that features in Thomas Heggen's novel *Mr. Roberts* was an AK, a noncombatant cousin of the AKA.

Heggen's novel catches something of the spirit of the "Gator Navy," as the amphibious force is called, in the period during and after the Second World War. Then as now, its ships were specialized, their form grimly followed function and they were as plain as dumpsters. The Navy did not generally dress them up in pennants for display. During the 1950s, in the Sixth Fleet's own Mediterranean, while the cruisers and supercarriers basked in the sunshine of Rapallo and Villefranche, the amphib gator ships were elsewhere: Bari, Patras, Izmir. Much time was spent practicing amphibious assaults on beaches in Turkey, Crete, or Sardinia.

Like hotels, colleges, and prisons, ships have their particular informing atmosphere. And despite the navy's mode of slate-gray uniformity, each vessel had qualities that could be isolated and analyzed. To lifers, career petty officers, the first question about a ship was often: "Is she a good feeder?" Eating was the principal pleasure available at sea. Good cooks were prized.

This is a review of Randy Shilts, *Conduct Unbecoming* (see chapter 18 in this volume). Reprinted with permission from *The New York Review of Books.* Copyright © 1993 Nyrev, Inc.

* * *

The personnel clerk who typed the orders transferring me from radio school to my new ship was a fellow New Yorker. We fell into conversation and he told me I was going to a problem ship.

"They're always falling off ladders," he said.

During the 1950s, discipline in the U.S. Navy was tight and fairly effective. Nevertheless, a ship was essentially its crew. Certain ships were dominated, prison-style, by cliques of sailors—sometimes men from the same tough town—who enforced a code of their own below decks. It has to be said that this was not universal, but everyone heard the stories. Such a ship's officers might be only vaguely aware of the systems that prevailed in the enlisted quarter. Masters-at-arms and senior petty officers either looked the other way or, like crooked cops, made some political accommodations with the de facto leadership. Certain captains naively approved, seeing a form of rough democracy, crude peer pressure that furthered cohesion.

Taking up my new billet, I was assigned to bunking space of the deck division because there were no bunks then available in the radio gang's sleeping quarters. At that time, men assigned to each of the ship's divisions bunked in the same compartment. The sleeping arrangements then consisted of "racks" four or five high from the deck, sheets of canvas stretched within metal rectangles and secured to the bulkhead by lengths of chain.

One day during our first week at sea I went below to arrange my gear in the deck division's compartment and encountered Flem (not, as they say, his real name), a third-class boatswain's mate, who was goldbricking below decks while better men worked topside. He ran a little tailoring and pressing shop in a tiny locker off one of the passageways. Seeing me settle in, Flem assumed I was a new seaman in his notoriously tyrannized deck division, thus his inferior in rank and with my fortunes at his disposal. He was a small, freckled man, round, neckless, and thick-featured. With his slack smile and shifty eyes he looked like a lying witness at a country murder trial.

When Flem introduced himself he made no offer of shaking hands, itself a considerable insult. He told me a few things I already knew about how tough life was aboard that particular AKA and how much tougher he could make it. He told me I looked like "tender gear" to him. "Tender gear" was a common navy expression, dating back to the good old days. It was applied to sailors of youthful appearance, when imagined as passive partners in prison-style, "facultative" homosexuality or as the victims of rape.

(This phrase was one of many homoerotic terms current in the navy. Like them, it could be used insultingly, ambiguously, or good-naturedly as in: "Carruthers, I'm so horny you look like tender gear to me." A man's reputation for wit, something useful and valued, could ride on the quality of the rejoinder.)

But Flem wasn't my buddy and he wasn't kidding. He wasn't starry-eyed with affection either. That night I thought it prudent to take a spare bunk chain to bed with me. Some time during the dead of night he woke me up with a lot of prods and heavy breathing. So we ended up fighting up and down the faintly lit compartment. A few men were awake and silent or laughing; I was new, nobody much cared. In those days I was always blundering into fights only to be reminded that it wasn't like the movies, to be amazed by the strength and determination of my opponent. Although drunk, Flem had the energy of an insect and, apparently, great single-mindedness.

But I was younger, stronger, and sober, my reputation on a new ship was at stake, and I had the chain. I was also considerably embittered. The youthful appearance that aroused lust in Flem seemed to make any woman I had the temerity to approach dismiss me as a Sea Scout. Flem went into the head to wash the blood off himself, cursed me out from a distance, and crept back to the tailor shop where he lived. The next day his face was swollen and covered with welts as though he had landed on his chin in poison ivy. The worse Flem looked the better for me, since every enlisted man aboard soon knew the story.

A few days later, we were off Gibraltar and I went past his shop and he said something to me I couldn't hear. I doubled back, lest it be thought he could mock me with impunity.

"How's that?"

He stood beside the presser, looking down at a blue jumper on the pad.

"You cried just like a cooze," he said, still not looking at me. I had an immediate anxiety that he was speaking for effect, trying to make anyone within earshot believe things had turned out differently. But there was no one around, so I went on my way. Appearances were everything.

I didn't want to think I had cried during engagement but it occurred to me that I might well have. I didn't care for the picture the reflection summoned forth, me whacking Flem repeatedly with a bunk chain, weeping away "like a cooze."

I was surprised by the memory of my difficulties with Flem some time last year when I was about to engage in a public discussion on the subject of sexual harassment. I had originally approached the issue as an examination of conscience, looking back on my relations with women over the years.

Flem and I were not romancing the wilder shores of love, we were acting out an old dirty sea story that must go back to the Phoenicians and has more to do with power, cruelty, strength, and weakness than with any kind of attraction. I'm sure Flem felt about the same fondness for me that he felt for his favorite farm animal back home. Flem today, if he's alive, retired in his trailer among the palmettos, is unlikely to regard himself as "gay." I think it very likely he thoroughly opposes the notion of gays being able to serve in the military.

A second bit of reminiscence about my time in service. About two and a half years after the business with Flem, I was serving aboard a different ship, also an AKA. By this time I was a petty officer myself, feeling very experienced and salty. The ship had just returned to the States from a long voyage that had kept it at sea for many weeks at a time and away from the United States for the better part of a year. Evenings at sea or on duty nights in port when we could not go ashore, a group of us, junior petty officers, took to gathering on the ship's fantail or in the shipfitter's shop. We were would-be intellectuals, of about college age, on average twenty-one or twenty-two. We met to smoke and talk and hang out. We liked progressive jazz and thought the *Playboy* philosophy was pretty hot stuff.

It was 1958, the year after *On the Road* was published. We were all short-timers, a few months shy of our discharges; the Road seemed to be waiting for us. Moreover, we found in the navy an inexhaustible fund of humor and buffoonery. Everything about it—from the hats we shared with Donald Duck to the grotesque locutions of the Uniform Code of Military Justice—struck us as risible. Without question, we got on some people's nerves. We were presently to learn the nature of the nerves we got on.

One evening while I was in New York on leave and on my way to the Central Plaza for an evening of jazz with my date I was arrested by a couple of plain-clothes New York cops on a charge of being absent without leave. I was not in fact AWOL. Nevertheless I was turned over to the New York military police headquarters in Hell's Kitchen where I spent several hours leaning against a wall on my finger tips trying to persuade an MP sergeant to call my ship in Norfolk. Eventually the sergeant did, the ship's duty officer confirmed my leave status, and I was released.

My false arrest had been part of the shockwave from a purge touched off by some incident in the Naval District. Foolish inquisitions and malicious informing were being promiscuously encouraged. Someone had told the executive officer about our gang of malingerers in the shipfitter's shop. It seemed that we were planning to found a motorcycle gang to be named the Weird Beards. It would have its headquarters near the Bethlehem Steel Yards in Staten Island. It would engage in unlawful activities and actions prejudicial to good order. Its members would carry arms and be dangerous. They would worship Satan, harass Christians, use marijuana, and, conveniently, be homosexual.

This was all amusing in every regard save one—that the navy in those days was obsessed with in-service gangs and homosexuality and tended, on not much evidence and without much formality, to lock alleged violators in the bowels of Portsmouth Naval Prison for years and years. The report of my being AWOL (based, needless to say, on some fantasy spun in the shipfitter's shop) seemed to speak most urgently to those obsessions.

The executive officer panicked and ordered the immediate arrest of everyone mentioned in the report. He must have imagined us already on the highway, darkening the horizon, mincing into Harley shops, torching roadside chapels. Some people came back in chains.

We discovered that lockers had been broken into, letters removed, possessions rifled through and, of course, occasionally stolen unofficially. I happened to own a paperback called *Immortal Poems of the English Language,* which I subsequently spotted on a master-at-arms desk in the ship's brig. Evidence, for sure. The MAA handed it back to me as though he were afraid there was semen on it.

In the aftermath, when the whole thing fell apart, the exec apparently felt silly. He would even show up in the shipfitter's shop to be pals, making us all stand to attention and upset our coffee. When I applied to college, being under twenty-one, I needed a signature on my application from a "parent or guardian." I was directed to the exec who signed it and gave me a nice letter to go with it, not a word about homosexual motorcycle gangs or anything like that.

"Of course," he said, chuckling "I'm not really your guardian."

"No, sir," I said.

Had I the naivete to report Flem during the first incident, I would have seen many a sour face and disgusted expression of which I, not Flem, would have been the object. I would have branded myself a pussy, a snitch, and quite possibly a homosexual. A man was expected to cope. Not quite conversely, if Flem had been able to coerce me into accommodation, shipboard opinion would have despised me, not him. A lingering tradition would have excused him, not legally but morally. The navy preferred not to know about the potential for forcible sodomy but could work itself into a moralizing dudgeon over rumors of subversion, with poetry as evidence. And as surely as today's charges of kindergarten child abuse tend to incorporate accusations of witchcraft, subversive notions in the navy were profoundly associated with homosexuality.

2

Whether or not the preceding sad story has a moral, it reflects the shabby and sordid way the armed forces have approached homosexuality in the ranks over the years, This is the subject of Randy Shilts's long book, *Conduct Unbecoming: Lesbians and Gays in the Military, Vietnam to the Persian Gulf.* Shilts's business here is advocacy, and he writes in favor of the right of gays and lesbians to serve in the U.S. armed forces. His arguments seem to grow more reasoned and less strident as the book proceeds, and he has a good reporter's instinct for the core of a story. He begins, somewhat irrelevantly, by invoking the Sacred Band of Thebes and George Washington's silk tights, but the cumulative effect of *Conduct Unbecoming* is a clear indictment of the morally confused and weak-minded policy that has prevailed so far.

If there is a single reference point against which the whole of *Conduct Unbecoming* may be viewed it is the report he cites, one officially entitled the "Report of the Board Appointed to Prepare and Submit Recommendations to the Secretary of the Navy for the Revision of Policies, Procedures and Directives Dealing with Homosexuals." This classified document, known less ponderously as "The Crittenden Report," might well surprise today's Congressional zealots for a 100 percent he-man heterosexual military. Shilts quotes from and summarizes it at length. The board writes:

> There is no correlation between homosexuality and either ability or attainments. Whether or not public opinion holds homosexuality to be synonymous with degeneracy, the fact remains that a policy which long remained contrary to public opinion could not but have an adverse effect on the navy.

Elsewhere the panel concluded:

> A nice balance must be maintained in changes of policy to ensure that public sensibilities are not offended in any attempt to promote a forward-looking program in recognition of the advances in the knowledge of homosexual behavior and treatment, nor can there be any intimation that homosexual conduct is condoned. It is not considered to be in the best interests of the military departments to liberalize standards ahead of the civilian climate; thus in so far as practicable it is recommended that the navy keep abreast of developments but not attempt to take a position of leadership.

Drawing on testimony from a variety of experts, the report generally refutes every truism behind the ban on homosexuals: There are "many known instances of individuals who have served honorably and well, despite being exclusively homosexual." The notion that gays were security risks was "without sound basis in fact. . . . No intelligence agency, as far as can be learned, adduced any factual data" (to support this conclusion). In fact, "there is some information to indicate that homosexuals are quite good security risks."

The report goes on to recommend that discovered homosexuals no longer be less than honorably discharged. It refers to the concentration of homosexuals in certain specialties—the medical services, the women's branch—as known facts of life, and it ends by suggesting, Shilts writes, that the navy " 'keep abreast' of social attitudes toward homosexuality."

This extraordinary document was prepared not, as might be thought, in preparation for a Clinton presidency but during the second Eisenhower administration, in 1957. Like all those bottles of ketchup we heard about but never saw, a crucial part of this wisdom was apparently tucked away somewhere in one of the navy's subtropical depots and forgotten. The absurd homosexual purges, which continue to the present day, very often have more to do with perception than with discipline. They concern the way the services see themselves as being seen, rather than the way in which they really see themselves or the way they actually are. Years later the military would indignantly deny the very existence of the Crittenden Report and only persistent application of the Freedom of Information Act retrieved it from the caves of the Pentagon.

There are many personal stories in *Conduct Unbecoming,* maybe a few more than the reader can keep track of. One of the saddest occurs over and over again, the pattern repeating itself as names and precise circumstances change: A young person, often a teenager, joins the service. In the course of enlistment that person discovers himself or herself to be gay. Service conditions provide the opportunity for an affair, not infrequently the first. Discovery follows and arrest and then terrorizing interrogations by the squalid keyhole cops of the military investigative services. There are the usual threats of disgrace: the prisoner's parents will be told, her home-town neighbors, his high-school coach, the boyfriend or girlfriend back home, and so on. And as often as not it seems, even after the victim destroys the remains of his or her own self-respect by naming names, the threats are made good. Then, the Crittenden recommendation notwithstanding, the subject is usually released into civilian life with a bad discharge, humiliated, sometimes traumatized for life.

This comes about, Shilts demonstrates, as a result of a routine procedure, the turning over of suspects to the military investigative services, whose livelihood has always been charges of homosexual behavior. Like the medieval church remanding heretics to the secular arm, commanding officers have dispatched accused personnel to the mercies of these agencies, of which the civilian-manned Naval Investigative Service is the most notorious. Shilts records an observation current in the fleet.

> Call the NIS [Naval Investigative Service] and tell them you've got a dead body and the agents may show up in the next week or so. Call and say you've got a dead body and you think the murderer was homosexual and the agents will be there in thirty seconds.

The stories Shilts marshals about the NIS are harrowing. Most harrowing of all is its attempt to blame the explosion in the USS *Iowa* gun turret on a fabricated gay relationship, in support of which it ruthlessly doctored circumstantial evidence and posthumously blackened the name of a sailor killed in the explosion.

The navy could have done with a better, wiser, and more humane investigative service because its ships were not without problems. In recounting the case of a 1980 anti-lesbian purge aboard the USS *Norton Sound* that was instigated by the complaint of a female sailor, Shilts describes post-Vietnam War conditions at their nadir: a ship utterly out of control, undisciplined, rife with dope dealing, loan sharking, violence, and tension between every identifiable group, racial, sexual, or otherwise. Anyone who has ever served aboard a U.S. Navy ship will know the sort of floating hell such a vessel can be. The USS *Belleau Wood*, an amphibious ship whose admittedly gay crew member Allen Schindler was murdered last year, seems to have supported similar conditions.

Until the middle of the 1970s, the military succeeded in living with the kind of contradictions that only a prestigious bureaucracy, with good public relations, can resolve. It was well aware that its ranks contained homosexuals, whose presence it often tolerated out of expedience. From time to time it would arrest and sacrifice one, *pour encourager les autres* [to encourage the others], a process of culling meant to demonstrate that the armed services were still part of Middle America.

During the Vietnam War, the numbers of homosexuals the military was shocked to detect in its ranks mysteriously diminished. Shilts asserts that during that war, draft boards were instructed to demand "proof" from inductees who claimed to be homosexual, proof which would not only be embarrassing but would make anyone who supplied it criminally liable in almost all of the United States. In other words, like society in general, the services dealt with homosexuality in an inconsistent, arbitrary way, entirely on the military's own terms.

But the world was changing, and after the Vietnam War the military was no longer so prestigious nor were its public relations so effective. A wave of activism was washing away old arrangements. In March 1975, a career air force sergeant with twelve years' service named Leonard Matlovich, Jr., wrote a letter to the secretary of the air force via his commanding officer. Matlovich had an outstanding record; he was the kind of senior noncom who makes the services work, a wounded veteran of Vietnam, a wearer of the Bronze Star. One can only imagine the foreboding that ascended the chain of command with this document.

"After some years of uncertainty," Matlovich wrote, "I have arrived at the conclusion that my sexual preferences are homosexual as opposed to heterosexual. I have also concluded that my sexual preferences will in no way interfere with my air force duties, as my preferences are now open. It is therefore requested that those provisions in AFM39-12 relating to the discharge of homosexuals be waived in my case."

The U.S. military had been overtaken by what might be called the American Factor. The most moralizing and legalistic country on earth, the land where everybody is responsible for everything although nobody is responsible for anything, was about to quarrel with itself. With its customary moral valor, the military looked wildly about for a moment, then sided with what appeared to be the respectable element. Its instincts were conservative and it wanted nothing more than to appear respectable. The air force initiated discharge proceedings against Matlovich, invoking AFM39-12, the very ordinance he had challenged. But as of March 6, 1975, the days of arbitrary punishment and arbitrary tolerance were numbered.

Any story whose subject is social change in America will consist in large part of legal detail, and *Conduct Unbecoming* is no exception. The book sets forth scores of cases and describes scores of proceedings and procedures, from discharge hearings to sessions of the Supreme Court. The case of Leonard Matlovich is one of many. Yet it is an informing thread running through the period under discussion, and there are few accounts in the book more poignant. Shilts sentimentalizes Matlovich to some degree but the sergeant's naive idealism and his unhappy fortunes are actually the stuff of drama. In 1980, discouraged by Reagan's election, he accepted a substantial cash settlement from the air force, failed to prosper in civilian life, and died of AIDS in 1988.

Shilts also describes a case with a happier outcome, that of Perry Watkins, an African American who told his Tacoma draft board in May 1968 that he was gay. It being 1968, his draft board told him otherwise: there were no gay blacks of military age in Tacoma in the year of the Tet offensive. Watkins went into the army and liked the life. His female impersonations became the hit routine of every army entertainment, and each time he was presented with a form demanding that he state his sexual preference he declared himself gay. So it went for sixteen years of army service until finally, during the Reagan years, his status was challenged and he was discharged. Watkins sued. In 1990, the U.S. Court of Appeals ordered his reinstatement and the administration appealed. Finally, in November of the same year, twenty-three years after his surreal visit to the Tacoma draft board, the U.S. Supreme Court found for Watkins and ordered him all pay and allowances.

Press accounts of gays in the military have tended to concentrate on homosexual men. In reality, the impact, both in numbers and on the military ambiance, has always been greater on the female side. On the whole a greater proportion of lesbians than male homosexuals have sought military careers. As Shilts makes plain, many have served with particular success. His narrative follows the paradoxical fortunes of a number of lesbians who, while turning in above-average professional performances, have run afoul of the military's social instincts. In some cases, trouble developed as a result of tension between lesbians and male personnel; sometimes there were complaints from nongay women who felt intimidated by lesbians. But the most famous case recounted here is that of Miriam Ben-Shalom, a lesbian who openly revealed her sexual preference upon graduation from drill-sergeant's school and was discharged from the army reserve in 1971 as a result. After literally decades of litigation, Ben-Shalom's administrative discharge was upheld by the Supreme Court in 1990.

By then there were many cases in the courts and the legal situation continued to seesaw. At one point in the Matlovich proceedings Judge Gerhard Gesell of the federal district court in Washington called on the military to take "a more discriminating and informed approach" to the issue but found against Matlovich on technicalities. The judge added: "It seems to the court a tragedy that we must confront—as I fear we will have to unless some change takes place—an effort at reform through persistent, insistent, and often ill-advised litigation."

But persistent litigation is the American way. By the nineties the services had tried to tighten the court-worthiness of their regulations. The armed forces had seen their first in-service AIDS case at Letterman Army Hospital in San Francisco in July 1982, a factor that would alter both the arguments and the underlying reality. But it was plain by the election of 1992 that the services' traditional and irrational methods of dealing with homosexuality had worn away. President Clinton's compromises may be less than the total vindication some activists have called for, but no amount of resistance will bring back the old system.

Various foreign military establishments have their methods of dealing with gay personnel and Shilts approvingly cites some of the more reasonable. But foreign examples are not necessarily useful. The United States has the largest and most active gay rights movement in the world, one completely committed to the right of gays to serve. Gay rights organizations in most other countries—even countries with civil rights laws that protect gays—are not as prominent. In Europe most gay rights organizations are ipso facto antimilitary and inhabit a different world than their armed services. Military service is not one of their priorities.

Charles Moskos, a sociologist at Northwestern University who testified before the Senate Armed Services committee, has pointed out the flaws in basing assumptions on foreign examples.

"More gays in the military have come out of the closet in the American military," Moskos writes, "where homosexuality is proscribed than in those countries (e.g. Israel, Germany, Scandinavia) where it is technically allowed." In those forces where gays are unrestricted, most gay members nevertheless remain in the closet. A distinction must be made, Moskos says, "between de jure and de facto treatment of gays."

Regarding Israel, often cited for its tolerance, Moskos says flatly: "No declared gay holds a command position in a combat arm anywhere in the IDF [Israeli Defense Forces]."[1] The situation in France, which nominally admits gays to its service, is suggested by the diffident language employed by two French military sociologists: "In the military [homosexuality] is shrouded in a kind of silence that does not express embarrassment, but a complete lack of interest. The clue may be that most homosexuals are screened or self-selected out."[2]

The situation in Britain, whose forces are governed by restrictions more or less equivalent to those of the United States, seems to be a reverse of the French position; legal prohibition but discreet selective tolerance at Her Majesty's Pleasure.

"The practice," according to an article in *Society*, "is not to act unless they call attention to themselves. Indeed, if their orientation becomes known but they are not openly engaged in homosexual behavior, they might be counseled and warned against misconduct, rather than discharged." Last spring, the RAF [Royal Air Force] discharged Sergeant Simon Ingram after he openly declared himself gay. "Everyone in the RAF has been helpful and supportive," he said. "I'm even going to have a proper leaving party. But the system doesn't change. My career is in ruins. . . ."[3]

It would be a mistake to assume that there are no problems for gays in services that technically do not discriminate. Plainly, many foreign military establishments function by way of arrangement, in which the de jure regulations cover some form of de facto accommodation. This may well prove the case in Australia and Canada, which recently responded to gay rights pressure by ending discrimination in their services.

What all this suggests is simply that every country's military is a reflection of its society. Our continuously divided society has always sought to accommodate different social elements according to the strict letter of the law. We are not good at creating "understandings" because so many of us understand entirely different things. No other country has anything like the polarization between progressive and conservative forces that exists in the United States. No other country has, at the same time, equivalents of either our strong gay rights movement or our militant religious right. The religious right is not without influence in that section of society from which the military is recruited. As Pat Buchanan is fond of saying, "The wars are fought by Catholics and Baptists." Certainly no other country has witnessed anything like the endless hours of testimony, defiance, rhetoric, moralizing, and accusation that have piled American court records on this one subject to the height of the Tower of Babel.

Plainly Bill Clinton was naive to think that he could lift the restrictions against gays in the military with the stroke of a pen. A sample of the arguments being drawn up by military experts opposed to ending the gay ban can be seen in the Spring issue of *Parameters,* the U.S. Army War College quarterly. An article there, by Major R. D. Adair and Captain Joseph C. Myers, is called "Admission of Gays to the Military: A Singularly Intolerant Act." [See chapter 22 in this volume.]

Adair and Myers attack even the "Don't ask, Don't tell" proposal calling it "remarkable hopeful" and also legally unenforceable.

> The [policy] begs an obvious question: Is the lifestyle of sexual orientation or whatever term might be used in an Executive Order or Act of Congress legitimate or not? If it is, then why delimit anyone's rights that flow from that lifestyle?

The article goes on to ask about homosexual marriages in the service. Would gay spouses be able to use PX facilities? Would they be assigned government quarters? "Would officers' and noncommissioned officers' spouses' clubs open themselves to the significant other of homosexual members?"

They pursue the issue into the sphere of affirmative action: "Within a very short period after the new policy's implementation we could well see tacit floors, quotas, and other affirmative action devices to assure that homosexual personnel get their 'fair share' of benefits."

Adair and Myers offer these prospects as a reduction to absurdity. In fact, they are questions that the military may well have to answer in the real world. The signs are clear. Political pressure from the White House and the Congress, legal mandates from the courts, will before very long compel the military to cope with the question of how to incorporate openly gay people into its ranks.

If the proponents of gay rights cannot get everything they require for their constituency, neither can Major Adair and Captain Myers have the world back as it was. Some kind of mutual accommodation will be required, unlikely as the prospect may seem. One of the defiant letters from gays cited in *Conduct Unbecoming* is from an enraged hospital corpsman, protesting antigay discrimination aboard his ship. "I will no longer live a second, secret life," the corpsman writes, "because the navy has seen fit to adhere to an antediluvian, Judeo-Christian posture that no longer and never was congruent with social realism [*sic*]."

But to what extent can the Catholics and Baptists (not to mention Jews) be called upon to abandon their "Judeo-Christian posture"? And to what extent can gays be asked to abandon their gay identity? The U.S. military lacks a grand heraldic or aristocratic tradition. Our army is and always was a "people's army" to a greater degree than that of any other major power. Our informing military totem is the Minute Man, the plough-jockey turned soldier. The military establishment is common ground; it does in fact belong to all Americans just as Shilts claims it does.

In this country, we are not good at subtle arrangements. We tend to get everything in writing, which would seem to make difficult any accommodation between two deeply self-righteous points of view. It may be that we will need to exercise considerably more flexibility in applying the letter of the law and the regulations that will eventually succeed the ones announced by Secretary Aspin. Problems, if they arise, will have to be worked out locally, company by company, vessel by vessel. Conditions like the ones that prevailed aboard the *Norton Sound* cannot be permitted because no accommodation can survive in such an atmosphere. It will be necessary to enlist the consent of all parties to abide by certain guidelines, just as in the past sailors signed the ship's articles as an earnest [statement] of their intention to be governed by the necessities of a vessel at sea.

This, of course, is what Major Adair and Captain Myers would call "remarkably hopeful"; it's easier said than done. In smaller units, where people know each other, provision can be made for everyone's attitude. In the impersonal atmosphere of large installations and supercarriers, it's very difficult to maintain such things as consent and mutual understanding. But the simple fact is our forces are not like other countries' forces; they serve a litigious, volatile country that worships Possibility and they will have to work it out somehow.

It will call for strict discipline, high morale, and some assistance from that Power whom Bismarck once claimed has a special providence for fools and the United States.

3

In the late summer of 1991, while the navy was preparing to grapple with the latest strategies of gay liberation in the wake of the Persian Gulf War, some of its wholesomely heterosexual young aviators—and a few older ones—were preparing for Tailhook '91. If the name sounds faintly risqué, nothing in the

Tailhook Association's published summary of its September "symposium" suggests anything other than huffy-puffy rightmindedness.

> By the time the event ended with a farewell brunch on a Sunday morning, the Tailhook Association knew to a certainty that the Naval Aviation Symposium had realized its full potential. With a varied, objective assessment of the first victory in a full-scale war in half a century, America's fleet aviators departed with enhanced pride in their profession and in themselves.

At the end of the summary, the author's boundless self-satisfaction leads him to echo the immortal Voltaire. "In summary, if the United States Navy did not already have access to a Tailhook Association, there would be every good reason to create one."

Not a word about "butt-biting." Nothing about "ball-walking." No reference to the unfortunate mooning episode in which the mooners managed to moon right through the window, sending broken glass and very nearly some of their number down on the Las Vegas Hilton's swimming pool. And not a whisper about the ninety separate "indecent assaults" that the revelers chalked up, giving the sleuths of the Naval Investigative Service an unaccustomed exercise on the straight side of the street.

The assaults were mainly endured by women who ran a "gauntlet" of scores of drunken young men, who happened to be naval and marine corps aviators. A couple of visiting British pilots seem to have participated as well. In the "gauntlet" the women were lured into a narrowing corridor, surrounded, and then generally felt up, pinched on the breasts and buttocks, and otherwise groped and insulted. In the light of day, a few women claimed they enjoyed it. Others "blew it off" and dismissed the drunken aviators as "jerks." But a great many were thoroughly terrified and seriously feared for their safety. The "gauntlet" was repeated over the several nights of the symposium, growing in relative violence. Its victims included navy wives and strippers, hired bartenders and local college students lured to the event by handbills. It also included many young female navy officers.

Besides the gauntlet and "ballwalking" (a naval jollity in which a drunken man parades with his trouser so adjusted that his testicles are exposed), symposium activity included, according to the Department of Defense investigators, "streaking," "mooning," "leg shaving," and "chicken-fighting." Chicken fighting is an aquatic contest more consensual than the gauntlet, in which two young women in a swimming pool, mounted on the shoulders of naval aviators, attempt to remove each other's bathing suits.

No fewer than thirty-five admirals attended the hi-jinks in Las Vegas, though no one seems to have been in charge. The presence of the secretary of the navy appears not to have sobered the mood. Not until Lieutenant Paula Coughlin, an admiral's aide, complained to her boss, did the incidents begin to become an issue.

Coughlin's boss, Admiral John W. Snyder, Jr., was the commanding officer of Patuxent River Naval Air Test Center, an extremely desirable and influential posting. Unfortunately for his career, he took no action on Coughlin's complaint. When she saw that she was getting no satisfaction from the admiral, Coughlin made her beef official. This involved NIS, whose investigators, so zealous in the pursuit of gays, found themselves stymied by a conspiracy of silence. Their investigation produced few names. They also seemed to have overlooked the presence at Tailhook '91 of Navy Secretary H. Lawrence Garrett III.

Finally, to preempt what she believed was a covert campaign to destroy her reputation, Coughlin went to the press, that ruthless but imperfect agent of redress. The ensuing carnage was terrible. Secretary Garrett was revealed as being in Las Vegas in '91 and ordered by the White House to resign. Admiral Snyder was transferred to a far less prestigious billet—"The kind of thing," an officer said, "where they leave a pistol on the table and everybody leaves the room." An assistant chief of naval operations being groomed for a position among the Joint Chiefs of Staff was made to retire at a reduced rank. The Defense Department was compelled to commence a more thorough investigation, one which still continues.

The Tailhook Association, a curious organization to facilitate contacts between naval officers and civilian contractors, saw its semi-official sponsorship by the navy withdrawn. Its conventions were a true feminist's nightmare, a macho revel of the actual military industrial complex itself, slack jawed, booze-swilling, and sexually predatory. The pilots who took part in Tailhook '91 were mainly young males aged twenty-one to twenty-six. What happened was partly the result of alcohol and partly a function of that atavistic antifemaleness that seems to lurk in the hearts of surprisingly many men.

There was a note of possible cheer for social progress here, however. At the press conference announcing the result of the Tailhook report, Admiral Frank B. Kelso, chief of naval operations, declared: "Tailhook brought to light the fact that we had an institutional problem with women . . . it was a watershed that brought about social change."

And two of the officers who had their buttocks pinched and fondled were men.

NOTES

1. Charles Moskos, "Treatment of Gay Men and Lesbians in Other Militaries" (statement presented to the Committee on Armed Services, U.S. Senate, April 29,1993).

2. Profs. Bernard Boene and Michel Martin, quoted in David R. Segal, Paul A. Gade, and Edgar M. Johnson, "Policies and Practices Regarding Homosexuals in the Military: A Cross-National Perspective," *Society* (November–December 1993).

3. *The Independent,* August 5, 1993.

Part Five

Homosexuality and Religion

25

Letter to the Bishops of the Catholic Church on the Pastoral Care of Homosexual Persons

Joseph Cardinal Ratzinger

1. The issue of homosexuality and the moral evaluation of homosexual acts have increasingly become a matter of public debate, even in Catholic circles. Since this debate often advances arguments and makes assertions inconsistent with the teaching of the Catholic Church, it is quite rightly a cause for concern to all engaged in the pastoral ministry, and this Congregation has judged it to be of sufficiently grave and widespread importance to address to the bishops of the Catholic Church this Letter on the Pastoral Care of Homosexual Persons.

2. Naturally, an exhaustive treatment of this complex issue cannot be attempted here, but we will focus our reflection within the distinctive context of the Catholic moral perspective. It is a perspective which finds support in the more secure findings of the natural sciences, which have their own legitimate and proper methodology and field of inquiry.

However, the Catholic moral viewpoint is founded on human reason illumined by faith and is consciously motivated by the desire to do the will of God our Father. The Church is thus in a position to learn from scientific discovery but also to transcend the horizons of science and to be confident that her more global vision does greater justice to the rich reality of the human person in his spiritual and physical dimensions, created by God and heir, by grace, to eternal life.

It is within this context, then, that it can be clearly seen that the phenomenon of homosexuality, complex as it is, and with its many consequences for society and ecclesial life, is a proper focus for the Church's pastoral care. It thus requires of her ministers attentive study, active concern and honest, theologically well-balanced counsel.

Reprinted from *The Vatican and Homosexuality: Reactions to the "Letter to the Bishops of the Catholic Church on the Pastoral Care of Homosexual Persons,"* edited by Jeannine Gramick and Robert Nugent (New York: Crossroad Publishing Co., 1988), pp. 1–10.

3. Explicit treatment of the problem was given in this Congregation's "Declaration on Certain Questions Concerning Sexual Ethics" of December 29, 1975. That document stressed the duty of trying to understand the homosexual condition and noted that culpability for homosexual acts should only be judged with prudence. At the same time the Congregation took note of the distinction commonly drawn between the homosexual condition or tendency and individual homosexual actions. These were described as deprived of their essential and indispensable finality, as being "intrinsically disordered," and able in no case to be approved of (cf. n. 8, § 4).

In the discussion which followed the publication of the Declaration, however, an overly benign interpretation was given to the homosexual condition itself, some going so far as to call it neutral, or even good. Although the particular inclination of the homosexual person is not a sin, it is a more or less strong tendency ordered toward an intrinsic moral evil; and thus the inclination itself must be seen as an objective disorder.

Therefore, special concern and pastoral attention should be directed toward those who have this condition, lest they be led to believe that the living out of this orientation in homosexual activity is a morally acceptable option. It is not.

4. An essential dimension of authentic pastoral care is the identification of causes of confusion regarding the Church's teaching. One is a new exegesis of Sacred Scripture which claims variously that Scripture has nothing to say on the subject of homosexuality, or that it somehow tacitly approves of it, or that all of its moral injunctions are so culture-bound that they are no longer applicable to contemporary life. These views are gravely erroneous and call for particular attention here.

5. It is quite true that the biblical literature owes to the different epochs in which it was written a good deal of its varied patterns of thought and expression (*Dei Verbum* [*The Word of God*] 12). The Church today addresses the Gospel to a world which differs in many ways from ancient days. But the world in which the New Testament was written was already quite diverse from the situation in which the Sacred Scriptures of the Hebrew People had been written or compiled, for example.

What should be noticed is that, in the presence of such remarkable diversity, there is nevertheless a clear consistency within the Scriptures themselves on the moral issue of homosexual behavior. The Church's doctrine regarding this issue is thus based, not on isolated phrases for facile theological argument, but on the solid foundation of a constant biblical testimony. The community of faith today, in unbroken continuity with the Jewish and Christian communities within which the ancient Scriptures were written, continues to be nourished by those same Scriptures and by the Spirit of Truth whose Word they are. It is likewise essential to recognize that the Scriptures are not properly understood when they are interpreted in a way which contradicts the Church's living Tradition. To be correct, the interpretation of Scripture must be in substantial accord with that Tradition.

The Vatican Council II in *Dei Verbum* 10, put it this way: "It is clear, therefore, that in the supremely wise arrangement of God, sacred Tradition, sacred Scripture, and the Magisterium of the Church are so connected and associated that one of them cannot stand without the others. Working together, each in its own way under the action of the one Holy Spirit, they all contribute effectively to the salvation of souls." In that spirit we wish to outline briefly the biblical teaching here.

6. Providing a basic plan for understanding this entire discussion of homosexuality is the theology of creation we find in Genesis. God, in his infinite wisdom and love, brings into existence all of reality as a reflection of his goodness. He fashions mankind, male and female, in his own image and likeness. Human beings, therefore, are nothing less than the work of God himself; and in the complementarity of the sexes, they are called to reflect the inner unity of the Creator. They do this in a striking way in their cooperation with him in the transmission of life by a mutual donation of the self to the other.

In Genesis 3, we find that this truth about persons being an image of God has been obscured by original sin. There inevitably follows a loss of awareness of the covenantal character of the union these persons had with God and with each other. The human body retains its "spousal significance" but this is now clouded by sin. Thus, in Genesis 19: 1–11, the deterioration due to sin continues in the story of the men of Sodom. There can be no doubt of the moral judgment made there against homosexual relations. In Leviticus 18:22 and 20:13, in the course of describing the conditions necessary for belonging to the Chosen People, the author excludes from the People of God those who behave in a homosexual fashion.

Against the background of this exposition of theocratic law, an eschatological perspective is developed by St. Paul when, in I Cor. 6:9, he proposes the same doctrine and lists those who behave in a homosexual fashion among those who shall not enter the Kingdom of God.

In Romans 1:18–32, still building on the moral traditions of his forebears, but in the new context of the confrontation between Christianity and the pagan society of his day, Paul uses homosexual behavior as an example of the blindness which has overcome humankind. Instead of the original harmony between Creator and creatures, the acute distortion of idolatry has led to all kinds of moral excess. Paul is at a loss to find a clearer example of this disharmony than homosexual relations. Finally, I Tim. 1, in full continuity with the biblical position, singles out those who spread wrong doctrine and in v. 10 explicitly names as sinners those who engage in homosexual acts.

7. The Church, obedient to the Lord who founded her and gave to her the sacramental life, celebrates the divine plan of the loving and life-giving union of men and women in the sacrament of marriage. It is only in the marital rela-

tionship that the use of the sexual faculty can be morally good. A person engaging in homosexual behavior therefore acts immorally.

To choose someone of the same sex for one's sexual activity is to annul the rich symbolism and meaning, not to mention the goals, of the Creator's sexual design. Homosexual activity is not a complementary union, able to transmit life; and so it thwarts the call to a life of that form of self-giving which the Gospel says is the essence of Christian living. This does not mean that homosexual persons are not often generous and giving of themselves; but when they engage in homosexual activity they confirm within themselves a disordered sexual inclination which is essentially self-indulgent.

As in every moral disorder, homosexual activity prevents one's own fulfillment and happiness by acting contrary to the creative wisdom of God. The Church, in rejecting erroneous opinions regarding homosexuality, does not limit but rather defends personal freedom and dignity realistically and authentically understood.

8. Thus, the Church's teaching today is in organic continuity with the scriptural perspective and with her own constant Tradition. Though today's world is in many ways quite new, the Christian community senses the profound and lasting bonds which join us to those generations who have gone before us, "marked with the sign of faith."

Nevertheless, increasing numbers of people today, even within the Church, are bringing enormous pressure to bear on the Church to accept the homosexual condition as though it were not disordered and to condone homosexual activity. Those within the Church who argue in this fashion often have close ties with those with similar views outside it. These latter groups are guided by a vision opposed to the truth about the human person, which is fully disclosed in the mystery of Christ. They reflect, even if not entirely consciously, a materialistic ideology which denies the transcendent nature of the human person as well as the supernatural vocation of every individual.

The Church's ministers must ensure that homosexual persons in their care will not be misled by this point of view, so profoundly opposed to the teaching of the Church. But the risk is great and there are many who seek to create confusion regarding the Church's position, and then to use that confusion to their own advantage.

9. The movement within the Church, which takes the form of pressure groups of various names and sizes, attempts to give the impression that it represents all homosexual persons who are Catholics. As a matter of fact, its membership is by and large restricted to those who either ignore the teaching of the Church or seek somehow to undermine it. It brings together under the aegis of Catholicism homosexual persons who have no intention of abandoning their homosexual behavior. One tactic used is to protest that any and all criticism of or reservations about homosexual people, their activity and lifestyle, are simply diverse forms of unjust discrimination.

There is an effort in some countries to manipulate the Church by gaining the often well-intentioned support of her pastors with a view to changing civil statutes and laws. This is done in order to conform to these pressure groups' concept that homosexuality is at least a completely harmless, if not an entirely good, thing. Even when the practice of homosexuality may seriously threaten the lives and well-being of a large number of people, its advocates remain undeterred and refuse to consider the magnitude of the risks involved.

The Church can never be so callous. It is true that her clear position cannot be revised by pressure from civil legislation or the trend of the moment. But she is really concerned about the many who are not represented by the pro-homosexual movement and about those who may have been tempted to believe its deceitful propaganda. She is also aware that the view that homosexual activity is equivalent to, or as acceptable as, the sexual expression of conjugal love has a direct impact on society's understanding of the nature and rights of the family and puts them in jeopardy.

10. It is deplorable that homosexual persons have been and are the object of violent malice in speech or in action. Such treatment deserves condemnation from the Church's pastors wherever it occurs. It reveals a kind of disregard for others which endangers the most fundamental principles of a healthy society. The intrinsic dignity of each person must always be respected in word, in action, and in law.

But the proper reaction to crimes committed against homosexual persons should not be to claim that the homosexual condition is not disordered. When such a claim is made and when homosexual activity is consequently condoned, or when civil legislation is introduced to protect behavior to which no one has any conceivable right, neither the Church nor society at large should be surprised when other distorted notions and practices gain ground, and irrational and violent reactions increase.

11. It has been argued that the homosexual orientation in certain cases is not the result of deliberate choice; and so the homosexual person would then have no choice but to behave in a homosexual fashion. Lacking freedom, such a person, even if engaged in homosexual activity, would not be culpable.

Here, the Church's wise moral tradition is necessary since it warns against generalizations in judging individual cases. In fact, circumstances may exist, or may have existed in the past, which would reduce or remove the culpability of the individual in a given instance; or other circumstances may increase it. What is at all costs to be avoided is the unfounded and demeaning assumption that the sexual behavior of homosexual persons is always and totally compulsive and therefore inculpable. What is essential is that the fundamental liberty which characterizes the human person and gives him his dignity be recognized as belonging to the homosexual person as well. As in every conversion from evil, the abandonment of homosexual activity will require a profound collaboration of the individual with God's liberating grace.

12. What, then, are homosexual persons to do who seek to follow the Lord? Fundamentally, they are called to enact the will of God in their life by joining whatever sufferings and difficulties they experience in virtue of their condition to the sacrifice of the Lord's Cross. That Cross, for the believer, is a fruitful sacrifice since from that death come life and redemption. While any call to carry the cross or to understand a Christian's suffering in this way will predictably be met with bitter ridicule by some, it should be remembered that this is the way to eternal life for *all* who follow Christ.

It is, in effect, none other than the teaching of Paul the Apostle to the Galatians when he says that the Spirit produces in the lives of the faithful "love, joy, peace, patience, kindness, goodness, trustfulness, gentleness, and self-control" (5:22) and further (v. 24), "You cannot belong to Christ unless you crucify all self-indulgent passions and desires."

It is easily misunderstood, however, if it is merely seen as a pointless effort at self-denial. The Cross *is* a denial of self, but in service to the will of God himself who makes life come from death and empowers those who trust in him to practice virtue in place of vice.

To celebrate the Paschal Mystery, it is necessary to let that Mystery become imprinted in the fabric of daily life. To refuse to sacrifice one's own will in obedience to the will of the Lord is effectively to prevent salvation. Just as the Cross was central to the expression of God's redemptive love for us in Jesus, so the conformity of the self-denial of homosexual men and women with the sacrifice of the Lord will constitute for them a source of self-giving which will save them from a way of life which constantly threatens to destroy them.

Christians who are homosexual are called, as all of us are, to a chaste life. As they dedicate their lives to understanding the nature of God's personal call to them, they will be able to celebrate the Sacrament of Penance more faithfully and receive the Lord's grace so freely offered there in order to convert their lives more fully to his Way.

13. We recognize, of course, that in great measure the clear and successful communication of the Church's teaching to all the faithful, and to society at large, depends on the correct instruction and fidelity of her pastoral ministers. The bishops have the particularly grave responsibility to see to it that their assistants in the ministry, above all the priests, are rightly informed and personally disposed to bring the teaching of the Church in its integrity to everyone.

The characteristic concern and good will exhibited by many clergy and religious in their pastoral care for homosexual persons is admirable, and, we hope, will not diminish. Such devoted ministers should have the confidence that they are faithfully following the will of the Lord by encouraging the homosexual person to lead a chaste life and by affirming that person's God-given dignity and worth.

14. With this in mind, this Congregation wishes to ask the bishops to be especially cautious of any programs which may seek to pressure the Church to change her teaching, even while claiming not to do so. A careful examination

of their public statements and the activities they promote reveals a studied ambiguity by which they attempt to mislead the pastors and the faithful. For example, they may present the teaching of the Magisterium, but only as if it were an optional source for the formation of one's conscience. Its specific authority is not recognized. Some of these groups will use the word "Catholic" to describe either the organization or its intended members, yet they do not defend and promote the teaching of the Magisterium; indeed, they even openly attack it. While their members may claim a desire to conform their lives to the teaching of Jesus, in fact they abandon the teaching of his Church. The contradictory action should not have the support of the bishops in any way.

15. We encourage the bishops, then, to provide pastoral care in full accord with the teaching of the Church for homosexual persons of their dioceses. No authentic pastoral program will include organizations in which homosexual persons associate with each other without clearly stating that homosexual activity is immoral. A truly pastoral approach will appreciate the need for homosexual persons to avoid the near occasions of sin.

We would heartily encourage programs where these dangers are avoided. But we wish to make it clear that departure from the Church's teaching, or silence about it, in an effort to provide pastoral care is neither caring nor pastoral. Only what is true can ultimately be pastoral. The neglect of the Church's position prevents homosexual men and women from receiving the care they need and deserve.

An authentic pastoral program will assist homosexual persons at all levels of the spiritual life: through the sacraments, and in particular through the frequent and sincere use of the sacrament of Reconciliation, through prayer, witness, counsel, and individual care. In such a way, the entire Christian community can come to recognize its own call to assist its brothers and sisters, without deluding them or isolating them.

16. From this multifaceted approach there are numerous advantages to be gained, not the least of which is the realization that a homosexual person, as every human being, deeply needs to be nourished at many different levels simultaneously.

The human person, made in the image and likeness of God, can hardly be adequately described by a reductionist reference to his or her sexual orientation. Everyone living on the face of the earth has personal problems and difficulties, but challenges to growth, strengths, talents, and gifts as well. Today, the Church provides a badly needed context for the care of the human person when she refuses to consider the person as a "heterosexual" or a "homosexual" and insists that every person has a fundamental identity: the creature of God, and by grace, his child and heir to eternal life.

17. In bringing this entire matter to the bishops' attention, this Congregation wishes to support their efforts to assure that the teaching of the Lord and his Church on this important question be communicated fully to all the faithful.

In light of the points made above, they should decide for their own dioceses the extent to which an intervention on their part is indicated. In addition, should they consider it helpful, further coordinated action at the level of their National Bishops' Conference may be envisioned.

In a particular way, we would ask the bishops to support, with the means at their disposal, the development of appropriate forms of pastoral care for homosexual persons. These would include the assistance of the psychological, sociological, and medical sciences, in full accord with the teaching of the Church.

They are encouraged to call on the assistance of all Catholic theologians who, by teaching what the Church teaches, and by deepening their reflections on the true meaning of human sexuality and Christian marriage with the virtues it engenders, will make an important contribution in this particular area of pastoral care.

The bishops are asked to exercise special care in the selection of pastoral ministers so that by their own high degree of spiritual and personal maturity and by their fidelity to the Magisterium, they may be of real service to homosexual persons, promoting their health and well-being in the fullest sense. Such ministers will reject theological opinions which dissent from the teaching of the Church and which, therefore, cannot be used as guidelines for pastoral care.

We encourage the bishops to promote appropriate catechetical programs based on the truth about human sexuality in its relationship to the family as taught by the Church. Such programs should provide a good context within which to deal with the question of homosexuality.

This catechesis would also assist those families of homosexual persons to deal with this problem which affects them so deeply.

All support should be withdrawn from any organizations which seek to undermine the teaching of the Church, which are ambiguous about it, or which neglect it entirely. Such support, or even the semblance of such support, can be gravely misinterpreted. Special attention should be given to the practice of scheduling religious services and to the use of Church buildings by these groups, including the facilities of Catholic schools and colleges. To some, such permission to use Church property may seem only just and charitable; but in reality it is contradictory to the purpose for which these institutions were founded, it is misleading and often scandalous.

In assessing proposed legislation, the bishops should keep as their uppermost concern the responsibility to defend and promote family life.

18. The Lord Jesus promised, "You shall know the truth and the truth shall set you free" (John 8:32). Scripture bids us speak the truth in love (cf. Eph. 4:15). The God who is at once truth and love calls the Church to minister to every man, woman, and child with the pastoral solicitude of our compassionate Lord. It is in this spirit that we have addressed this Letter to the Bishops of the Church, with the hope that it will be of some help as they care for those whose suffering can only be intensified by error and lightened by truth.

26

Toward an Understanding of the Letter "On the Pastoral Care of Homosexual Persons"

John R. Quinn

Widespread attention was given recently to a document from the Congregation for the Doctrine of the Faith entitled "Letter to the Bishops of the Catholic Church on the Pastoral Care of Homosexual Persons" (1986). A good deal of comment was negative, especially on the part of those who read the document as condemnatory of homosexual persons.

At the outset, it should be noted that the document is in the form of a letter and is addressed to the bishops of the Catholic Church. It is not addressed to the general public and, consequently, is not written in popular, everyday language but in technical, precise language. On the one hand, this contributes to the clarity of the document, yet, paradoxically, it also contributes to its obscurity. Clear, technical language is not likely to be understood correctly by those who are not familiar with it.

In assessing the letter, we should note that it has been approved, as theologians say, *in forma communi*. This means that although Pope John Paul II has approved the document, it is not a document of the pope but a document of the Congregation for the Doctrine of the Faith. Nevertheless, it is an authentic teaching of the Holy See, and for this reason it carries weight apart from the merit of its intrinsic arguments precisely by reason of the formal authority of the Apostolic See. It is an act of the teaching Church and cannot be regarded simply as just another theological opinion.

Having an objective understanding of such a document according to the mind of the Church is important. Hence it is appropriate to ask: What kind of assent does such a document require? An examination of the letter reveals that

Reprinted from *The Vatican and Homosexuality: Reactions to the "Letter to the Bishops of the Catholic Church on the Pastoral Care of Homosexual Persons,"* edited by Jeannine Gramick and Robert Nugent (New York: Crossroad Publishing Co., 1988), pp. 13–19. Reprinted by permission of the author.

it contains affirmations of different kinds. For instance, some affirmations are of a doctrinal nature and represent the constant teaching of the Church. An example of this kind of affirmation would be the statement: "It is only in the marital relationship that the use of the sexual faculty can be morally good. A person engaging in homosexual behavior therefore acts immorally" (no. 7).

On the other hand, there are affirmations that are not of a doctrinal nature but pertain more or less to the realm of social commentary. An example of this kind of affirmation would be that "[When] homosexual activity is consequently condoned, or when civil legislation is introduced to protect behavior to which no one has any conceivable right, neither the Church nor society at large should be surprised when other distorted notions and practices gain ground, and irrational and violent reactions increase" (no. 10). Clearly these are different kinds of affirmation that do not call for the same measure of assent. The former is a witness to the constant moral teaching of the Church. The latter is a judgment about the social effects of certain ways of thinking or acting.

Given this necessary distinction, the document as such does not claim to be *de fide*. It is not a dogmatic definition. Still, as an authentic teaching of the magisterium it does lay claim to internal and respectful assent, particularly in those matters that are doctrinal in character and witness to the constant teaching of the Church.

CENTRAL MORAL AFFIRMATIONS

The central moral affirmation of the letter is: "It is only in the marital relationship that the use of the sexual faculty can be morally good. A person engaging in homosexual behavior therefore acts immorally" (no. 7). Of course, in virtue of this principle, those who commit adultery or who engage in heterosexual behavior before marriage also act immorally.

This principle is based on two biblical foundations. The first is the creation narrative in Genesis in which man and woman are created as complementary, each destined for the other. This reveals God's plan for creation. The differentiation of the sexes is meant for the union of the two in the service of life and love. The second foundation of the letter's teaching is found in three Old Testament and three New Testament texts that explicitly condemn homosexual acts. The understanding of these texts has been a constant in the moral tradition of the Church. The most recent biblical scholarship also supports this understanding. For instance, Richard B. Hays, writing in the *Journal of Religious Ethics* (Spring 1986), makes a detailed analysis of the first chapter of Romans. He concludes that the condemnation of homosexual acts is here beyond question and that this is the consistent stance of the Scriptures.

Consequently, the Church cannot be faulted for its teaching on the grounds that such teaching is in conflict with Scripture or with the best contemporary exegesis. It should be clear from these indications that those who entertain the hope that the Church will alter its moral teaching on homosexuality or that it can be forced to do so through various forms of pressure are soaring into the realms of fantasy.

SCOPE OF THE LETTER

Given the clarity of its moral teaching, what is the scope of the letter? Its second paragraph begins: "Naturally, an exhaustive treatment of this complex issue cannot be attempted here." Hence the letter itself indicates that its scope is limited; some things are left unsaid.

Furthermore, the word *complex* is used twice in the same paragraph, indicating that the subject is not dealt with easily. For this reason, it states that the Church requires of its ministers "attentive study, active concern and honest, theologically well-balanced counsel." It further states that "the Church is thus in a position to learn from scientific discovery." In other words, there is more to be learned at the empirical level. Nevertheless, the moral teaching of the Church, based in the Scriptures, must be the basis of understanding "the phenomenon of homosexuality, complex as it is."

POSITIVE AFFIRMATIONS

Because the letter was reported in such a negative way and created such a bitter reaction in some areas, I believe it will be helpful to point out some of its many positive aspects. Among the positive affirmations found in the letter are these:

"The particular inclination of the homosexual person is not a sin" (no. 3).

"Homosexual persons are often generous and giving of themselves" (no. 3).

"It is deplorable that homosexual persons have been and are the object of violent malice in speech or in action. Such treatment deserves condemnation from the Church's pastors wherever it occurs . . . [and] the intrinsic dignity of each person must always be respected in word, in action, and in law" (no. 10).

"What is essential is that the fundamental liberty that characterizes the human person and gives him his dignity be recognized as belonging to the homosexual person as well" (no. 11).

"The characteristic concern and good will exhibited by many clergy and religious in their pastoral care for homosexual persons is admirable and, we hope, will not diminish" (no. 13).

"A homosexual person, as every human being, deeply needs to be nourished at many different levels simultaneously. . . . The human person, made in the image and likeness of God, can hardly be adequately described by a reductionist reference to his or her sexual orientation. . . . Today the Church provides a badly needed context for the care of the human person when [it] refuses to consider the person as a 'heterosexual' or a 'homosexual' and insists that every person has a fundamental identity: the creature of God and, by grace, his child and heir to eternal life" (no. 16).

THE LETTER AND PASTORAL PRACTICE

The letter's doctrinal and biblical analysis is complemented by its treatment of pastoral practice. Having ruled out homosexual acts as contrary to the teaching of Scripture and of God's plan for creation, the letter quotes a 1976 document on sexual ethics: "Culpability for homosexual acts should only be judged with prudence" (no. 3).

Then for the first time in a magisterial document, the letter admits the possibility that the homosexual *orientation* may not be "the result of deliberate choice" (no. 11). And having noted this, it continues: "Here, the Church's wise moral tradition is necessary since it warns against generalizations in judging individual cases."

The reason for avoiding generalizations is: "In fact, circumstances may exist, or may have existed in the past, that would reduce or remove the culpability of the individual in a given instance; or other circumstance may increase it" (no. 11).

What is to be avoided is "the unfounded and demeaning assumption that the sexual behavior of homosexual persons is always and totally compulsive and therefore inculpable."

The pastoral stance, then, is to uphold the Church's teaching and, within that framework, to be cautious in judging culpability—avoiding the extremes of saying that there is always culpability or that there is never culpability.

THE HOMOSEXUAL ORIENTATION

The section of the letter dealing with the homosexual orientation has created one of the most negative reactions. It states; "Although the particular inclination of the homosexual person is not a sin, it is a more or less strong tendency ordered toward an intrinsic moral evil; and thus the inclination itself must be seen as an objective disorder" (no. 3).

This is philosophical language. The inclination is a disorder because it is directed to an object that is disordered. The inclination and the object are in the same order philosophically. But "the particular inclination of the homosexual person is not a sin" (no. 3).

In trying to understand this affirmation, we should advert to two things. First, every person has disordered inclinations. For instance, the inclination to rash judgment is disordered, the inclination to cowardice, the inclination to hypocrisy—these are all disordered inclinations. Consequently, homosexual persons are not the only ones who have disordered inclinations. Second, the letter does not say that the homosexual person is disordered. The inclination, not the person, is described as disordered. Speaking of the homosexual person, the letter states that the Church "refuses to consider the person as a 'heterosexual' or a 'homosexual' and insists that every person has a fundamental identity: the creature of God and, by grace, his child and heir to eternal life" (no. 16). Consequently, the document affirms the spiritual and human dignity of the homosexual *person* while placing a negative moral judgment on homosexual *acts* and a negative philosophical judgment on the homosexual *inclination* or orientation, which it clearly states is not a sin or moral evil.

Why was the letter written? A variety of concerns lay behind and led to the writing of the letter. The letter itself mentions some of them. The increasing public debate about homosexuality, the enunciation of positions that are incompatible with the teaching of the Church, the increasingly positive appraisal of the homosexual orientation used as a basis for a positive appraisal of homosexual acts. But still another source of concern for the Church is that certain militant elements appear to be posing a threat to family life. The Church is fearful of the trivialization of sex and of the trivialization of its relationship to marriage and the family. While the Church does not place all homosexuals in one category, it does want to diminish the harmful effects of some homosexual groups and individuals.

HOW SHOULD HOMOSEXUAL PERSONS BE TREATED?

We may find an answer to this question in several documents of the magisterium. I would begin by applying the words of Pope Paul VI in *Humanae Vitae* to homosexual persons. He said: "To diminish in no way the saving teaching of Christ constitutes an eminent form of charity for souls. But this must ever be accompanied by patience and goodness, such as the Lord himself gave example of in dealing with men. Having come not to condemn but to save, he was indeed intransigent with evil, but merciful toward individuals. In their difficulties, may [homosexual persons] always find, in the words and in the heart of a priest, the echo of the voice and the love of the Redeemer" (no. 29).

Pope John Paul II, addressing a group of bishops from the United States during their ad limina visit (5 September 1983), said:

> In particular, the bishop is a sign of the love of Jesus Christ: He expresses to all individuals and groups of whatever tendency—with a universal charity—the love of the Good Shepherd. His love embraces sinners with an easiness and naturalness that mirrors the redeeming love of the Savior. To those in need, in trouble and in pain, he offers the love of understanding and consolation. . . .
>
> As a sign of Christ's love, the bishop is also a sign of Christ's compassion, since he represents Jesus the High Priest who is able to sympathize with human weakness, the one who was tempted in every way we are, yet never sinned. The

consciousness on the part of the bishop of personal sin, coupled with repentance and with the forgiveness received from the Lord, makes his human expression of compassion even more authentic and credible. . . .

The bishop, precisely because he is compassionate and understands the weakness of humanity and the fact that its needs and aspirations can only be satisfied by the full truth of creation and redemption, will proclaim without fear or ambiguity the many controverted truths of our age. He will proclaim them with pastoral love, in terms that will never unnecessarily offend or alienate his hearers.

And the bishops of the United States wrote in their 1976 pastoral letter "To Live in Christ Jesus?": "Some persons find themselves through no fault of their own to have a homosexual orientation. Homosexuals, like everyone else, should not suffer from prejudice against their basic human rights. They have a right to respect, friendship, and justice. They should have an active role in the Christian community. Homosexual activity, however, as distinguished from homosexual orientation, is morally wrong. Like heterosexual persons, homosexuals are called to give witness to chastity, avoiding, with God's grace, behavior that is wrong for them, just as nonmarital sexual relations are wrong for heterosexuals. Nonetheless, because heterosexuals can usually look forward to marriage, and homosexuals, while their orientation continues, might not, the Christian community should provide them a special degree of pastoral understanding and care" (no. 52).

CONCLUSION

Moral norms provide vectors for human behavior and development. Some people reach the minimum and stop. Others move on toward the heights. Others plod along and find it a slow and tedious journey marked by setbacks. Not all measure up perfectly to these norms at all times. But without moral norms it would be a darksome journey. It would be a chaotic journey if the Church's moral teaching were so fluid as to change with every change of viewpoint in secular society.

Pope Paul VI's words, addressed to an international congress in 1970, apply equally well to the struggles of the homosexual person:

It is only little by little that the human being is able to order and integrate his multiple tendencies, to the point of arranging them harmoniously in that virtue of conjugal chastity wherein the couple finds its full human and Christian development. . . . Their conscience demands to be respected, educated, and formed in an atmosphere of confidence and not of anguish. The moral laws, far from being inhumanly cold in an abstract objectivity, are there to guide the spouses in their progress. When they truly strive to live the profound demands of holy love, patiently and humbly, without becoming discouraged by failures, then the moral laws . . . are no longer rejected as a hindrance, but recognized as a powerful help.

The final portion of Richard Hays's article, to which I made reference earlier, is most useful. He says: "Certainly any discussion of the normative application of Romans 1 must not neglect the powerful impact of Paul's rhetorical reversal in Rom. 2:1—all of us stand 'without excuse' before God, Jews and Gentiles alike, heterosexuals and homosexuals alike. Thus, Romans 1 should decisively undercut any self-righteous condemnation of homosexual behavior. Those who follow the church's tradition by upholding the authority of Paul's teaching against the morality of homosexual acts must do so with due humility."

27

A View from the Pews

Margaret Susan Thompson

In 1982 two students in my United States women's history course at Syracuse University—both bright, self-identified feminists—knocked nervously at my office door. "I don't know how to say this," stammered one of them, "but someone in the class is spreading the rumor that you're a lesbian." Both young women smiled tentatively, pleadingly. "Reassure us," they said with their eyes. "Tell us it isn't so!"

I looked at them and said calmly, "Oh?" At first they seemed taken aback, and then they looked even more imploringly than before. There was a moment of silence, until I asked, "Well, what do you expect me to say? [I knew what they *wanted* me to say.] Did you expect anger? Denial? [Yes!] Proud assertion of heterosexuality—of 'normalcy' [Yes, YES, *YES!*]"? Again there was silence—this time, mingled with signs of shock, even fear. Finally, when they realized that I was not going to say any more, the two students turned and left.

Later in that same term, after several class sessions in which lesbianism had figured prominently, I asked them if they could begin to understand why I had responded as I did on that earlier occasion? Why had I not acquiesced to their need for reassurance about my sexual identity? I think they did understand the points I had tried to make: that the label of "lesbian" should not be perceived as pejorative and that *any* negative response to their original plea would have been implicit endorsement of homophobia. I think they understood and left my office this second time with a little less homophobia than they had before. But the lesson was only half-learned, I discovered later, as word reached me through a third student, that the other two had interpreted my

This article first appeared in *The Vatican and Homosexuality: Reactions to the "Letter to the Bishops of the Catholic Church on the Pastoral Care of Homosexual Persons,"* edited by Jeannine Gramick and Robert Nugent (New York: Crossroad Publishing Co., 1988), pp. 149–56. Reprinted by permission.

explanation as oblique evidence of my "straightness," and that they were spreading the news accordingly through the class.

The third student, the one who told me that affirmation of my "normality" was being circulated, was a close friend of the other two. She was also a lesbian—something of which the others were unaware. She had never revealed this essential dimension of her identity with these supposed friends because she was afraid that their response would be rejection. I don't know if her assumption was justified; I'd like to think that it was not, but I can't do so with any confidence.

It's five years later now. Has anything changed? One thing that has changed is that, thanks to a couple of well-attended lectures in a subsequent course on religion and politics, as well as a 1986 arrest for civil disobedience at Griffiss Air Force Base under the auspices of our local chapter of Pax Christi, I am now known on campus not only as a feminist but also as a committed Roman Catholic. In a lot of ways, this makes me more unusual than my being a feminist; practically no one on the Syracuse faculty is explicitly "religious," and overt expressions of faith are hardly everyday events. But the upshot has been that quite a large number of students, not all of them Catholic by any means, have come to me to talk about matters of conscience and faith. They know I'll listen and won't laugh at them, and also that I won't view them as freaks for having such thoughts in the first place. Consequently, I think I've seen some aspects of my students that probably few of my colleagues have seen, and my understanding of my own role and responsibilities has been significantly deepened and altered. As a teacher, as a feminist, and as a person of faith, I now believe that my responsibilities to my students go well beyond the merely academic.

The implications of these responsibilities present a constant and difficult challenge. Specifically, I am forced almost daily to confront the substance of my own beliefs as well as those of my students; I am forced to ask questions of myself, even as I try to answer theirs. And the dilemma is particularly acute when the issues that get raised relate to institutional church teachings with which I cannot myself agree. How do I deal with students' doubts? How do I deal with my own? Can I present a vision of faith to those who come to me for help that is both personally honest and truly "Catholic"?

I have no definitive answers to any of these questions. But I think that they are important and probably not too unusual. I'm not a theologian, and I'm not in any way a church "professional." In fact, I have no specific training in counseling, psychology, or even sociology (not even a single course!). Thus the only "Catholic" or even human perspective I can offer is that of a "person from the pews," of one who is trying to live explicitly as a Christian in the walk of life in which I find myself. I am, in short, your basic lay person—the person to whom most institutional church teachings presumably are directed, the person for whom "scandal" is supposed to be avoided, the person whose voice is rarely heard in either official or unofficial ecclesial circles.

It's important, I think, to emphasize my typicality, rather than any distinctiveness to my insights or experiences. Like about 57 percent of the self-identified Catholic laity in the United States, I attend mass weekly in a local parish and I try to pray daily. Beyond that, I serve on my parish council, was in a Renew group, lector occasionally, and serve as a Eucharistic minister. After a few alterations in language, I have no problems reciting the Nicene Creed, and I even (if only occasionally) go to confession. I am *not,* in other words, some sort of aberrant radical!

Similarly, the Catholic students who come to talk with me are *not* those who have completely given up. These are the ones who *want* to believe, who think there is a God and who, if given the choice, want to feel comfortable worshiping in the tradition of their upbringing. They come to me, I think, rather than (or in addition to) a chaplain, because they want reassurance from the "ranks," and not simply from someone whose Catholic commitment is professional. They want to believe that it is possible to be a Catholic in the "real" world, to be a member of a Church that is demanding as well as inspirational. But they have doubts. And the more serious and thoughtful they are, the more doubts they are likely to have.

Within the past year or so, many things have happened to exacerbate those doubts. The censuring of the Vatican 24,* Charles Curran, and Archbishop Hunthausen; a synod on the laity whose delegates were all bishops; a celibate hierarchy that seems obsessed with matters of reproduction; and overrepresentation of Catholics among Iran-Contra operatives are all problems that concern and trouble my students. Individuals tend, of course, to care more about some of these matters than others. But almost without exception, every one of the young people who has approached me since Halloween of 1986 has raised the issue of the Vatican letter on homosexuality. For some, this has become the sort of catalytic question that birth control posed twenty years ago. For others, it is merely another example of institutional judgmentalism in the area of sexuality. For a few—the lesbian and gay—it has led to a pivotal religious crisis. The surprising thing is that practically no one, including the straight majority, has found herself or himself untouched. And, without exception, every one of these students has challenged the letter's teaching and has asked the sorts of difficult questions to which I can give no satisfactory answers.

What is somebody who thinks of herself as a *teacher* supposed to do? This sense of helplessness merely compounds my own incomprehension and anger at a document I do not understand and cannot accept. Perhaps the only good that has come from all this is an enhanced appreciation of the notion of faith as "mystery" and as an essence beyond reason and knowing. Yet that is a little too abstract for the young people before me, who want something both more and less than inchoate (and incompetent) philosophizing. So I listen, and

*The Vatican 24 was the name given to two dozen American nuns who publicly argued that not all Catholics consider abortion wrong. (Eds.)

speak only occasionally, and sometimes find myself drifting off into that fantasy land of the powerless: a dream world in which I can imagine that someone *else* has to struggle with my situation. What if that someone else were the pope, or Cardinal Ratzinger, or any of those nameless, faceless, male celibates in the bowels of the Vatican Congregation for the Doctrine of the Faith? In the unlikely event that any of them found themselves in the company of my students, how would *they*—how *could* they—respond?

I think of a serious would-be physician, who asked me why Roman officials seem bent upon ignoring both the entire body of scientific knowledge that suggests sexual orientation is inborn and not acquired *and* the theological implications of that knowledge. If sexuality is a factor of birth, he wonders, why would an omnipotent God deliberately create "disordered" people? And, assuming that they *are* "disordered," with inclinations that must not be realized, why would such a God not simultaneously also give them the gift of celibacy? Does this mean that God intentionally places people in impossible situations? Is this the God of the Gospels?

And how do I respond to the student who has never really thought much about gay and lesbian sexuality, and who is even willing to consider the idea that such activity may be "wrong," but who still can't deal with the harshly punitive tone of the Vatican letter? "I thought Jesus came for sinners," this one muses. "Wouldn't he then reach out to them with love?"

In walks a bright and deceptively quiet freshwoman. Enrolled in a research seminar intended for juniors and seniors, she is determined to prove herself. The general theme is religion in America; she wants to explore some dimension of modern Catholic dissent, and it's clearly more than an intellectual exercise. "My Italian grandmother would be horrified if she knew what I was doing but she'd be more horrified if she knew *why* I was doing it," the young woman confides. "I simply can't take things for granted anymore. I can't deny being a Catholic, but I want to *understand.* How can such a beautiful Church do such ridiculous things to its own body?" Ultimately she decides to focus on the Vatican 24, after rejecting her initial plan to examine homosexuality. "I can at least see merit, some validity, in the Church's opposition to abortion, if not to dialogue," she said. "But I simply can't get inside their heads on this other thing. *What,*"she demanded to know, "is their *problem?*"

A young woman who described herself to me as "aggressively heterosexual feminist," said the Vatican letter had accomplished something constructive. For the first time, she felt a kinship with lesbians and gays, common victims with her of patriarchal contempt. She *wants* to go to church, but how can she worship meaningfully in such an irrational milieu, where only celibate men are presumed to speak with authority? For her, this allegedly "pastoral" letter may be the straw that breaks the camel's back and may ultimately force her to pursue her spiritual search outside the Catholic tradition. "It's not what I want," she says. "Is it possible that God *wants* me to leave the Church and is just using this as the tool to kick me out?"

The telephone rings. It is a friend of mine, a mother of several children including a twenty-one-year-old daughter who is about to return home from the 1986 cross-country Peace Walk. This woman of tremendous faith, one of those who is always there for the homeless and the hungry and the other victims of the world, is agonizing over how to "be there" for her own daughter, a lesbian. "She's already so disillusioned with the institutional Church and now this. What can I say to her? Is there anyone around here she can *talk* to? Is it right for me to urge her to keep hanging in to an institution that seems determined to condemn her? Can I continue to hang in?" I give her a couple of names, promise to pray, and feel completely incompetent.

I think of my own parents. When I was growing up, they welcomed so many different kinds of people into our home that I could never figure out what "normal" was supposed to mean, unless it was supposed to mean everybody. Looking back, I realize that two of their closest friends were a lesbian couple and that the two men who shared a house and sometimes visited were probably gay. All I knew then was that they were friends, that they were nice people, and that my parents apparently enjoyed their company. I thank God for bringing these supremely normal and loving individuals into my life at an early age. I have never had to contend with the sorts of fears and speculations that result from isolation or ignorance. I'm sure my friend raised her children in exactly the same way. She has no regrets, I know, but she is angry.

When Christmas comes, I hear as always from one of my dearest college friends, not a Catholic. After years of insecurity and loneliness, she's now one of the most *complete* human beings I know. She writes of a new and exciting job, of renovations on the house, of a stepson at an Ivy League college and two other children doing well. She sends "greetings from Penny," her lover of nearly ten years and the natural mother of these children; they are off to spend the holidays with my friend's parents. I think of how unhappy this woman was before she fully understood and accepted her sexuality, and rejoice in the contentment she knows now. Her postscript reads, "Still can't understand you and your Church. Explain it to me sometime, okay?" I put the card aside, realizing how irrelevant Ratzinger's epistle is to her life. I find myself rejoicing in the fact that she's not Catholic.

The card from a gay friend is not so joyful. Born a Catholic, he and his lover of seven years find themselves "longing to go to midnight mass tomorrow, but probably won't; the 'Vatican Rat's zinger' leaves too bitter a taste, and Eucharist is impossible." He says they will gather with some close friends to welcome Christmas, but that "it just won't be the same. My head tells me that this is not of God, but my heart is broken. Can you see me as an Episcopalian?"

After the holidays classes resume. I read more and more articles about gay-bashing and accelerating open racism on college campuses. I remember the reaction of one among many Reagan supporters in my class on the American presidency in 1984. When asked how he (incidentally, a Catholic) could vote for the president's reelection in light of his appalling record on civil rights, the young man looked at me in astonishment and said, as if to someone completely obtuse, "What are you talking about? *I'm* not black!" Can I wonder at such arrogant self-righteousness when cardinals define AIDS as the "vengeance of God against queers," when the Vatican states that violence directed against gays is somehow "their own fault," and when those who *minister* to lesbians and gays are kicked out of their religious orders, lose their jobs, and/or have their priestly faculties revoked?

Meanwhile, one of our most compassionate diocesan priests responds to a reporter's question about the Vatican letter with respectful and obviously well-considered reservations. The newspaper reports his remarks accurately, along with his statement that he had attended a locally held workshop on gay and lesbian ministry in the fall *before* the letter was promulgated. Some, at least, do not regard this as indicative of priestly determination to minister effectively to all people. Within two weeks, a letter arrives in the Syracuse chancery from New York's Cardinal John J. O'Connor who, after acknowledging that he has no right to interfere in the internal affairs of another diocese, asks our bishop to "investigate" this priest's activities and to "set him straight." Upon investigation, it turns out that the letter was prompted by O'Connor's receipt of a "clipping sent anonymously in an envelope with a Syracuse postmark." And I wonder, doesn't a "prince of the Church" have better things to do with his time? Nothing came of this little incident insofar as that priest was concerned. But our now retired ordinary has been replaced by the former vicar general of New York, while an auxiliary with lots of local support, and who had attended the same workshop as a means of expanding his own pastoral understanding, is today still an auxiliary.

If what I have written appears to be merely a collection of random reflections, it is probably a better representation of my own experience than something more organized might be. Neither my life nor my faith, apparently, are intended to fit into clearly explicable patterns. I try to cope, and try to respond to others, and find both those things very difficult.

I am left with the question of what to say to my students. With each one I encounter, I come away more and more convinced of the reality of their desire for faith—*Catholic* faith—and more and more frustrated by my inability to give them useful answers. Like them, I would like to be able to look to official leaders for actual leadership; like them, I come away unable to believe that their teachings reflect either incarnate reality or the will of God. I tell them, and believe, that "we are the Church," and that the Spirit speaks to us as truly and validly as it does to Vatican bureaucrats. I tell them to hang in, and that it is possible to be a practicing Catholic and still dissent from what is not part of the doctrinal core of the faith. I say all this as much to myself as to them, and wonder if any of us can buy it. I go home at the end of the day, increasingly convinced that what is *truly* disordered here is not the sexual orientation of about 10 percent of the People of God, but rather the pharisaic legalisms of the bunch of insular patriarchs who purport to represent a messiah of love and compassion.

If I and my students are to find an answer, we will find it in God and not in these men. My Bible opens to what has become for me a beacon of hope, the story of the Canaanite woman. She is an alien, a lay person, and a woman, and yet she dares to approach Jesus for help. The disciples—institutional ancestors, we are told, of the hierarchy of today—beg Jesus to tell her to shut up and go away. He ignores her and then calls her a dog. This beautiful woman, so marginal a figure that we are not even told her name, persists. She pleads not for herself but for her daughter. And ultimately Jesus sees the light. He calls her a "woman of great faith" and rids her daughter of the demon. The woman disappears; we never hear of her again. But she remains the only person in Scripture who does one extraordinary thing: she is the only one who changes Jesus' mind.

I tell my students that this is an easy story to miss. Despite its appearance in two of the four Gospels, it arises in the Sunday readings only once in three years (and in mid-August, when they're likely to be on vacation!). I refuse to allow my nascent paranoia to let me believe this is deliberate, and yet. . . . It is a revolutionary incident, and who could blame a defensive hierarchy from trying to keep it from us?

If the bishops can see themselves in "apostolic succession" to these disciples, then we powerless and nameless lay people can surely claim this anonymous and prophetic woman as one of us. Marked by faith, fearlessness in faith, persistence, and compassion, her determination changed not only Jesus' mind but salvation history. She tells those of us with nothing that we have nothing to lose, so we may as well take risks and confront religious authority, even God.

But she also holds out hope. While demanding of us the courage to ask each member of the institutional magisterium if he can honestly present himself to us as representing Christ if he is not open to personal conversion, she holds out the possibility that even radical change is both possible and legitimate. Her prayer, after all, *was* answered. And so we, her daughters and sons, can pray with her to be rid, once and forever, of the demon.

28

The Christian Community
and the Homosexual

Carlyle Marney

"Homosexual" is an adjective, not a noun. It describes, in part, as adjectival-modifier, a person the dominant trait of whose *sexualis* inclines him to seek the satisfaction of his sexual drives in relationships with persons of his own sex. Who is he?

"He" is a gentle and receptive Sunday school teacher forty years ago who never did me anything but good. "He" is a pastor for many productive years who never knew his label until he was thirty. . . . "He" is a young, frightened, mother-dominated, timid rebel with a Ph.D. in history who twists his hands as he tells me how he dreads today's visit to his psychiatrist. "He" is beautiful, and thirty, and a friend of mine since *she* was fourteen years old and discovered that her musical gifts were but vehicle for other "gifts," but had courage even then to talk about it. "He" is a young groom being married to an exquisite girl, but so like her in his physical traits as to cause me then to wonder and make me now ashamed that I performed a ceremony over his abortive attempt to be heterosexually whole. "He" is a swarm of pretty boys admiring their organ teacher's power. "He" is a student whose father has met the crisis . . . by buying him a plane. "He" is a towering 6-foot-4, 240 pounds of dark Spanish-Indian who once cornered me in a narrow Argentine elevator, stuck between floors. "He" is a battered, tooth-loosened victim of "homosexual-panic" in his first-time partner at the bus station men's room.

And, "he" is victim, too, of all the standard Christian reactions. "He" is the schoolteacher French-horn player a posse of parents ran out of town; "he" is the director of a church youth center whom the deacon board gave no time to get his clothes. "He" is the half-dozen hidden-to-most in the room when a veteran pastor protested vigorously the creation of a "halfway house" in church because

This is an edited version of an article that first appeared in *Religion in Life: A Christian Quarterly of Opinion and Discussion* 35, no. 5 (Winter 1966).

it would attract "deviates and other sinners" of whom he seemed inordinately frightened. "He" was the fellow next door at prep school, branded, shipped off, and ruined by that stout and pudgy and righteous fellow whose incensed morals were terribly inadequate to control his own profligacy, but who told me proudly that he would always yell again if ever he even had a "suspicion." . . .

In most classic Protestant ethics the subject is ignored. At best, treatment consists of desensitizing the victim with information, convincing him with ethics, changing his mannerisms, changing his friends, and telling him to go with girls.

I must take more seriously two . . . works by . . . capable Protestant theologians, Karl Barth (in *Church Dogmatics*)[1] and Helmut Thielicke (*The Ethics of Sex*).[2] In the main my remarks constitute a critique and a rejection of the main base of the best-made approach to this problem by the popular and able Thielicke.

Barth's application of I-Thou to male-female can be helpful, is helpful, but nowhere do I find him taking with real seriousness the way *sexualis* is constituted genetically or experientially. Nor does he allow for the psychic repercussions of overt victimization in a person's history. Everywhere I must reject his notion of male-female as separate categories fundamental in creation—and so with Thielicke.

I feel—unless I stereotype too broadly—a kind of German and male clumsiness in both Barth and Thielicke when they talk of maleness and femaleness. They talk as if men were males and women were females, when each, as a matter of universal experience, is *both* to some extent. What they call a *structural* difference between male and female is not this clear. . . .

The first words of Thielicke's first chapter head contain an idea I believe to be fatal for his argument and destructive of any real help from his book. "The Duality . . ." it begins. Unless the German means something other than duality, we are at once in trouble.

On page 3 of this influential book Thielicke casts his lot with Holy Scriptures, Babylon Gemara, and Karl Barth (three incredible authorities) by using some technically correct anthropological material. But when he is ready to talk of homosexuality he has already created such a duality that any real bipolarity of sexuality becomes a homosexual trait. He speaks as if this immanental bisexuality were an acquired homosexual trait. He writes as if the "norm" to which the homosexually inclined man is bound is discretely, clearly *male*.

My quarrel with these experts is in Barth's assumption (almost everywhere repeated) that sexual differentiation is an axiom of biblical anthropology; that apart from (and prior to) this differentiation there is no humanum; that each sex has an indelible character.

Is there a true duality? Does biblical anthropology rest on this? Is sex a primal difference? Is man really dual?

Biblical anthropology begins *by seeing both sexes in one*—Adam. Sex difference is not a duality; it is a bipolarity—each specimen. There is a "prior state" in which male and female are present in one. Everyone is "homosexual" in that he participates (incorporates) in the other. It is not a sex difference that is constitutive of humanity, else Adam is not human. Eve represents a primeval separation, but not an original separation. There is no structural differentiation but only a pragmatic biological separation of function in relation.

What would constitute a duality? If each were so distinct as to make confusion of the sexes impossible? If each exhibited traits never present to the other? If either could be complete with no vestige of the other? If neither were complementary to the other? If either could reproduce without the other? If neither could compensate for the absence of the other? Or conversely, if neither could substitute for the presence of the other? If either could find his opposite in the other? But complementation is not duality.

On the contrary, male and female are so alike as to be essentially the same. There is a difference but not a duality. . . . Maleness and femaleness are biological devices, not psychic equipment of a determinative nature. *And sex is a continuum of maleness-femaleness in each specimen, not a discrete entity in either.* Sex "traits" are so culturally determined that the axial situation can shape any sexual response from eunuch to nympho in any given infant, regardless of his biological equipment. And none is all male or purely female. Each is both from 99–1 or from 1–99, while 70–30 in favor of maleness makes a good stout burgher of the male variety. In every *fundamental* sense male and female are the same. The "duality" of male and female is not dual. We are not this discrete. To be human, male or female, is essentially homogenous. There is not enough real difference psychically, emotionally, or physically. To be male or female is biologically one of nature's smart packaging gimmicks, but she derived it from an original oneness which remains. Whatever the original oneness biologically, cell division is a convenient mechanism, not a structural differentiation, and the note of duality is not high enough to have been the original phylogenetic harmony. To say it were so would be to make procreation the aim of existence, and this note also is too low in the scale to contain the chord of man's full meaning. Thielicke's exegesis of Eden does not get at it. What is said in the Hebrew word *woman* is not helper, or helpmeet, or even partner! The word means the answerer, the filler-upper, the rest of, the one who stands before in the posture of receptivity ready for union. She is the rest of the one from whom she was taken and he misses her until they find their sameness, until they find they are the same. The one.

This insistence on duality which does not understand bipolarity in each is only half my quarrel with Thielicke's standpoint. I offer now a serious objection. There is no Christian community possible as an outgrowth of his treatment of homosexual themes.

The chapter on homosexuality in *The Ethics of Sex* runs to twenty-three pages and is very properly entitled "The Problem of Homosexuality." At no single point, in spite of his apparently gracious personal attitude toward those who have the problem, does Dr. Thielicke get past the "problem." . . .

Notably missing: Any communion within and understanding by community (only pastors, really); any transcendence of the trap into which a homosexually inclined person feels himself thrown, any recognition that personhood is really a prospect; and worse, any community of responsibility for dispensing *grace*. Thielicke does not really allow his "problem" to take its place with other offenses in St. Paul's list. Homosexuality, for Thielicke, is still a separate offense to God and against "Nature."

In fine, Thielicke and Barth, more than one would think in the case of two such gracious persons, still make the old Protestant-legal gestures. The person who is homosexually oriented is a *they*, a *them*. There is no identifying. Thielicke is never tempted. He is male. There is no we-ness, or us-ness, and this all derives from the mistake about duality. . . . He stands himself within an ordered, structured, discretely bounded maleness and talks like this:

"the constitutionally predisposed homosexual"
"his somewhat abnormal constitution"
"the person so constituted by fate"
"the endrogenous and therefore incurable cases"
"the fundamental and created determination of the two sexes"
"his irreversible situation"
"homosexual needs, slippery ground, minimal chances, possible exception, those who are *ready*, universal aversion ineradicably embedded . . ."

And worse—"endrogenous *habitus*." And still worse—how can any man ever accept "the burden of this predisposition" as a "divine dispensation"? And the great impossible therefore of all therefores: "The homosexual must be willing to be treated or healed so far as this is possible; he must, as it were, be willing to be brought back into the 'order,' to be receptive to pastoral care." This helps! The help is overpowering—anybody who knows a genuine lover of his own kind must laugh like hell.

No writer I have read makes less of a person and more of an object of the bearer of this sexual adjective "homosexual." This thingifies us all. The writer has some real dreads here and is typical therefore of Protestant sex mores. The chapter is an ultimate rejection. Where can we go? Can the church's grace for homosexuals ever be limited to those who wish to change, or come to us, or seek help? If so, we are out of business. . . .

I have no hope of going beyond my betters, of transcending the legalism of the fathers, and worse, I see no hope for Christian communion to have anything to say about our main topic unless my main objection to Thielicke can be dealt with. There is no Christian community short of that we-ness or us-ness I miss in Thielicke, and most everywhere else.

We will have to become and become known as a community of responsible involvedness. But this has not been our stance or station. We keep making objects out of sinners of various kinds. My teacher here is Jean-Paul Sartre: "We 'normal' people know delinquents only from the outside, and if we are ever 'in a situation' with respect to them, it is as judges or entomologists: we were astounded to learn that one of our bunkmates had stolen from the regimental cash box or that the local storekeeper had drawn a little boy into the back of the shop." Not involved ourselves, the thief or the deviate is a spectacle, a specimen of something. Except for *good* homosexuals: "The good homosexual is weaned away from his vice by remorse and disgust; it is no longer part of him. He was a criminal but no longer is."

This, just this, has been our stance. Sartre goes on: "The homosexual must remain an object, a flower . . . an automaton that hops about in the limelight, anything you like except my fellow man, except my image, except myself. For a choice must be made; if every man is all of man, this black sheep must be only a pebble or must be me." Here is the area of our difficulty. Over against all our separateness the Christian community must adopt a we-ness, a corporate responsibleness. And we can do this only as we identify ourselves too.

That is to say further: *We will have to become and become known as a community of the guilty and of guilt—real guilt.* This is the genius of the saint of sinners, Genet. "He refuses to be a pebble; he never sides with the public prosecutor; he never speaks to us *about* the homosexual, *about* the thief, but always *as* a thief and *as* a homosexual. His voice is one of those that we wanted never to hear; (he does not analyze disturbance, he communicates it)." Here we Christians have to join Genet, our brother. Only if we forgo our divinity as spectators, only as we participate instead of seeing, only as we know our common guilt as homos and heteros, all, is there redemption for each or any. And this is our guilt—that men have been objects to us, that we have been objects to ourselves. "Man," says Marx, "is an object to man." True. But I am also subject—and guilty. If we can share each other's merit we can share the weight of our crimes.

Guilt? There is no question about the common offenses of Christians. It's a question of the community's competence to deal with guilt at all. Or is our sexuality such as leaves us no more responsible than the little boar pigs I have seen using the cool mud as a receptacle for their strivings? Are we pigs and not guilty, or men and guilty? There is a control and a discipline to be sought by all of us guilty ones, but not in a single direction. And who could be a better example of maturity and discipline than the known and respected person of homosexual inclination who can live as well as any priest in his continence or any unmarried woman in her chastity? He could teach us all how to bear our guilts and to separate genital-act from sex. The Christian community *needs* this witness, and properly graced (equipped to be gracious) the community can create this witness from among its present constituency, for as Paul said to his jailer, "We are all here—do yourself no harm."

All of which is to say that *the Christian community has to become and become known as the community of grace. . . .*

In the community, of responsible involvedness, which is a community of guilt and of grace, we see grace at work when we transcend the "them" and the "they." . . . Where all are transgressors, who is the guilty? And this is grace.

The basic phenomenon in nearly all our personality problems is an inability to love. Let us treat the homosexual inability to love just as we treat our own. Let us have more grace for ourselves. . . .

But again, what if everyone lived as a homosexual? And the old utilitarian ethic won't answer, either. The community of guilt and grace has to ask: What if everyone practiced *coitus interruptus*; what if everyone had a doctor who would abort; what if everyone practiced abstinence; or what if all were bachelors and continent?

But isn't homosexual relationship the sin against nature? *So is any other aggression,* grace answers. But what about that point at which others are harmed? And grace has here its hardest time—for aren't we all harmed harmers? Every careless truck driver, every saloon keeper, every operator of a nursery school for children harms the innocent! Just here, in this split between grace and guilt, there is seen the emergence of a *community of compassion.*

A community of compassion is a group that has faced and come to know its own makeup. . . . We would be a community that knows its own vulnerability. How close each of us came or will come to one extreme or the other! The ward of a French orphan society, says Sartre, taught by the military neither to read nor write but to kill—and so, abused all his life, did kill—said to the court: "I'm a wild animal. The public prosecutor has asked for my head and he'll probably get it. But if he had lived my life he might be where I am now and if I had lived his, I might be prosecuting him."

The community of compassion is not terrified. It can look into this abyss, for it knows its margins. And because we are men of compassion we can hear the suffocating child in every form of so-called perversion. For, of Genet, Sartre has said, "A person is not born homosexual or normal. He becomes one or the other according to the accidents of his history and his own reaction to those accidents. I maintain that inversion is the effect of neither a prenatal choice nor an endocrinian malformation nor even the passive and determined result of complexes. *It is an outlet that a child discovers when he is suffocating."* Compassion knows from the power of its own sexual innards, how incompetent we all are to face opportunity without succumbing. There are situations in which my id would ride my little superego into the ground, which means I have had to terminate some counseling because of *my* problems, not the "others."

This says, too, that in the community of compassion and grace there is some moral competency for a mutual control. In the community of responsible involvedness, where a we-ness and us-ness involves us in a communion of guilt, we need each other, and thereby discover ourselves to be in a community of God's grace.

NOTES

1. Karl Barth, *Church Dogmatics* (Edinburgh: T&T Clark, 1936–1977), 3:2.
2. Helmut Thielicke, *The Ethics of Sex,* trans. John Doberstein (New York: Harper and Row, 1964).

29

Homosexuality and the Church

Paul Duke

There is no more volatile or sensitive issue in our day than homosexuality. We all approach this subject not only with opinions or convictions but with deep and dark levels of emotional response, far beyond the rational. When we speak to each other on any complex issue, we expect disagreement; but [with] this issue we risk something deeper than disagreement. Before it's over, I may say something to offend almost everyone. My willingness to speak to this issue is in part an act of trust in your capacity to listen and to ponder and to form your own judgments.

Why am I doing this? Because I have felt *called* to do it. For some years I have known that I should, and have wrestled with the question of how and when. But one day early this year, on February 2, to be exact, I made a commitment to Christ to do it now.

There's something you should know at the outset. I first came to reflect on this subject not by reading books or engaging in academic discussion, but by the way of personal relationships with Christians who were struggling with their own homosexuality. When you're a pastor, some people will come and tell you their secrets. For me it began in my first part-time pastorate in rural Shelby County, Kentucky, and I have had pastoral relationships with Christians of homosexual orientation ever since. I have prayed, thought, and read a great deal on the issue, but my learning began as I listened to and observed and loved particular people for whom this is not another issue but a powerful personal reality.

So let me start with this question. What is your mental image of homosexual people? When I say *homosexual,* what kind of person comes to mind? The militant activist, wearing leather, screaming obscenities? Someone looking for

A pastoral conversation, Kirkwood Baptist Church, Kirkwood, Missouri, May 1993. Reprinted by permission of the author.

partners in a park or public restroom? A child molester? Flamboyantly effeminate men? Mean-looking women? If so, your image needs revising. Those types are out there—you might have seen some at the protests and parades. But these I don't know. The people I've met of homosexual orientation look just like heterosexual people. They lead quiet lives, have the same concerns that everyone has, aren't out to molest anyone or seduce anyone. They work; they go to church; they pray; they love their families. There's a sexual aspect to their lives, but as with most of us, it's not the main part of who they are.

This is only one reason that I will insist: the word *homosexual* should never be used as a noun. It's an adjective. The noun is *person*. The adjective *homosexual* defines one and only one aspect of a person. No matter what value judgments are to be placed on homosexual orientation or behavior, we start here: we are speaking of real human beings who are like all human beings.

What do we know about homosexuality? There is a very great deal that we do not know, and we ought not to speak more simply than our knowledge will allow. Let me point to some of the complexities.

In the first place there is no clear line between homosexuality and heterosexuality, as if we could say all these people are in one group and all the rest are in the other. All of us to some extent are both male and female. This is true spiritually and biologically. (As just one example, we men have varying amounts of estrogen in our bodies, and as we grow older, our estrogen increases.) It varies from person to person how the brain is organized according to masculine or feminine ways of being. There is a striking biblical image of this gender blendedness. Before Eve was created there is no reference to Adam being male; it's as if there was a human entity before the sexes were differentiated that was somehow both. Our sexual duality is primal but not original. (Marney*) We all, in varying ways, bear both genders in ourselves.

Studies show that there is a broad continuum of heterosexual and homosexual inclinations. That is, there are people who have never had a sexual *thought* in their lives that involves their own gender. There are other people who have never had a thought in their lives that involves the opposite gender. In the middle there are a great many people who have had on some occasion a sexual fantasy about someone of their own sex. As for behaviors, there are largely heterosexual people who have an incidental homosexual history, or considerable homosexual history. There are largely homosexual people with various amounts of heterosexual history, or with no heterosexual history at all. So how do you define a homosexual person? This is one reason why the statistics are so contradictory. The Kinsey Report said, that about 10 percent of the population is homosexual. A recent study says it's closer to 1 percent. Both studies are flawed. The numbers are somewhere in between. Part of the problem is that a great many people in varying degrees have had inclinations and/or behaviors that are both heterosexual and homosexual.

---

*See chapter 28 in this volume.

What about the issue of choice? Do people take up homosexual ways by choice? Some do. Some are experimenters, sexual adventurers, who turn to homosexuality as a kinky recreation. Others are profoundly lonely people, longing for someone to love them; and unable to find anyone of the opposite sex who will, they turn for comfort to the arms of someone their own gender. Some people are bent by abuse. I have known women who were early in life sexually abused by men, who now recoil from the love of any man and who long only for the love of women.

But some people, for physiological reasons we are only beginning to understand, are from their earliest recollections drawn exclusively toward the thought of intimacy with their own gender. The studies we have are not conclusive. But there is evidence that prenatal hormone flow can be a factor in the organization of the brain. And a portion of the hypothalamus that pertains to sexual drive is apparently smaller in many homosexual men than it is in heterosexual men. (It's about the same size as a heterosexual woman's.) No one can say with confidence yet what this means or doesn't mean. And there are surely social components and personal components as well. But the evidence points to a physiological biological component in the homosexuality of some people. For what it's worth, there is also evidence from the animal kingdom that many species of mammals produce a rather constant percentage of individuals manifesting homosexual behavior.

I will tell you that I personally have no doubts that some homosexual people have absolutely no choice about their sexual orientation. By *orientation*, I mean their own exclusive inclination to desire. Questions of conduct aside, their *desire* from the beginning is exclusively toward their own gender. I have known such people, and it is wrong to ever use of them the phrase: "sexual preference." For them, it's not a preference. With them we speak of "constitutional homosexuality" or "homosexual orientation."

What about homosexual behavior? If we wanted to draw a line between homosexual orientation and homosexual behavior, where would we draw it? Genital intercourse is homosexual behavior. Most of us when we think of homosexuality think genitally. But let me ask you this: What is heterosexual behavior? "What is a heterosexual act? A glance? A wink? Holding hands? Watching someone walk by and being attracted? Touching someone on the arm? Embracing?" Bruce Hilton raised those questions for me and then asked this one: "Is it the practice of homosexuality when one man pats another affectionately on the rump?" Not if one of them is a first base coach and the other is a baseball player who just hit a single.[1] We would like to draw some clear lines about behavior. Behavior is complex. Some Christians with exclusive homosexual orientation are asking legitimate questions about how we define homosexual behavior.

All of this is to say that some real people are asking us to think about homosexuality in ways that are not simplistic, because the issues have many, many layers. Think of the church's response to homosexuality. A place to begin is to recognize that many of us subscribe to some false notions or misperceptions about homosexuality. Let me name a few common misperceptions.

It is false to say that all people who experience attraction to someone of their own gender are constitutionally homosexual persons. As previously noted there is a broad continuum of heterosexual and/or homosexual predispositions, feelings, and behaviors. There are people who from their earliest recollections and for all their lives desire intimacy only with their own gender. We refer to these people as having a constitutional homosexual orientation. But there are many people as well who experience an occasional or situational attraction to someone of their own gender who are not constitutionally homosexual This is quite common and may be especially common among adolescents or young adults.

Now in our culture, which in the first place is obsessed with sex and in the second place has an oversimplified either/or view of heterosexuality and homosexuality, this sets up a dangerous equation. A young man has a sexual fantasy about another man and leaps to the conclusion: "I must be gay." A young woman forms a deep, emotional bond with another woman and finds herself having sexual desires and she thinks, "I'm lesbian." This is false, and it's the source of some horrible confusion and anxiety in many who are young and sometimes leads them to tragic choices. In a great many of us there is at least a latent bisexual capacity. This capacity isn't sinful; it's natural; it's developmental; it passes away. So I offer this pastoral word especially to you who are young. If you experience a sexual attraction to someone of your own sex, please don't leap to the conclusion that you are now defined as a homosexual person. Don't act on it, don't panic over it. Many have been there who don't stay there. If you have questions about it, talk to an adult you can trust. It's not a terrible secret, you can talk about it. Don't believe the modern myth that all people are locked in to either heterosexuality or homosexuality. A great many people as their sexuality develops are a great deal more complicated than that.

Another myth that too many of us still hold is that all homosexual persons somehow choose their orientation or could choose to change their orientation. This is absolutely false, but it's important enough to reiterate. There are people involved in homosexual behavior who do so by choice. And we all as sexual creatures can make choices about our conduct. But for a great many homosexual persons, the orientation of their desire was not chosen and cannot be unchosen. There is a growing body of evidence that constitutional homosexuality is biologically determined. Genetics may well be a factor. Prenatal hormone flow may well be a factor in the sexual organization of the brain. I am persuaded, as most people are who look at the evidence, that many people are born with a fixed orientation toward homosexuality. They do not choose their drive or desire any more than those of us who are heterosexual choose ours. It is cruel to condemn or accuse or belittle human beings for what they are and did not choose.

Yet another myth that rises from this one is that parents are somehow to blame for the homosexuality of their children. Some disciples of Sigmund

Freud observed that many of the homosexual men they saw had domineering mothers and passive, emotionally absent fathers, and we've been running all the wrong ways with this ever since. There may well be family factors in the ... [homosexuality] of some.

There are certainly cases where sexual abuse in the home has led to what is called situational homosexuality. But if constitutional homosexuality is biologically determined it is nobody's fault. We now understand, for example, that the frequent instance of emotional distance in a father of a homosexual young man is not the cause but the result of the homosexuality. The boy is different and the father doesn't know how to relate, so he withdraws and perhaps the mother steps in to compensate. If you have a son or daughter who is homosexual, I have this pastoral word for you. It's not your fault. It's not their fault. It is a mystery, a largely biological mystery. It just happens. And when it does, in this world the burdens are heavy enough on everyone without adding false burdens of blame.

A final misperception held by many of us is that all homosexual persons are promiscuous. It isn't true. It is true that in our country and many others there is an absolutely degenerate gay and lesbian subculture. It's a pornographic subculture. Multiple partners and one-night stands are the rule. Many in this group have sex with hundreds of people, perhaps a thousand in a lifetime. This subculture is obscene and exploitive, and its representatives are the ones who are usually on camera the longest in what are called the Gay Pride Parades. We cannot help but abhor what these people have chosen to become, though I believe *we* bear some responsibility for what they have become. To this we will return.

My present point, however, is that many in the church have singled out the degenerate subculture and dishonestly proclaimed: these are the Homosexuals. I recently watched a horrible videotape, put out by a conservative group and widely distributed to churches, that shows extended scenes of public homosexual perversion, then cuts to alleged experts denouncing that all homosexuals do this and they all have so many partners and the vast majority are engaging in such and such. And it all gets labeled: "The Gay Lifestyle." That's unforgivably dishonest. What they're describing is the degenerate, promiscuous lifestyle. There are countless homosexual men and women who have nothing to do with that "lifestyle," and are as appalled by it as anyone is. To take the crowd who have sunk to the lowest and to lump all homosexual men and women into that picture is a vicious lie. It's like saying, let me show you what heterosexuals are like and pointing to the people who make pornographic films. It's a disaster that so many homosexual people in our culture are promiscuous, but they don't have to be. And there are many who live with a deeper sense of morality and a higher sense of faithfulness than a great many heterosexual people do.

Now having named some of the myths that distort our thinking about the fact of homosexuality, it's time for us to make a confession. There has been a lot of hatred in the world, and a lot of hatred in many of us toward homosexual people. There is a heart-breaking degree of harassment, belittlement, and hate-crimes committed against people whose orientation is homosexual. These are facts you need to know. In the United States, at least one hundred homosexual people are murdered each year by heterosexuals because of their sexuality. Each year, up to one thousand are attacked severely enough to be hospitalized. An interesting thing happened in Houston two years ago. Members of the homosexual community complained to the police of frequent attacks. The Houston Police didn't believe them but the cries for help kept coming. Finally the police agreed to send out decoys—male officers in civilian clothes, walking in pairs. In that one week, four of the decoy officers were attacked, two of them with baseball bats. In that one week a dozen people were arrested for attempted assault.

The history of violence against homosexual people is sordid. In Europe for centuries homosexual people were routinely put to death. Let us never forget that the slur "faggot" comes from the practice of burning homosexual people alive.

To be homosexual can be especially dangerous in the high schools. In many schools kids who are gay or suspected of being gay are beaten by classmates. In all schools they are teased and called names and ostracized. No wonder that a recent federal study revealed that suicide among gay teenagers is two to three times higher than among other teens. We could add to the casualty count the high number of homosexual persons who are lost to drug and alcohol abuse.

Whose fault is this? It's the fault of us all. It's the fault of any of us who make jokes about gay people, who insult them with the use of demeaning names. It's the fault of us who are silent when others do these things or when they publish lies about what homosexuality is. And it's the fault of us who don't provide a safe place and a caring response to those of homosexual orientation. Who knows how many hundreds of thousands of lives have been lost—to violence, to suicide, to drugs, to promiscuity, to AIDS, to shattered self-esteem, to life forever outside the doors of the church—because we have participated in or by silence colluded with the demeaning and the ostracizing of homosexual people. In this respect there is blood on the hands of the church. And that's what has driven me more than anything ease to talk with you as I am doing. I have had a vision of Christ at the judgment asking, "Why were you silent?" Why has the church abandoned these children of God to despair and to death? When people are lost and dying by the millions you don't pontificate about sexual morality, you reach out to them, you give them a safe place, you listen, you talk, you love with the love of Christ.

Why haven't we? We're afraid. Many of us are afraid of something in the homosexual person because we're afraid of something in ourselves. There is no other way to explain the irrational rage of so many people against homosexual people apart from the fact that we're terrified of something in our own sexuality that we don't want to face. That's the meaning of the word *homophobia*. It's a word that perhaps is overused and misused but it stands for a real demon among us that rises from the depths of our own unresolved sexuality.

Perhaps we're afraid for other reasons too. Some say they're afraid of "the gay agenda"—that if we are open at all, these people will take over the country and the schools; they'll teach it in schools as an alternate "lifestyle"; they'll corrupt our children; they'll tempt our children to be homosexual. Others are more simply afraid that if we open up on this issue, we'll appear to condone what we feel to be wrong.

I can't address all those fears here. Some of them are unfounded. Our children won't become homosexual persons because they see others who are. Others of these fears may represent some legitimate concerns about proper boundaries. The point is that it's possible to oppose some particular behaviors and practices and policies while opening up some radically new space in the heart for homosexual people, entering into new kinds of relationships with them, granting them dignity and respect, the openness of friendship, the acceptance of love.

This much I do know. Fear is always wrong. If what moves us most is fear, we are lost. For fear is the opposite of love, and our gospel proclaims that perfect love casts out all fear. Love puts our fears aside and makes the center of our calling to find people where they are, to embrace them and walk with them as Jesus would. The church must build some walls and the church must build some bridges, but the bridges come first. The church's first and last call is to evangelize, and that's what I'm after here.

The psychologist James B. Nelson has outlined four classical ways that heterosexual people respond to homosexual people. Let me name them and ask you to locate what your own attitude has been and what you think your attitude might be.

The first level of response is called the Rejecting-Punitive. Those who hold this view believe homosexuality has no place and should be punished. All who commit hate-crimes hold this view, as do those who deliberately ostracize and who support laws that punish private, consenting adult sexual practice.

The second level is called Rejecting-Nonpunitive. Homosexuality is viewed as being always wrong, but homosexual persons can be treated with forgiving grace. We don't like it, we don't approve and we say so. We stand apart. But we live and let live.

A third position is called Qualified Acceptance. Here we take the view that homosexuality is tolerable *if* it is irreversible and *if* the relationship is monogamous. We may be troubled by homosexual behavior but we view the stable, faithful homosexual relationship as a lesser evil than a homosexuality that is promiscuous.

A final position is called Full Acceptance. This view places homosexuality on a par with heterosexuality. The sins of of exploitive, hurtful, or promiscuous sex are equally condemned in homosexuality and heterosexuality. But where the love is faithful and caring, both forms are equally accepted and blessed.

Where do you locate your own response to homosexuality: Rejecting-Punitive, Rejecting-Nonpunitive, Qualified Acceptance, or Full Acceptance? I will tell you that I know committed Christians in each of the last three positions. I refuse to advocate any of these positions as *the* Christian response. I hope we are all past the Punitive-Rejecting response which in my view is un-Christian. But it is possible to hold any of the other three with integrity and good faith. It is even possible to build a biblical case for each of the three. We can disagree on which response is most faithful and still be faithful together in what matters most about reaching out to our homosexual friends and family members and neighbors.

But as you ponder your own response, I will give you one word of counsel. If your position is that every single form of homosexual behavior is wrong, as many Christians do as the safest and most traditional way to read the biblical texts, be very careful how you express your opposition to the behavior. The motto most often is: "We hate the sin and love the sinner." Think very carefully before you say it. For no matter what you think you mean, the two words that always get heard in that sentence are *hate* and *sinner.* There's a lot of sin in my life that is truly hateable. But if you tell me how much you hate my sin, what feels hated is me. Truth is . . . I don't know how to separate the sin from the sinner. Do you? And the truth is that all of us sinners matter infinitely more to God than our sin does. So God came in to welcome sinners and to die for us, saying not a word of his hatred of our sin, but laying down his life in love. Grieve the sin that you see. With Christ, let something in you die for the sin that you see. But make it most of all plain to all your fellow sinners how deep and unconditional is the love of Christ for them, as it is for you.

Now I want to raise the issue of change. To what degree is it possible for a person of homosexual orientation to change? On one level the answer is: in the grace of God we can all change. We have a gospel of transformation. We may be powerless to change ourselves, but the power of God can help us turn away from our sins, change our habits, get free from addictions, bring new discipline and purpose to our lives. In Christ, we can all change.

Does Christ change us in every conceivable way? No. Some of our circumstances that we may wish could be changed and earnestly ask God to change, God does not. Surely in the realm of conduct, by faith and by discipline we can be transformed. But in aspects of our biological being, miraculous change isn't given so often. This is the case with constitutional homosexual orientation. Where the brain from birth is homosexually organized, a change in basic orientation is not likely to occur.

There are conservative Christian groups all over the country who do what they call "reparative therapy" with homosexual people. They claim to have changed thousands of homosexual persons into heterosexuals. I've read some of what they say. Interestingly, they are Freudians, who seem to believe that homosexuality happens only because of unhealthy relationships with significant adults. They work on healing those relationships; they teach and they pray and many of their clients move into heterosexual marriage. I have no doubt that situational homosexuality can be healed in this way. Can it happen for constitutional homosexuality? The testimony of most of the men who have been through the program and are married is that their fantasies are still about men. Many of their marriages fail. Apparently their behavior can be controlled, but their orientation remains.

It is dangerous for the church to speak naively of how God can deliver anyone from homosexual orientation. I know homosexual persons who have prayed desperately again and again to be delivered from their orientation and it doesn't come, which only multiplies their guilt and despair. Tony Campolo, the conservative evangelical Baptist, says he knew of a case where a simplistic theory of deliverance expounded by a preacher drove a young man to suicide. "The preacher had told him that if he were a Christian whom God loved, then God would answer his prayers for deliverance and turn him into a heterosexual This young man prayed hard and to no avail. He concluded that if Christians whom God loves were delivered from their homosexual orientation, then he must not be a Christian whom God loved." In his despair, he blew his brains out.[2]

It's not just prayer that has been tried. In earlier times the medical profession bent its full force toward "curing" homosexuality. Lesbian women were forced to have hysterectomies and estrogen injections, to no avail. Gay men were forced to undergo lobotomies, electrical shock, castration, and various kinds of aversion therapy, *none* of which could be shown to change their sexual orientation.

It's time we showed more humility in the presence of realities we don't understand. We mustn't insist on change or hold out hopes for change where God does not promise change. No matter how hard I pray, God won't make me tall, or make me a woman, or make me black, or make me young again. What would be nice is someone to help me accept the fact, and deal with the limits of being a short little middle-aged white guy. This is part of the church's mission with people of homosexual orientation—helping them accept the fact and deal with the limits.

What do we say to homosexual Christians about the limits? After the welcome, after the listening, after prayers and perhaps the tears and perhaps some laughter together too, after breaking bread together, what does the church say about how the life is lived?

I think it's rather important that homosexual Christians talk to the rest of us about how the life is lived. The conversation can't consist of the heterosexual majority in the church lecturing the homosexual minority in the church about what is right. Homosexual Christians are fully legitimate voices of Christ in the church. Mature homosexual Christians have wrestled deeply with the issue of sexual obedience and fairness under God. The church should let them say what they know.

Many of them would speak to us a strong word about celibacy. Can we in the church still speak to each other about the high call and the discipline of celibacy? Unequivocally, yes. There are many homosexual Christians and heterosexual Christians who live powerfully—sometimes painfully, but powerfully—in this discipline. They have much to teach us all. In this sex-obsessed culture, celibacy is misunderstood and often maligned, but it is an ancient and honored way. It is the clearest biblical alternative we have to marriage. It is far more possible than our culture makes it out to be. It isn't easy. But it is a worthy way of being faithful. It is a witness. It is a way that scripture and the church commend.

I need to stress that the most powerful word about celibacy in the church will have to come from the celibate. It is a fact concerning how authority functions among us now in the West, as much as we may lament and regret it, that words from on high simply cannot function now as in the past. In the Western world and in the Western church, the chief source of *functional* authority now is experience. We noncelibate preachers holding up the standard of celibacy will simply not be heard as we once were heard. Celibate homosexual and heterosexual Christians will have to speak of the struggles, the discipline, the disappointments, and the fulfillments of that form of discipleship.

Some homosexual Christians will commit themselves to celibacy and fail. What do we do? We meet them with forgiveness as we have been forgiven. We give them our patient support and our empathetic encouragement. Some may well say to us: "Look, we can't do it. What's more, we don't believe we should. We believe we can express our faithfulness best in a committed monogamous relationship to a single life partner, and that's what we're doing." How would we respond to that? With bafflement perhaps? With disappointment perhaps? But perhaps even here with a new measure of grace. It is not absolutely certain that scripture forbids all forms of homosexual love. Even if we think that it does, can we grant the possibility that some committed Christians read scripture otherwise and find a way to honor them with acceptance?

Certainly we can agree that it's far better for homosexual persons to live in a stable lifetime relationship than in multiple secretive promiscuous affairs. One reason that so many homosexual persons sink into this is that they have no community of accountability to support them in a more faithful commitment. Those of you who are married, think of this. Suppose that your marriage all these years were a secret. Suppose no one knew of your commitment to your spouse. Suppose no one had any expectations of your marriage; no one knows and no one cares. Now think of all the times that your marriage has been painful, difficult, frustrating. With no community of accountability at all, how many times do you suppose you might have quietly left each other and found another partner? That's how it is for homosexual people. For heterosexual people in marriage, there's a community that keeps us in check and gives us support. It makes a lot of difference.

Now imagine a homosexual person who has come to the conclusion that celibacy is an unliveable option. None of us would question that it's better for him or her to have a committed, caring lifetime relationship with one partner than to go from one relationship to another. But here's their problem. Who's going to give any support, any encouragement, any accountability to help that relationship be as faithful as it can be? This is the bind that we put homosexual people in. We don't want to hear about it. We don't want to look at it. We condemn it. Be celibate or leave. No wonder so many homosexual people are angry, no wonder so many act out their rage in self-destructive promiscuity. Who can be faithful in any respect without a faithful community of support? We abandon them to unbearable loneliness or to the one community that will accept them, which may be the community in which anything goes.

Which is why some Christian groups—even some theologically very conservative groups—permit and even encourage monogamous same-sex relationships. Jack Pantaleo is a fundamentalist evangelical Christian who runs such a group called Evangelicals Concerned. He says, "The problem isn't homosexuality. It's gluttony, it's sexual addiction." You may not think any homosexual behavior is right. But there is something more important than being right and guarding what we think of as right. Is it possible to tolerate—and more than tolerate—in some real measure to support—arrangements with which we may not be comfortable but that offer a chance of some faithfulness and some witness to love?

Whatever your position on monogamous, lifetime homosexual relationships may be, I encourage you to put something ahead of it. Put compassion first, put your evangelical witness to the grace of God toward all persons first. If it's change in people's conduct that we desire, let us remember how changes in conduct occur. Did you straighten out your life and turn from all your sins and get all your priorities in order and then start coming to church? No. You came into the community of Christ, you were welcomed and loved and you listened and you prayed and Christ began to do his patient and gracious work with you, clothing you week by week and year by year with your new nature. This is how the church becomes an instrument of the Spirit's transformation of human lives toward freedom and holiness. Not by checking credentials at the door, but by embracing all who enter as they are.

I do dream of this. I dream of a church where people are safe to tell all their secrets. I dream of a church where no one has to struggle alone with who he or she is or with what he or she desires. Where those who find themselves with homosexual orientation can say so and be answered with empathetic love and prayers and support. Where parents of homosexual children can tell of their pain perhaps and tell of their love. Where no one has to hide and slowly, quietly die of loneliness in the house of God, but awaken to the welcoming, strengthening arms of the church, like the arms of Christ. Can we do that? Can we *not* do that and be the church of the living Christ?

Tony Campolo tells of a pastor friend in Brooklyn who got a call one day from the undertaker. A young man had died of AIDS. Some other ministers had been called to do the funeral and wanted nothing to do with it. This pastor said yes.

The pastor told Campolo that when he got to the funeral home there were twenty-five or thirty homosexual men waiting. They were in the room with the casket, just sitting as if they were frozen in their chairs, staring straight ahead with glassy eyes. The pastor read some scripture, said some prayers, and made a few remarks. When the service was over he and the young men got in their cars and followed the hearse to the cemetery. There at the graveside he prayed the prayers of committal, said a benediction and turned to leave.

Then he realized that all the men were still standing frozen in their places, all with blank expressions on their faces. He walked back to the grave and asked if there was anything more he could do for them.

One of them spoke. He said, "Will you read the Twenty-third Psalm? When I got up this morning to come to this funeral, I was looking forward to hearing the Twenty-third Psalm. I figured they always read the Twenty-third Psalm at funerals. You didn't read the Twenty-third Psalm."

The pastor read the Twenty-third Psalm. When he finished, another man spoke. He said, "Read the part that says there is nothing that can separate us from the love of God." So he read from the eighth chapter of Romans how neither death nor life nor principalities nor powers nor anything at all will be able to separate us from the love of God which is in Christ.

The pastor said that when he read to those men how nothing could separate them from the love of God, he saw for the first time some signs of emotion on their faces. Then one after another, they made requests for him to read their favorite passages of scripture. He stood there for almost an hour reading scripture to those men before they got back in their cars and headed home.

They had the longing, the deep longing for the living Word of God. Most people do, especially in the presence of death. Many of them even had memories of portions of that Word, given to them long ago in a church. But for years they hadn't felt welcome in a church, and they were starving.

The church has a great many things to say to homosexual people. We have stories to tell; we have news to share; we have faith, hope, love, and all the gifts of the Christ community to give, including words about discipline and discipleship and holiness of living. We have much to say to them, and much also to learn from them. But none of it can be heard, none of it learned, none of the word of Christ can get through, none of the freeing and transforming gift can be given, as long the church's posture toward homosexual people is defensive or judgmental or recoiling in repugnance or fear.

Let's look deep into our hearts. Let *us* repent of all that keeps us from our bravest and clearest witness to the outreaching loving of Christ and the power of his resurrection to bring us all home.

NOTES

1. Bruce Hilton, *Can Homophobia Be Cured?* (Nashville: Abingdon Press, 1992), pp. 46f.
2. Anthony Campolo, *20 Hot Potatoes Christians Are Afraid to Touch* (Dallas: Word Pub., 1988), p. 111.

30

The Loving Opposition

Stanton L. Jones

When I confront the issue of homosexuality, I do not immediately think of the theology of human sexuality, of Christian sexual ethics, or of matters of church order. To think about homosexuality is to think about people—people whom I have known as acquaintances and a few well enough to love.

I think of Tom, who begged me to help him regain his Christian faith and stop both his compulsive pursuit of anonymous sexual encounters and his seduction of teenage boys. Before I really had a chance to know him, Tom announced that he did not want to control himself any longer. He later wrote me in shocking and angry detail of his immersion into the rough leather world of the gay bathhouses and alleys of San Francisco. Tom is now dead of AIDS.

I think of Gail, a lesbian in a monogamous relationship, who speaks with passion of her Christian faith, but who worships a god who accepts and affirms the "god force" within us all. She argues that the true Christian faith does not get bogged down in repentance and forgiveness but is empowered by love of any kind. Gail felt her lesbianism should not entail a denial of her right to experience motherhood. She had several friends donate sperm so she could be artificially inseminated with no ties to a father. Gail gave birth to a baby whom she loves deeply.

I think of Fred, who was homosexually molested by an older brother as he was going through puberty. He subsequently threw himself for six long years into a highly promiscuous gay subculture. He experienced no attraction to women. When Christ claimed his life, he immediately forsook his homosexual behavior in simple obedience to what he perceived to be the call of God. After a couple of years of costly discipleship and growth, Fred felt called by God to marry Debbie, and she him, in full knowledge of his problem. Only

From *Christianity Today* 37, no. 8 (July 19, 1993). Reprinted by permission of the author.

toward the end of their engagement did he begin to experience any sexual attraction to her whatsoever. Now, after fourteen years of marriage, much prayer and counseling, Fred feels almost completely healed of his homosexual inclinations. He feels that the heart of his homosexual struggle was a desperate longing for the love and affirmation of his father and a deep insecurity about his own manhood.

I think of Peter, who began experimenting with homosexuality at a seventh-grade Bible camp. This early experience confirmed his suspicion that he was different. His high school and college years were filled with furtive homosexual experiences followed by agonized repentance, prayer, and weeks or months of trying to deny his homosexual feelings. He married Denise at the end of college, never telling her of his homosexual feelings. He secretly hoped the sexual experiences of marriage would cause his homosexual attractions to go away. Fifteen years later, when Denise discovered evidence of his homosexual affairs, both of their lives blew apart. Peter is now living in the gay community, feeling that he made every possible effort to change and that his calling now is to live as a gay Christian man in a monogamous relationship, though he has yet to achieve such a relationship and no longer attends a church. Denise is consumed with rage and feels utterly betrayed.

I also think of Mark, a single Christian businessman. He has known of his homosexual inclinations ever since he has been aware of any sexual feelings whatsoever. In his mid-twenties, Mark sporadically acted out his homosexual feelings in adult bookstores and public washrooms. He looks back on these experiences with a mixture of shame, revulsion, and lust. The depth of Mark's commitment to Christ and to costly discipleship is staggering. Mark has not acted on his homosexual wishes for over fifteen years. But his pain is enormous. He oftentimes feels that he lives a twilight existence in the church—a church that does not know how to relate to single people, that acts in revulsion to the very idea of someone being homosexual, a church where he is pestered repeatedly as to why he does not marry, a church in which he longs for intimate fellowship but in which the opportunities for honesty are few and far between.

These are the faces before me as I write of a Christian response to homosexuality. And these are the faces we need to remember as we ask, Why do Christians think homosexual acts are wrong? Why is it an important issue? And what are we to do?

WHY ARE HOMOSEXUAL ACTS WRONG?

When asked why they think homosexual behavior is wrong, many Christians reply simply, "Because the Bible says it is!" The Bible does indeed condemn homosexual acts every time they are mentioned. But many Christians are unprepared for the revisionists' arguments for rejecting all the major biblical texts as either irrelevant or misunderstood.

This is a thumbnail sketch of what one will hear from critics of the traditional view:

They argue that Leviticus 18:22, 20:13, and Deuteronomy 23:18, which condemn male homosexual behavior, are irrelevant because they do not address today's homosexual lifestyles. These passages occur in the midst of a discussion of God's disapproval of the fertility cults in the pagan communities surrounding the Israelites. The only kind of homosexual behavior the Israelites knew, it is argued, was homosexual prostitution in pagan temples. That is what is being rejected here and not the loving monogamous gay relationship of persons of homosexual orientation today.

The Genesis 19 story of Sodom and Gomorrah is alleged to be irrelevant because it is a story of attempted gang rape, which was an indicator of the general wickedness of the city. The homosexual nature of the gang rape is seen as an irrelevant detail of the story.

Romans 1 is often reduced to being a condemnation solely of heterosexual people who engage in homosexual acts. They rebel against God by engaging in what is unnatural to them. This passage has no relevance today, it is argued, because modern homosexuals are doing what is natural to them and thus not rebelling against God.

In I Corinthians 6:9 and I Timothy 1:10, the Greek words that are often translated as referring to homosexual practices are said to be unclear and probably describe and forbid only pederasty, the sexual possession of an adolescent boy by an older adult man of the elite social classes.

Some of these criticisms have an element of legitimacy, but most evangelical biblical scholars concur that every one of them goes too far. The critics are right, for instance, in dismissing the view that homosexual preoccupation was the most heinous sin of Sodom and Gomorrah. Ezekiel 16:49–50 says, "Now this was the sin of your sister Sodom: She and her daughters were arrogant, overfed and unconcerned; they did not help the poor and needy. They were haughty and did detestable things before me. Therefore I did away with them" (NIV [New International Version]). Materialistic America in general, and not just the gay community in particular, is uncomfortably similar to this description of Sodom's sins. We are quick to condemn those we are uncomfortable with but slow to judge ourselves.

But Leviticus, Romans, I Corinthians, and I Timothy are relevant and binding. Archaeological studies confirm that the ancient world knew of homosexual desire and practice, even if the concept of a psychological orientation was not present. Thus it is striking that *every time homosexual practice is mentioned in the Scriptures it is condemned.* There are only two ways one can neutralize the biblical witness against homosexual behavior: by gross misinterpretation or by moving away from a high view of Scripture.

Important as they are, these passages are not the cornerstone of the Christian stance that homosexual action is immoral. The core of Scripture's negative assessment of homosexual practice is the positive biblical vision of sexuality, which applies equally to homosexual persons and to heterosexual, men and women, adults and children.

To have a truly Christian view of our own sexuality, we must understand the four great acts in God's drama, the epic poem of God's saving work. We destroy our understanding of the script if we mix up the order of the acts.

Act 1 is Creation. If we do not understand ourselves *first* as divine handiwork, created in God's image, everything else will be distorted.

Act 2 is the Fall, the reality of which much contemporary liberal scholarship denies. The Fall twists and ruins everything but does not destroy the imprint of Creation.

Act 3 is Redemption in and through Christ. Christ is at work in those who love him, redeeming them and the world.

The final act is Glorification, the expected final consummation, the blessed hope.

The Christian view of sexuality must be understood within this biblical drama. For instance, in I Timothy 4:1–5 Paul deals with the sexual views of a protognostic group whose teachings denied Creation, exaggerated the Fall, and distorted the proper view of Redemption. In particular, they despised marriage because they saw sex as evil.

To this, Paul said: "The Spirit clearly says that in later times some will abandon the faith and follow deceiving spirits and things taught by demons. Such teachings come through hypocritical liars, whose consciences have been seared as with a hot iron. They forbid people to marry and order them to abstain from certain food, which God created to be received with thanksgiving by those who believe and who know the truth. For everything God created is good, and nothing is to be rejected if it is received with thanksgiving because it is consecrated by the word of God and prayer.

From this we can get Paul's understanding of marriage and sex. Paul's grounding is that God created marriage and sex. Everything God created is good (Act 1). But notice that what God created to be good has to be cleaned off; it has been dropped in the mud—that is, the Fall (Act 2). Through Christ sex can be redeemed (that is what *consecration* means) by being received with thanksgiving through "the word of God and prayer" (Act 3). We must start with Creation, recognize the Fall, and participate in Redemption.

The heart of Christian sexual morality is this: God made sexual union for a purpose—the uniting of husband and wife into one flesh in marriage. God uses sexual intercourse, full sexual intimacy, to weld two people together (I Cor. 6:16). God has a big purpose in mind for sex because he has a big purpose for marriage—something bigger than simply a means for us to get our sexual needs met, have fun, have kids, and not have to be lonely.

In Ephesians 5 we learn more of what this bigger purpose is. According to Paul, marriage is to model concretely here on earth what God wants in the relationship between Christ and his bride, the church. Jesus, is one with the Father, and he tells us that we can be one with him. We are utterly different from God, but he wants to unite with us (I Cor. 6:17). This reality can be uniquely modeled on earth through the union of two different kinds of human beings, male and female. Marriage is a living parable, a concrete symbol, that models for the world the mystical union of Christ and his people. According to God's original design, marriages have grand, even cosmic, meaning. And this meaning remains regardless of how pathetically short we fall of that grand design.

Interestingly, the scientific evidence supports this. If it is God's intent that sexual intercourse is to bond two people together for life in marriage, what would we expect the effect of premarital sex and cohabitation to be? Those actions should make marriage less likely to work. And that is what the facts show (especially in a recent study reported by Andrew Greeley in his book *Faithful Attraction*) The more premarital sex people have, the more likely they are to have affairs in marriage; the less likely they are to have optimal sexual relationships in marriage; and the less likely they are to be satisfied with their marriages. Numerous studies over decades have shown that people who cohabit before marriage are more likely to divorce. All of the ways we humans foul up God's design have long-term negative consequences.

If marriage occupies this place in God's plan, and if sex is so important to God's plan for marriage, we can see the vital importance of obedience to God's standards for sexuality. Sex is a gift, but it is a gift we can abuse. God's intent is that sex be used rightly inside and outside of marriage. Inside of marriage, its proper use is for pleasure, procreation, and as something to be shared lovingly and with gratitude to build up the unity of the couple. Outside of the marriage of a man and woman, the proper use of sex is to honor God by costly obedience in living a chaste life. Through this difficult commitment, we learn to value obedience over gratification and to serve God instead of serving our own lusts. Heterosexual or homosexual, the call of Christ is the same: if you find yourself unmarried, God wants you to live a chaste life.

But isn't this unfair to the homosexual person? The heterosexual single at least has the chance of marriage. The person with homosexual longings has no such chance. He did not choose to have the feelings and inclinations he does. Is it fair to Mark to argue that God is calling him to a life of chaste singleness? Is it fair to Gail to suggest that God would have her forgo motherhood because she is not married?

First, let us acknowledge that few people choose to have homosexual inclinations. The evidence suggests that genetic factors, possibly operative through brain differences, may give some a push in the direction of homosexual preference. Disordered family relationships that leave people confused at a deep level about their sexual identity seem also to play a major role. In addition, early homosexual experiences of seduction or abuse may play a role as the stories of Fred and Peter illustrated earlier. And many lesbians, especially, seem to have been the targets of sexual abuse by men earlier in life, leaving them with deeply impaired abilities to trust or feel close to men later.

But the existence of inclinations, orientations, or preferences have little to do with God's moral call upon our lives. Social science is finding many powerful factors that shape character and influence morally laden choices. Alcoholism, anxiety-proneness, ill-temperedness, and even the propensity to violence are made more likely by the presence of genetic and family variables. Is it unfair, then, for God to hold up sobriety, and moderation, trust and faith, self-control and patience, restraint and respect, as moral values?

No, because God is the Maker, the one who sets the design. And though God is perfectly just, he never promised to be fair by human standards. We are saved by grace, but in the race that Paul talks about—the race to press on to the high calling of Christ—some of us start further back in the pack than others, further back from the ideal. But that does not make the goals that God ordains illegitimate or nonbinding.

While one ideal, heterosexual marriage, is not an option for the homosexual Christian without a large dose of divine healing, the other ideal, chaste singleness, is open and accessible. And that ideal of chaste singleness holds out the possibility for true integrity and beauty, as the models of Jesus himself, Paul, and many other saints show. The fact that such chastity is difficult for homosexual persons is of little moral consequence, as it is also difficult for heterosexuals. The difficulty should be dealt with pastorally, not by changing the moral standard.

And so, the Christian vision for sexuality and marriage is our foundational reason for rejecting homosexual action as a legitimate moral option. A warning, though: many gay Christians will simply deny that this is the binding Christian view. Many advocates of a liberalization of the church's ethical stance suggest that the only element of the Bible or of the Christian tradition that is binding upon all people is the general call to manifest in any relationship the kinds of loving characteristics that are described as being important in marriage—sacrificial love, honesty, and so forth. Gay relationships, it is argued, can do this as well as straight.

The first problem with this argument is that it does not truthfully reflect the Christian tradition. It is ultimately irrelevant whether or not homosexual couples can be just as loving, faithful, or monogamous as heterosexual couples. God has a distinctive purpose for sex and for marriage, a purpose that necessitates a heterosexual union.

Second, the revisionist's argument simply does not match reality. For example, male homosexuality tends to be strongly associated with promiscuity: The famous Bell and Weinberg study (*Homosexualities*) suggested that about a third of gays have had over one thousand sexual partners in their lifetimes. Very few gays are in committed, long-term relationships; Bell and Weinberg found that less than 10 percent of gays are in such relationships. Those who are in stable relationships do not tend to be sexually monogamous. McWhirter and Mattison (*The Gay Couple*) found that 0 percent of the one hundred stable male couples they studied were sexually monogamous after being together for five years. The authors of that study, themselves a gay couple, said that to be gay is to be nonmonogamous, and that monogamy is an unnatural state that some gay men attempt because of their internalized homophobia; so when you finally grow to accept your own gayness, you shed monogamy like a butterfly sheds a cocoon.

It may be that the homosexual community cannot embrace monogamy because homosexual sex can never produce what God made sex for. They turn instead to promiscuity and perversions to create sexual highs. The gay community calls these perversions "high-tech sex." Many know of oral and anal sex, but fewer know of commonly, though not universally, practiced activities such as sadomasochistic practices of inflicting pain on a partner during sex, group sex of all kinds, and more extreme distortions. When sex outside of God's will does not do what God made it to do, many people, gay and straight, search for some way to make sex deliver an ever bigger electric charge, the elusive ultimate orgasm, that can somehow make up for the absence of what sex was meant to create: unity.

In summary, persons of homosexual inclination are under the same moral call as we all are—to respond to the offer of divine mercy and forgiveness through the gift of Jesus Christ, to offer our lives as the only gift we can give in return. If we love him, we will obey his commands. And his will with regard to our sexuality is either that we live chaste lives of dependence upon him, or that we strive to build a marriage that models Christ's love for the church before the watching world, aided by the uniting gift of sexual intercourse. All of us should strive anew to live by this holy standard.

WHY IS THE ISSUE IMPORTANT?

Homosexual acts are like every other sin: They violate God's express will and distort God's creational design. Just as much fire from our pulpits should be aimed against greed, pride, racism, lack of compassion, and spiritual lukewarmness as against homosexual behavior. The best estimates today suggest that 1 to 3 percent of the population engage in homosexual acts (*not* the 10 percent that badly biased research once suggested). In this light, why should homosexuality be a special concern for the church?

There are three reasons why this issue is important, and none of them has anything to do with homosexual people being especially bad or disgusting.

First, the church's historically high view of the authority of Scripture is threatened by efforts at revising the church's position on homosexuality. As was argued earlier, the only way to neutralize the biblical witness against homosexual behavior is either grossly to misrepresent the Bible or to undermine its authority. The apologists for the "gay Christian" movement tend to do both.

While claiming to be staunchly within the Christian tradition, revisionists terribly distort biblical sexual ethics. In his book *Come Home! Reclaiming Spirituality and Community as Gay Men and Lesbians,* Presbyterian minister Chris Glaser says that *fidelity* does not mean being sexually exclusive and monogamous; *fidelity* really means only keeping your promises. So if a gay Christian companion promises to have only five other lovers per year, he is being faithful if he stays within those limits.

Episcopal biblical scholar William Countryman, in his book *Dirt, Greed, and Sex,* adopts a biblical theology that allows for homosexual practice, but he at least has the courage to admit that his method of interpretation also makes prostitution and sex with animals legitimate options for Christians (as long as such acts are done in love).

In her book *Touching Our Strength,* Carter Heyward, an Episcopal ethicist, suggests that heterosexual marriage enslaves women. She calls instead for loving sexual friendships; and there is no reason to limit these life-giving "godding" relationships to only one person or to one sex.

The majority group of the Presbyterian Special Committee on Sexuality, which authored *Presbyterians and Human Sexuality, 1991,* claimed that God's Word to us is those parts within the Bible that are just and loving, that liberate people and make them more satisfied and fulfilled; the rest is simply not God's Word. Therefore, since the prohibition against sex outside of marriage oppresses and frustrates single people and denies their sexual rights, the committee argued, then this could not be God's Word.

The second reason why homosexuality is an important issue is that what the Bible treats as an isolated *act* to be condemned (namely, people of the same gender having sex), our society treats as a fundamental element of personal *identity.* In this view, the people I described at the beginning are not people who engaged in certain acts or who have certain inclinations. Rather, they *are* homosexuals—gays and lesbians. Their sexual inclinations define most deeply who they are. If a sexual desire defines a person, then acting on that desire is essential to personhood. If we buy this logic, then to suggest that God does not want them to engage in homosexual acts is to insult their innermost beings.

The Christian response is to deny the legitimacy of defining a person by his or her sexual desires—or by any other fallen element of one's nature. In Christ, our identities are based on our status as God's adopted children. This is the foundation for understanding who we most truly are.

Paul teaches in Romans 6:16 that we do not just find or discover ourselves; rather, we build a moral and personal momentum by the choices we make. We are either becoming more a slave to sin or a greater slave to Christ. If what you mean by saying you are a homosexual is that you experience homosexual desire, that is reality. If what you mean by saying you are a homosexual is that your identity is defined by your gayness and that living out those sexual leanings is essential to your very nature, then your identity is misplaced; you are trying to build an identity on shifting sand.

It is for this reason that Christians must continue to strive to love the sinner but hate the sin, even though this saying drives the gay Christian community crazy. We can say and strive for this because we refuse to make homosexual behavior or preference the core of anyone's identity.

The third reason this issue is vital today is that there is unrelenting pressure on the church to change its historic stance. The revisionists present it as a simple issue: The church has evolved in rejecting slavery, racism, and sexism, and now it is time to stop its most deeply entrenched bigotry—homohatred, heterosexism, and homophobia.

But again we encounter a problem: We can only change our position on homosexuality by changing our fundamental stance on biblical authority, by changing our core view of sexuality, and by changing the meaning and character of Christ's call on our lives. The first two have already been addressed above; but we need to say more about the nature of Christ's call on our lives.

Christ is our perfect model of love and compassion, and we have much to learn from his love for sinners and participation in their lives. But he did not just ooze warm fuzzies; Christ also had the gall to tell others how to live their lives, to insist that his truth was the only truth, and to claim that he alone was the way to God. In short, Jesus was what many people today would call a narrow-minded bigot.

And we, the church, have been entrusted with proclaiming the message that we have received from him. When we do, we risk being called rigid and narrow-minded. We must face the reality that Christianity "discriminates." It says one path is the right way. Christians make a ridiculous set of claims: that an omnipotent God bothered to create and love us; that he let us and our forebears spit in his face in rebellion; that he chose a peculiar and unsavory primitive tribe to be his conduit for blessing; that he actually revealed what he wanted these people to believe and how they were to live; and that this God actually became a person and died for us to conquer sin and death on our behalf. That is a most unlikely story! But Christians are supposed to spread the news that this is *the* story, the only true story.

The church has, in each generation, been faced with new challenges, which are really new twists on old issues. The current movement to see gay persons as a social group that must be loved and accepted as they are is the latest form of an old challenge—the challenge to diminish the authority of God's revelation, to understand people on their own terms rather than by God's view of them, and fundamentally to amend the nature of Christ's call to take up our crosses and follow him.

WHAT ARE WE TO DO?

In this difficult time, there are two things that we must do. They are two things that do not naturally go together. We must exhibit the very love and compassion of Jesus Christ himself. And we must fearlessly proclaim the truth that Jesus Christ himself proclaimed and embodied.

The key to compassion is to see ourselves in another, to see our common humanity. This is what many of us cannot or will not do. A certain degree of natural revulsion to homosexual acts per se is natural for heterosexuals. All of us should be thankful that there are at least some sinful actions to which we are not naturally drawn. But a revulsion to an act is not the same as a revulsion to a person. If you cannot empathize with a homosexual person because of fear of, or revulsion to, them, then you are failing our Lord. You are guilty of pride, fear, or arrogance. And if you are causing others to stumble, you are tying a millstone around your own neck.

The homosexual people I know are very much like me. They want love, respect, acceptance, companionship, significance, forgiveness. But, like all of us sinners, they choose the wrong means to get what they want.

We, the church, have the opportunity to demonstrate, in our words and in our lives, God's love for the homosexual person. If we truly love, we act on that love. We must start by eradicating our negative responses to homosexual people. Stop the queer jokes and insults: they hurt others. We must deal with our own emotional reactions; we must decide to love. We must repudiate violence and intolerance toward persons of homosexual orientation. We must change the church so that it is a place where those who feel homosexual desire can be welcomed. The church must become a sanctuary where repentant men and women can share with others the sexual desires they feel and still receive prayerful support and acceptance.

Are you willing to pray with, eat with, hug and comfort, share life with a woman or a man who has homosexual feelings? Frequently, we already do but do not know it. Just as we share meals with gluttons, shop with the greedy, share with the vain, and vegetate with the slothful—and as others share life with us without knowing our hidden sins—so we share life, knowingly or unknowingly, with the homosexual. But we need to do so knowingly and lovingly.

Now the second part of our call—to speak the truth. If we truly love, we will not shrink from speaking God's view of homosexual behavior. Do not be deceived: increasingly today we are defined as unloving solely for viewing homosexuality as immoral, regardless of the compassion we exhibit. Nevertheless we must strive to be loving when we voice our opposition. Compassion in no way entails an acceptance of the gay lifestyle any more than it entails affirming an adulterer's infidelity.

As people with homosexual inclination follow our Lord down the narrow road, they can pray and hope for healing. There are two prevalent distortions about healing today. The first is the conservative Christian myth that a quick, sincere repentance and prayer for healing will instantly change the person. Thankfully, few spread this damaging myth today.

The more prevalent myth is that there is no hope for healing. Anyone who says there is no hope is either ignorant or a liar. Every secular study of change has shown some success rate, and persons who testify to substantial healing by God are legion. There is hope for substantial change for some in this life.

But while our ultimate hope is secure, we do not have certainty about how much healing and change is possible for any particular homosexual person. Some will never be healed in this life. We need to balance a Christian triumphalism with a theology of suffering, a recognition that we are a hurting and beaten-down race. We must not believe the world when it tells us there is an easy answer to everything, even when the speaker is a Christian. There is dignity and purpose in suffering. The Christian homosexual's witness is not invalidated by pain and difficulty. Christians trust that there is always a deeper purpose in suffering

Mark, my Christian brother who still longs for healing while he lives a celibate life, and many like him, needs to be assured by the church of the meaningfulness of his pilgrimage. We need to remember that Christians witness to their faith not just in their strength and triumph, but also in their brokenness. We can be Christlike in how we bear our sufferings. We all want to be triumphant ambassadors for Christ, but few of us are. Our homosexual brothers and sisters who follow our Lord into costly discipleship have much to teach all of God's people.

While challenges are nothing new for God's body on earth, they are nonetheless real challenges. This is an important moment for the church, with many denominations and institutions debating whether to change the church's traditional teaching on homosexuality. Those of us involved in the debate must remember that we can fail in two directions.

First, we can fail by compromising (and thus undermining) God's authoritative word, rejecting God's view of sexuality, and embracing a human-centered notion of costless acceptance. The challenge here is to resist the pressure and courageously articulate God's truth regarding sexuality.

Second, we can fail by saying the right things but in the wrong way. Too many Christians have let hate slip into their rhetoric on this issue. The challenge here is to be the loving opposition, to imitate our Lord, who chases down his sinful creatures with aggressively open arms while all the while saying no to our sins. We all need to repent of our arrogant and intolerant attitudes toward those whose struggles are different from ours. Our goal must be to become a community that embodies the welcoming grace and love of our Lord Jesus Christ.

REFERENCES

Bell, Alan P., and Martin S. Weinberg. *Homosexualities: A Study of Diversity among Men and Women*. New York: Simon and Schuster, 1978.

Countryman, Louis William. *Dirt, Greed, and Sex: Sexual Ethics in the New Testament and Their Implications for Today*. Philadelphia: Fortress Press, 1988.

Glaser, Chris. *Come Home! Reclaiming Spirituality and Community as Gay Men and Lesbians*. San Francisco: Harper & Row, 1990.

Greeley, Andrew. *Faithful Attraction*. New York: Tor, 1992.

Heyward, Carter. *Touching Our Strength: The Erotic as Power and the Love of God*. San Francisco: Harper & Row, 1989.

McWhirter, David P., and Andrew M. Mattison. *The Gay Couple: How Relationships Develop*. Englewood Cliffs, N.J.: Prentice-Hall, 1984.

Presbyterians and Human Sexuality, 1991. Louisville, Ky.: Office of the General Assembly, Presbyterian Church (U.S.A.), 1991.

31

Gayness and God:
Wrestlings of an Orthodox Rabbi

Yaakov Levado

I am an Orthodox rabbi and I am gay. For a long while I denied, rejected, railed against this truth. The life story that I had wanted—wife, kids, and a family that modeled Torah and *hesed**—turned out to be an impossible fantasy. I have begun to shape a new life story. This essay is part of that life story, and thus remains unfinished, part of a stream of consciousness rather than a systematic treatise.

It is hard to say how or when I came to know myself as a gay man. In the beginning, it was just an array of bodily sensations; sweaty palms and that excited sort of nervousness you feel around certain people occurred without awareness. The arrival of the hormonal hurricane left me completely dumbfounded. Just when my body should have fulfilled social expectations, it began to transgress them. I had no physical response to girls. But I was physically pulled, eyes and body, toward guys. I remember my head turning sharply once in the locker room for an athletic boy whom I admired. At the time, I must have noticed my body's involuntary movement, but it meant nothing to me. I understood nothing. How could I? I had no idea what it meant to be homosexual. "Faggot" or "homo" were words reserved for the boys hounded for being passive, or unathletic. None of this said anything about sexual attraction. There were no categories for this experience, no way to explain the strange muscle spasms, the warm sensation on my face, or the flutter in my chest. Not until years later, after countless repetitions of such events, did it slowly, terrifyingly, break through to my consciousness.

When other boys were becoming enraptured by girls, I found my rapture in learning Torah. I was thrilled by the sprawling rabbinic arguments, the

---

*I.e., steadfast love or loyalty. (Eds.)

Reprinted from TIKKUN MAGAZINE, A BI-MONTHLY JEWISH CRITIQUE OF POLITICS, CULTURE, AND SOCIETY. Subscriptions are $31.00 per year from TIKKUN, 251 West 100th Street, 5th floor, New York, NY 10025.

imaginative plays on words, and the demand for meaning everywhere. *Negiah,* the prohibition to embrace, kiss, or even touch girls until marriage was my saving grace. The premarital sexual restraint of the Halacha* was a perfect mask, not only to the world, but to myself.

My years in yeshiva were spectacular, in some measure because they were so intensely fueled by a totally denied sexuality. There were many *bachurim* (students) in the yeshiva whose intense and passionate learning was energized with repressed sexual energy. For me, the environment deflected sexual energy and generated it as well. The male spirit and energy I felt in yeshiva was both nourishing and frustrating. I do not know if I was alone among my companions or not. From those early years, I remember no signs by which I could have clearly read my gayness or anyone else's. I only know that I was plagued with stomach aches almost every morning.

Later, on one desperate occasion, beset with an increased awareness of my attraction to a fellow yeshiva student, I visited a sage, Rav Eliashuv, who lives in one of the most secluded right-wing Orthodox communities in Jerusalem. He was old and in failing health, but still taking visitors who daily waited in an anteroom for hours for the privilege of speaking with him for a few minutes.

Speaking in Hebrew, I told him what, at the time, I felt was the truth. "Master, I am attracted to both men and women. What shall I do?" He responded, "My dear one, then you have twice the power of love. Use it carefully." I was stunned. I sat in silence for a moment, waiting for more. "Is that all?" I asked. He smiled and said, 'That is all. There is nothing more to say."

Rav Eliashuv's words calmed me, permitting me to forget temporarily the awful tensions that would eventually overtake me. His trust and support buoyed me above my fears. I thought that as a bisexual I could have a wider and richer emotional life and perhaps even a deeper spiritual life than is common—and still marry and have a family. For a long while I felt a self-acceptance that carried me confidently into rabbinical school. I began rabbinical training with great excitement and a sense of promise. At the center of my motivations were those powerful rabbinic traditions that had bowled me over in my early adolescence. I wanted more than anything else to learn and to teach Torah in its full depth and breadth. I finished rabbinical school, still dating and carefully avoiding any physical expression and took my first jobs as a rabbi. There were many failed relationships with wonderful women who could not understand why things just didn't work out. Only after knocking my shins countless times into the hard wood of this truth was I able fully to acknowledge that I am gay.

It has taken a number of years to sift through the wreckage of "my life as I wanted it" to discover "my life as it is." It has taken more time to exorcise the self-hatred that feeds on shattered hopes and ugly stereotypes. I am still

---

*The entire body of Jewish law and tradition. (Eds.)

engaged in that struggle. I have yet to receive the new tablets, the whole ones, that will take their place in the Ark beside the broken ones. Rav Nachman of Bratzlav teaches that there is nothing so whole as a broken heart. It is in his spirit that I continue to try to make sense of my life.

Although much has changed in the past few years as I have accepted my gayness, much remains the same. I am still a rabbi, and I am still deeply committed to God, Torah, and Israel. My religious life had always been directed by the desire to be a servant of the Lord. None of that has changed. The question is an old one, merely posed anew as I strive to integrate being gay into my life. Given that I am gay, what is it that the God of Israel wants of me?

Of course, many will hear this as an illegitimate question—fallacious in thinking that the God of Israel can somehow accept and move beyond my gayness. Leviticus 18:23 instructs: "Do not lie with a male as one lies with a woman, it is an abhorrence." I do not propose to reject this or any text. For the present, I have no plausible halachic method of interpreting this text in a manner that permits homosexual sex.

As a traditionalist, I hesitate to overturn cultural norms in a flurry of revolutionary zeal. I am committed to a slower and more cautious process of change, which must always begin internally. Halacha, as an activity, is not designed to effect social revolution. It is a society-building enterprise that maintains internal balance by reorganizing itself in response to changing social realities. When social conditions shift, we experience the halachic reapplication as the proper commitment to the Torah's original purposes. That shift in social consciousness in regard to homosexuality is a long way off.

If I have any argument, it is not to press for a resolution, but for a deeper understanding of homosexuality. Within the living Halacha are voices in tension, divergent strands in an imaginative legal tradition that are brought to bear on the real lives of Jews. In order to know how to shape a halachic response to any living question, what is most demanded of us is a deep understanding of the Torah and an attentive ear to the people who struggle with the living question. Confronting new questions can often tease out of the tradition a *hiddush*, a new balancing of the voices and values that have always been there. There is no conclusive *psak halacha* (halachic ruling) without the hearing of personal testimonies, and so far gay people have not been asked to testify to their experience.

How can halachists possibly rule responsibly on a matter so complex and so deeply foreign, without a sustained effort at understanding? Whatever the halachic argument will be, we will need to know much more about homosexuality to ensure that people are treated not merely as alien objects of a system but as persons within it. Halachists will need to include in their deliberations the testimony of gay people who wish to remain faithful to the Torah. Unimagined halachic strategies, I believe, will appear under different conditions. We cannot know in advance the outcome of such an investigation. Still, one wonders what the impact might be if Orthodox rabbis had to face the questions posed by traditional Jews, persons they respect and to whom they feel responsible, who are gay.

There is one quasi-halachic issue I must address—that of choice. One of the mitigating factors in halachic discourse is the presence of free will in matters of law. A command is only meaningful in the context of our freedom to obey or disobey. Thus the degree of choice involved in homosexuality is central to the shaping of a halachic response. There is indeed a certain percentage of gay people who claim to exercise some volition in their sexual choices. But for the vast majority of gay people, there is no "choice" in the ordinary sense of the word. Gay feelings are hardwired into our bodies, minds, and hearts. The strangeness and mystery of sexuality is universal. What we share, gay or straight, is the surprising "queerness" of all sexual desire. The experience of heterosexuals may seem less outlandish for its being more common, but all sexual feeling is deeply mysterious, beyond explanation or a simple notion of choice.

The Halacha addresses activities, however, not sexual identities; thus, in halachic Judaism there is no such thing as a gay identity—there are only sexual impulses to control. The tradition describes all sexual desire as *yetzer ha'ra* (evil impulse), rife with chaotic and destructive possibilities. Heterosexual desire is redeemed and integrated back into the system through a series of prescriptions and prohibitions that channel sexuality and limit its range of expression. Confined within marriage, giving and receiving sexual pleasure, even in nonprocreative ways, is raised to the level of *mitzvah*.

Homosexual desire, in contrast, is not seen as redeemable and thus remains an implacable *yetzer ha'ra* that needs to be defeated rather than channeled. In this argument, gay people are treated as people with a dangerous and destructive sexual desire which must be repressed. The spiritual task of a gay person is to overcome the *yetzer ha'ra* which prods one to have erotic relations with members of the same sex.

The unfairness of this argument begins with the recasting of homosexuals as heterosexuals with perverse desires. The Torah is employed to support the idea that there is only one sexuality, heterosexuality. God confirms heterosexual desire, giving heterosexuals the opportunity to enjoy love and companionship. With the impossibility of another sexuality comes the implicit assumption that gay people can "become" straight and marry and indeed should do so.

This has in fact been the ordinary state of affairs for many, if not most, gay men and women throughout history. I know a number of gay (or bisexual) men who have married and sustain relationships with their wives. Of those, most have had an affair at some point which did not end their marriage. Two gay rabbis I know were married and are now divorced, and a third remains happily married, surviving recurrent bouts of depression and emotional exhaustion. What disturbs me most in this sometimes heroic attempt at approximating the traditional ideal is the cost to the heterosexual spouse.

* * *

While in my first rabbinical post, I decided to come out to an older rabbi and seek his advice. He counseled me to find a woman and marry. I asked him if I was duty-bound to tell her about my attractions to men and my general sexual disinterest in women. He said no. I was shocked to hear that it was all right to deceive a woman who could very easily be damaged by such a marriage. It made no sense to me.

Surely some heterosexual women might be willing to marry a gay friend who could provide children and be a wonderful father.

There have been rare instances of gay women and men who have worked out marriages where the "disinterest" was mutual. I struggled for a number of years to find such a woman, gay or straight, with whom to begin a family. Sometimes I still torment myself to think that this is all possible—when it is not. I still feel ripped apart by these feelings—wanting a woman at the Shabbat table and a man in my bed. If I am judged for some failure, perhaps it will be that I could not choose the Shabbat table over the bed, either for myself or for the forlorn woman who, after dinner, wants the comfort of a man who wants her back.

Having rejected this option, the standard Orthodox position is to require celibacy. Many recent articles and responsa regard gay sex as indistinguishable from adultery, incest, or bestiality. The heterosexual is asked to limit sexuality to the marital bed, to nonrelatives, to human beings; the homosexual is asked to live a loveless life. I have lived portions of my adult life as a celibate clergyman.While it can have spiritual potency for a Moses or a Ben Azzai, who abandoned sexual life for God or Torah, it is not a Jewish way to live. Always sleeping alone, in a cold bed, without touch, without the daily physical interplay of lives morning and night—this celibate scenario is life-denying and, for me, has always led to a shrinking of spirit. What sort of Torah, what voice of God would demand celibacy from all gay people? Such a reading of divine intent is nothing short of cruel.

Many gay people now and in the past have been forced to purchase social acceptance and God's love through a denial of affection and comfort, and, worse, a denial of self. Today many simply leave Judaism behind in order to salvage a sense of dignity and to build a life. This understanding of homosexuality leaves no sanctified option for gay people, no possibility of *keddusha* or *keddushin*.

I have come to understand my gayness as akin to my Jewishness: it is integral to my sense of self. I did not choose it, but it is mine. To try to escape it would be self-defeating. There is nothing left to do but celebrate it. Whether in or out of the given halachic rubric, I affirm my desire for a full life, for love, and for sexual expression. Given that I am gay, and cannot be otherwise, and given that I do not believe that God would demand that I remain loveless and celibate, I have chosen to seek a committed love, a man with whom to share my life.

But so little of life is carried on in the bedroom. When I indeed find a partner, what sort of life do we build together? What is it that the God of Israel wants of me in regard to family and community?

Struggling with God and with Torah as a gay person was just the beginning. To be Jewish is to be grounded in the continuity of the Jewish people as a witness—a holy people, a light among the nations—a blessing to all the families of the earth. How does a gay person help to shape the continuity of the Jewish people? The carrying forth of the Jewish people is accomplished by marriage and procreation. It is both a tool of the Abrahamic covenant and its most profound meaning statement.

We are a people on the side of life—new life, more life, fuller life. The creation story invited the rabbis to read God's blessing of "be fruitful and multiply" as a command to have two children, a male and a female. Every Jewish child makes the possibility of the Torah's promise of a perfected world more real, more attainable. Abraham and Sarah transmit this vision by having children. Often the portrayal of blessing includes being surrounded with many children. Childlessness is a punishment and curse in the tradition, barrenness a calamity.

Gay life does not prevent the possibility of producing or raising Jewish children, but it makes those options very complicated. Being gay means that the ordinary relationship between making love and having children is severed. This is a deep challenge to the structure of Judaism, since its very transmission is dependent on both relationship and reproduction. For Jews who feel bound by *mitzvot*, bound by the duty to ensure that life conquers death, the infertility of our loving is at the core of our struggle to understand ourselves in light of the Torah.

This problem, among others, lies at the root of much of the Jewish community's discomfort with gay people. To a people that was nearly destroyed fifty years ago, gay love seems irresponsible. Jews see the work of their lives in light of the shaping of a world for their children. By contrast, gay people appear narcissistic and self-indulgent. Gay people's sexuality is thus a diversion from the tasks of Jewish family and the survival that it symbolizes, and is perceived as marginal to the Jewish community because we are shirkers of this most central and sacred of communal tasks.

This challenge also has a moral chord which strikes deep into the problems of gay subculture. The tradition understood parenting as one of the major moral crucibles for human development. No judge could serve without first being a parent for fear that without the experience of parenting one could grasp neither human vulnerability nor responsibility. Being heterosexual carries one down a path that demands years of selfless loving in the rearing of children. While not all straight couples have children, and some gay couples adopt them, the norm is shaped less by choice and more by biology. Yet if gay people do not ordinarily fall into monogamous coupling and childbearing, how do we find our place in the covenant? And what of the moral training that caring for children provides, how do we make up for that? Is there another job to be done that requires our service to God and to the Jewish people? Of all the problems entailed in gay sexuality, this one looms for me, both spiritually and emotionally.

Although there is no obvious biblical resource for this dilemma, there are biblical writers who struggled to address God's will in very new social circumstances. Isaiah was one such writer who bridged the worlds before and after the Exile. Some familiar passages have become charged for me with new meaning. In these verses Isaiah is speaking to his ancient Israelite community and trying to convince them that God's covenantal plan for Israel is larger than they think. The covenant begins with Abraham and Sarah but has become much more than a family affair. He speaks to two obvious outsider groups in chapter 56, the *b'nai ha'nechar,* the foreigners of non-Israelite birth, and the *sarisim,* the eunuchs:

> Let not the foreigner say,
> Who has attached himself to the Lord,
> "The Lord will keep me separate from His people";
> And let not the eunuch say,
> "I am a withered tree."

In the Talmud, a eunuch is not necessarily a castrated male, but a male who is not going to reproduce for various reasons (*Yevamot* 80b). Why does Isaiah turn his attention here to the foreigners and the eunuchs? In the chain of the covenantal family, the foreigner has no past and the eunuch no future. They both seem excluded from the covenantal frame of reference. It is this "exclusion" that the prophet addresses:

> For thus said the Lord:
> "As for the eunuchs who keep my sabbaths,
> Who have chosen what I desire
> And hold fast to My covenant—
> I will give them, in My House
> And within my walls,
> A monument and a name
> Better than sons or daughters.
> I will give them an everlasting name
> Which shall not perish.

The prophet comforts the pain of eunuchs with the claim that there are other ways in which to observe, fulfill, and sustain the covenant. There is something more permanent than the continuity of children provides. In God's House, the achievement of each individual soul has account. A name in the Bible is the path toward the essence, the heart of being. It is passed on to progeny. But there is another sort of a name, a name better than the one sons or daughters provide. The covenant is carried forward by those who live it out, in the present. Loyalty to the covenant is measured in God's House in such a way that even if one's name is not passed on through children an eternal name will nonetheless be etched into the walls. Isaiah offers a place to the placeless, an alternative service to the person who cannot be part of the family in other ways:

> As for the foreigners
> Who attach themselves to the Lord,
> to be His servants—
> All who keep the sabbath and do not profane it,
> And who hold fast to my covenant—
> I will bring them to my sacred mount
> And let them rejoice in my house of prayer.
> Their burnt offerings and sacrifices
> Shall be welcome on My altar;
> For My House shall be called
> A House of prayer for all peoples."
> Thus declares the Lord God,
> Who gathers the dispersed of Israel:
> "I will gather still more to those already gathered."

So inclusive is God's plan for the Israel in the world that any foreigner can join. The notion of conversion, so obvious to us now, was a striking innovation for the generation of Isaiah. Conversion is about rewriting the past. Like adoption, conversion redefines the meaning of parents and family. Birth and lineage are not discarded. The central metaphor for Israel is still family. But Isaiah and later tradition open up another avenue into the covenant. Those with no future are promised a future in the House of the Lord; those with no past are nevertheless included in Israel's destiny.

God can only require the doable. A foreigner cannot choose a different birth, or the eunuch a different procreative possibility. Gay people cannot be asked to be straight, but they can be asked to "hold fast to the covenant." God will work the story out and link the loose ends as long as we hold fast to the covenant.

Holding fast to the covenant demands that I fulfill the *mitzvot* that are in my power to fulfill. I cannot marry and bear children, but there are other ways to build a family. Adoption and surrogacy are options. If these prove infeasible, the tradition considers a teacher similar to a parent in life-giving and thus frames a way that the *mitzvah* of procreation can be symbolically fulfilled.

Holding fast to the covenant demands that I seek a path toward sanctity in gay sexual life. The Torah has much to say about the way people create *kedusha* in their sexual relationships. The values of marriage, monogamy, modesty, and faithfulness which are central to the tradition's view of holiness need to be applied in ways that shape choices and lifestyles.

Holding fast to the covenant means that being gay does not free one from the fulfillment of *mitzvot.* The complexities generated by a verse in Leviticus need not unravel my commitment to the whole of the Torah. There are myriad Jewish concerns, moral, social, intellectual, and spiritual, that I cannot abandon. Being gay need not overwhelm the rest of Jewish life. Single-issue communities are political rather than religious. Religious communities tend to be comprehensive of the human condition. The richness of Jewish living derives in part from its diversity of attention, its fullness.

For gay Orthodox Jews, this imagination of engagement between ourselves and the tradition is both terribly exciting and depressing. Regretfully, the communities that embrace us, both gay and Jewish, also reject us. The Jewish community wishes that we remain invisible. The gay community is largely unsympathetic and often hostile to Judaism. There are some in the gay community who portray Judaism as the original cultural source of homophobia. More often, the lack of sympathy toward Jewish observance derives from the singlemindedness of gay activism. Liberation communities rarely have room for competing loyalties.

Gay synagogues have filled a void for many, providing a place of dignity in a Jewish community. This work is part of a movement toward a fuller integration in the larger Jewish community for which most gay Jews long. Gayfriendly synagogues may well point the way, modeling a community of families and singles, young and old, straight and gay that is in spirit much closer to my hopeful future imagination than anything yet.

Gay Jews who wish to be part of an Orthodox community will find very few synagogues in which there is some level of understanding and tolerance. Some gay Jews attend Orthodox services and remain closeted in their communities. It is crucial that Orthodox rabbis express a loving acceptance for known gays in their synagogues even if public legitimation is now impossible. Attacks on homosexuality from the pulpit are particularly painful to those who have remained connected to the traditional synagogue, despite the hardships.

I have hesitated until now to address the central halachic concerns of homosexuality. Real dialogue is necessary before such a process of responsa writing can begin. Still, it appears to many Orthodox Jews that in the case of homosexuality there is little use for dialogue in the face of such a clear biblical prohibition. A number of my colleagues and friends want very much to respond compassionately to gay people, but feel compelled to remain loyal to what they see as the unambiguous word of the Torah. Let me offer the possibility of an intermediate position to demonstrate that real listening may indeed give birth to new halachic strategies.

The Torah very specifically forbids anal intercourse between two men. If the Torah expressly forbids only this one form of sexual fulfillment, could we articulate a possible "halachic" form of gay loving that excludes anal intercourse but permits a loving physical and emotional relationship between two men or two women? After all, heterosexuality is not a free zone of activity for halachically committed Jews. For the sake of holiness, the Torah requires heterosexual couples to refrain from intercourse during menstruation. Why not offer such a sanctified option to gay men who wish to find acceptance in the halachic community?

For many gay men, this will not be a realistic choice. But until it becomes a real possibility, who knows who will agree to commit? Of course, this challenge to gay Jewish men will be sincere only if the halachic community then takes a lead in accepting the couples who commit in this covenantal fashion. (Lesbian women would be accepted without condition, because there is no Torah text that specifically prohibits their relationships.)

I offer this framework knowing that Orthodox Jews will protest that there are rabbinic prohibitions that invalidate it, and that many gay Jews will feel that it too severely limits the essence of gay lovemaking. Let it then simply demonstrate at least the beginnings of a language of discourse between the tradition as it now stands and the lives of gay people.

For the present, in regard to sexual behavior, I personally have chosen to accept a certain risk and violate the Halacha as it is presently articulated, in the hope of a subsequent, more accepting halachic expression. I realize that this is "civil disobedience." It is not the system itself which I challenge but its application to an issue that has particular meaning for me and for those like me. There is always the possibility that I am wrong. Ultimately, the halachic risks that I take are rooted in my personal relationship with God, Who I will face in the end. It is this faith that makes me both confident and suspicious of myself.

I have, admittedly, a rather privatized form of community. I am closeted and have chosen to write this essay in anonymity to preserve what is still most precious to me: the teaching of Torah and caring for my community of Jews. What concerns me most is neither rejection by the Orthodox community, nor the loss of my particular pulpit. Were I to come out, the controversy would collapse my life, my commitments, my identity as a teacher of Torah, into my gayness. Still, the secrecy and the shadowy existence of the closet are morally repugnant and emotionally draining. I cannot remain forever in darkness. I thank God that for the time being, the Torah still sheds ample light.

I have a small circle of friends, gay and straight, men and women with whom I share a sense of community. We are looking for other tradition-centered Jews who can help build a place that embraces both the Torah and gay people. Not a synagogue, not a building, but a place for all the dispersed who are in search of community with Israel and communion with God. In this place, this House of the Lord, now somewhat hypothetical and private, and soon, I pray, to be concrete and public, those of us who have withered in the darkness, or in the light of day have been banished, will discover our names etched upon the walls.

32

Homosexuality and
Family-Centered Judaism

Reuven Kimelman

The debate on homosexuality in the Jewish community has created two distinct camps. Opponents of homosexual behavior and especially homosexual commitment rites often rely on Scripture and the norms of religious law to substantiate their position. Proponents, for their part, frequently underscore the right of choice, the importance of "live and let live," and the plight of the homosexual. Unless common ground can be found, the debate threatens to be as divisive as the abortion issue, with both sides veiling over a chasm of deafness about their fundamental rights.

If some common ground is to emerge, it is more likely to emerge out of considerations of public policy than those of private morality. More people are likely to agree on the need to encourage and sustain the centrality of the family than on the impermissiblity of homosexual activities. Many opposed to any infringement of the private rights of the homosexual are still willing to encourage a policy of shoring up the status of the family. The policy question with regard to homosexuality is whether it in general and commitment rites in particular threaten the primacy of the normative family. The answer to this is significantly dependent upon the degree to which a laissez-faire position on human sexuality threatens the cohesiveness and privileged position of the family in religious life. If so, the right of choice, which rings so well to the democratic ear, might not ring as well for the future of family life.

The emphasis on choice is frequently at odds with law-based ethics since it tends to reduce ethical norms to preferences. It assumes that choice takes precedence over moral claims. Normative ethics, for its part, assumes that moral claims are prior to choice. Thus the good is to be chosen, rather than the

Reprinted from TIKKUN MAGAZINE, A BI-MONTHLY JEWISH CRITIQUE OF POLITICS, CULTURE, AND SOCIETY. Subscriptions are $31.00 per year from TIKKUN, 251 West 100th Street, 5th floor, New York, NY 10025.

chosen becoming good. Neither the authenticity of the intention nor the depth of the self transforms an act into a good, rather it is its alignment with the good independent of human choice. Since the inner depths of the self can as readily choose evil as good, no moral authority can be attributed to the promptings of the self alone. Indeed, more often than not it is through transcending the promptings of the self and the denial of its claims that the good is achieved.

In periods of ethical relativism, ethical issues tend to be reduced to other categories. A powerful tactic in the arsenal of ethical relativism is the displacement of the language of ethics by the language of medicine, aesthetics, and especially psychology. Evil becomes unhealthy, wrong becomes distasteful. The ultimate in the relativizing or trivializing of the ethical is its psychologization. The result of this reductionism is the categorization of ethical issues as matters of health and ethical objections as phobias.

Framing the issue of homosexuality more in terms of public policy than private morality means asking whether there is a Gresham's law of sexuality which would argue that as bad coinage drives out good coinage, so bad sex drives out good sex. Ascertaining whether valorizing homosexuality is at all detrimental to family-producing sexuality is at the heart of a public policy analysis. If it is, then the approval of a priori nonprocreative marriages as a class could tend to devalue the type of sexuality that leads to procreation.

The devaluation of procreative sex is not inconsequential. Without commitments of time, money, and emotions, there will be no family to speak of. The creation of families is a major investment. Because of the toil, anguish, and expense of raising children, societies concerned with their biological future extend special inducements for those assuming such responsibility. Within the larger polity, there are economic inducements such as tax deductions, tax-supported public education, tax write-offs, and tax deductions for interest on mortgage loans. Jewishly, the inducements include the reward of doing a *mitzvah*, genetic and cultural continuity, family and social expectations, and that joy of raising children called *nachas*.

It is clear that Jewish continuity is already threatened by too many singles not marrying and too many couples declining to invest in the future by replenishing themselves. It is precisely because of the hassles of real-life interactions that we must invest so much in order to sustain a family-focused culture. Contemporary mores militate against families thriving on their own.

The Jewish meaning of marriage is broader than the notion of human intimacy. By contributing to an ethos that sees the relationship as the sole end of marriage, we undermine efforts to persuade couples to assume their responsibility for the type of investment in the future that childbearing entails. Our credibility is compromised when we promote child-bearing families while sanctifying relationships which are inherently childless. The Jewish community has a vested interest in getting people to deal with their sexuality in a manner that is supportive of family and children. Indeed, its success is dependent

upon persuading its members to define their self-interest as including responsibility for others starting with spouse and children. In order that this message
be received unambiguously, the community must be wary of any factor that
adds to the process of relativizing the social and moral status of heterosexuality and the family. The alternative is a mixed message with all its attendant
ambiguities.

Childless marriages are different from those with children in their impact
on the partners and on society. It is the birth of a child that most fully validates
sexual partnership as a means of continuity. As the Talmud *Yevamot* (64a)
notes, a childless marriage brings about a withdrawal of the divine presence
(*shekhina*) from Israel, as it says, "to be a God to you and to your seed after
you" (Genesis 17:7); "Whenever your seed is after you, the *shekhina* dwells,
[whenever] there is no seed after you, upon whom will the *shekhina* dwell, on
wood and stones?" Apparently, there is a special divine concern for those
who invest in progeny. We rabbis are acutely aware of the impact of children
from our involvements in divorce cases. When there are children the sense of
tragedy is qualitatively different. The presence of children intensifies the feeling that marriage breakup frays the social fabric of community. There is of
course a considerable difference in having compassion for a couple who cannot have children as opposed to one that biologically was not meant to.

Contemporary technology and mores have widened the gap between sex
and love, childbearing and parenting. In specific cases this may accrue to the
benefit of all involved. Su...dering these links for a whole class of people, however, undermines the centrality of the family as the locus of love, sex, childbearing, and parenting. Judaism would be false to its own best insights were
it to become a partner to the dissolution of the family, its major contribution
to the civilization of humanity.

The building blocks of family are male and female. A man without a
wife, according to the Midrash *Genesis Rabbah* (17:2 and parallels), lacks
blessing, bliss, well-being, protection, and atonement. There is even the opinion there that a single male, unable to realize his full humanity, cannot be
called *adam*. Male-female interaction contributes to the stabilizing of gender
identity along with the flowering of masculinity and femininity. Although
they share much, the differences between the two should not be underesti-
mated. Masculine and feminine love are not identical. Besides the obvious differences, feminine love possesses a futurity that cannot easily be duplicated by
masculine love. Anatomically and psychologically, feminine love is more
bound up in creating a future than its masculine counterpart.

It is through commitment to the female that male sexuality lays claim to the
future. As George Guilder writes in his book *Sexual Suicide,* a man's "participation in the chain of nature, his access to social immortality, the very meaning of his potency, of his life energy, are all profoundly" bound up with a
woman's durable love. Traditionally, women have leveraged the male sexual
drive into domestication. Without channeling the sexual drive into family-

making we could become totally enmeshed in "nowness" with little thought of the future. It is precisely the link with the future inherent in heterosexual relations that allows glimmers of the transcendent to be refracted through human sexuality. When the Midrash *Genesis Rabbah* (9:7) notes that "were it not for the evil impulse, a man would not build a house, marry a wife, and produce children," it is expressing appreciation for the divine cunning in the use of our physical sensations to enhance our concerns for building a better tomorrow.

It is no wonder that the rabbis saw in a loving husband-wife relationship a fitting dwelling place for the divine presence. The Kabbalah went one step further by picturing the husband-wife relationship as capable of completing the circuit of divine electricity, as it were, that charges all of life. Since the unity of husband and wife is a source of special blessing, there is a linkage with the divine made possible through marriage. Indeed, it is precisely in the complementarity of husband and wife that humanity realizes the fullness of the divine image. Kabbalists described marriage as making possible a kind of connection to the Infinite. As such, it entitles one to don the mantle of infinity, the *tallit* (prayer shawl).

Family in contemporary Judaism serves to promote the ideal of monogamy. The multiple encirclings of the groom by the bride under the marriage chuppah can be understood as seeking to weld man's polymorphic sexuality to his wife. For civilization to succeed, male sexual impulses and psychology need to be subordinated to the long-term horizons of female psychology and biology. Through love of wife, husbands can achieve a futurity that many women are graced with biologically. This helps explain the fact that so many happily married men deep down believe, however they may loathe to admit it, that marriage has had a domesticating and civilizing effect on them. We males frequently become nurturers through our wives and in return extend their nurturing capabilities. Just contrast the statistics of the leisure activities and acts of violence of single men with their married counterparts. Thus despite the fragility of the contemporary husband-wife bond, it remains the most stable and lasting of chosen, nonbiological relationships. It is no wonder that Judaism has found no better civilizers than the life of Torah and a good family.

Marriage is more than the ratification of love between two people. It is the transformation of the love into a biological and social continuity and community that transcends the participants. Married love is an investment of faith in the future of the family, society, and humanity. For a couple, love for each other and children properly nurtured can lead to care for the community that supports them and to a willingness to work for a future to house them. Thus family involvement can lead to the expansion of both horizontal and vertical horizons. Horizontally, concern for the immediate family can lead to concern for community and ultimately for the extended human family. The mutual helpfulness that takes place within the family can set the pattern for such throughout society. Vertically, continuity is epitomized through having children. Anybody who has counseled a barren couple knows how much the absence of children can undermine the professed motives of marriage. Marriage both institutionalizes the desire for continuity and spurs it on.

At least since the first paschal offering upon the redemption from Egypt, biblical religion has invested in the family as its central vehicle of education and continuity. Ever since, this holiday of redemption has become the quintessential family holiday. It is clear that a religion committed to a multigenerational covenant to bring about the redemption will be inclined to invest in that agency that is intrinsically multigenerational. As no other biological community can so easily become a historical community as the family, so no other institution has the wherewithal to stretch from the first to the final redemption.

The two themes of redemption and family are linked, according to the Talmud *Sabbath* (31a), on the day of judgment. At that time, we are asked about trying to have children right before we are asked about awaiting the redemption. The sequence and juxtaposition of the two highlights their relationship and commonality. Both attest to long-term commitments. Indeed, the extended vision produced through having children can enhance the capacity for the long-term envisioning required for redemption. A perspective that limits itself to the self and its indulgences will tend to exclude both. Family, for its part, forces us to see ourselves in a larger context of meaning both within a generation of humanity and throughout the generations. Any effort that serves to undermine, whether intentionally or not, the primacy of the family is *eo ipso* inimical to the interests of religion and its vision of redemption. This may explain why the Talmud *Pesahim* (88b) cites the verse from Isaiah, "He did not create it a waste, but formed it for habitation," in support of the idea of *tikkun olam.** This weave of family, religion, and redemption stands behind the proclamation of the psalmist:

> He established a testimony in Jacob
> and appointed a law in Israel
> which He commanded our fathers
> to teach to their children;
> that the next generation might know them,
> the children yet unborn,
> and arise to tell them to their children,
> so that they should set their hope in God.
> (Psalm 78:4–7)

The focus on the family as the agent of continuity and therefore of redemption accounts for its centrality already in Genesis. Genesis is more than a series of episodes organized along chronological lines. On the level of ideas, it is unified by a sense that history is going somewhere and that its consequential participants are those that share this sense and express it in covenan-

---

*Eternal transformation. (Eds.)

tal terms. On the level of roles, it is unified not only by the presence of God, but also by that of the family.

The sense of family as expressed in biblical law and narrative underscores the bonds between husband and wife and parents and children. Much of the prohibited sexual activity serves to maintain and enhance these links by focusing on the exclusivity of these relationships. In addition to undermining the primacy of the family, same-sex activity has the potential of undermining the idea of sexual prohibitions. The fear is that the legitimation of loving homosexual relations is the first step to the legitimation of "loving" incestuous, pedophiliac, and adulterous relationships. Such is the slippery slope in today's sexual climate as it was apparently in antiquity. Accordingly, Rabbi Akiba in Talmud *Sanhedrin* (58a) derives the prohibition of incest, homosexuality, adultery, and bestiality all from different parts of the same verse, Genesis 2:24. To note that Torah is a reflection of culture without underscoring how often it was and remains a protest against the ethos of the day is to do a disservice to the biblical impact on human culture. In the same vein, Jewish political thought from Albo to Luzzatto opposed utopian schemes of social organization from Plato to Thomas More precisely on the issue of the inviolability of the family unit. The biblical sexual ethos with all its prohibitions is but the flip side of its commitment to the sanctity of the family unit.

Sociologically speaking, deviations from the norm come in clusters. One could easily imagine somebody contending that he is sexually functional only with other married women or his own daughters. There are now support groups for men with sexual appetites for children, of course only consenting (*sic*) children. Once feelings are accepted as the criterion for overturning a prohibition, every leak in the dike can become a flood. Moreover, if there is a market for promoting incestuous relations and the like, there will always be some health expert ready to publish a book on how loving, stable, incestuous relations are healthy for the participants. They are already appearing on television talk shows. Books that tout the benefits of extramarital relations for "healthy" marriages are readily available. Capitalistic cultures are most effective in producing suppliers for demands.

Those who advocate an abolition of the norms of the Torah frequently argue that the prohibition against homosexuality was based on health considerations and on the assumption that homosexuality was voluntary, neither of which any longer obtain. (The theory that the prohibition is due to an association with the pagan cult has been consigned to the dustbin of out-dated scholarly theories.) Whatever the health status of homosexuality or its etiology, it bears little on the issue of maintaining the privileged position of the normative family in Jewish life. Its impact is independent of its origin. Moreover, we lack the evidence to assess whether health considerations played any role in the Torah's prohibition. Those who claim to know have already made up their mind on the validity of the prohibition as those who ruled against the validity of *kashrut*

(Jewish dietary laws) a century ago had made up their mind on the Torah's assessment of health factors. There is also no evidence to suggest that homosexual behavior was condemned on the basis of choice. Indeed, the Talmud *Sanhedrin* (75a) roundly prohibits even for curative purposes a sexually sick man from having relations with a women who is otherwise prohibited to him. Note that it is not the sexual orientation, which may or may not be of one's choosing, that is subject to opprobrium, but its expression in behavior.

It is precisely the chosenness of the behavior that argues against any analogy with the *mamzer* (child born outside of marriage). If an analogy is in order, kleptomania may be an instructive one. Feeling that what is their own cannot have much worth, kleptomaniacs take things precisely because they belong to others. Notwithstanding our compassion for the low self-esteem that generates the characterological problem of kleptomania, we still cannot condone the stealing. In both cases. compassion for a person's orientation however involuntary does not entail approval of behavior. Moreover, even if judgments are to be mitigated because of duress, psychological pressure is still not the mitigating factor that physical coercion is.

Whatever the truth of the genetic origin of homosexuality, it is evident that social conditions enhance its expression, especially for borderline cases. Even the advocates of a neurobiological etiology are unable to identify those genes which carry, as it were, a homosexual code. The most that can be affirmed is that it is polygenic. Even those that argue for polygeny concede that biology is only part, however great, of the case. It is still not possible to achieve total correlation between genes or chromosomes and behavior in healthy people. Indeed, were it otherwise the spiritual dignity of humankind would be seriously questioned, for human beings would be nothing more than automatons of the body. Since no single factor accounts for its existence (all the more so for its expression), homosexuality is clearly multifactorial.

Gender distinctions are not absolute. Male and female represent the neurobiological and psychological poles of a continuum. Whereas moving from one pole to the other is rare, sliding along the continuum is more common, especially among the young, whose gender identity is still in formation. Such sliding may be as much a product of nurture as nature. Latent tendencies properly cultivated can become overt. Frequently all that is needed are role models and supportive surroundings. Much of the content of sexual roles results from observation and imitation of others. Certain environments encourage the expression of one predisposition over another. It is precisely because we understand our social codes to be the result of nature and design, human and divine, that we should see to it that Jewish life fosters environments that encourage optimal Jewish behavior.

Some people have considered leaving more liberal denominations for more conservative ones when the former legitimate homosexuality. To call this "homophobia" sheds no more light on the phenomenon than calling its alternative "heterophobia." People frequently join synagogues in search of a community of shared values in order to provide themselves and their children with a haven from the general culture. Common values are predicated on shared convictions about what is right and what is wrong, what is decent and what is obscene. Otherwise, there is no communal bonding. For a religious community to bond, it must also share a sense of what is noble and what is base, what is sacred and what is profane.

There are those who would prohibit rabbis from performing commitment ceremonies for homosexuals, but allow them to be present. Rabbinic presence at alternative lifestyle ceremonies, however, is not harmless if it serves to validate the lifestyle. The nonverbal message is that one lifestyle is as good as another. Prohibiting rabbis from the performance of such ceremonies while permitting their presence qua rabbi is disingenuous, since it connotes condonation if not approval.

Religious legitimation of extranormative sexual relationships threatens to undermine the privileged position of normative marriage. Such legitimation tends to equalize the status of the two, especially in the eyes of children. Instead of being a social ideal, family-centered marriage would become simply another alternative. Already a besieged institution, it is questionable whether its protective walls can withstand much more battering. Thus, Jewish family advocates should reserve sanctification ceremonies for rites of marriage between men and women.

REFERENCE

Guilder, George F. *Sexual Suicide.* London: Millington, 1974.

33

Family Values:
A Reply to Reuven Kimelman

Yaakov Levado

The image of the family as an institution in distress has become one of the most successful rhetorical tools used against gays. The claim is simple: Gay people, their relationships, and especially their committed relationships pose a deadly threat to the normative family. Reuven Kimelman . . . has marshaled the symbolic power of the family for American Jews to encourage the continuing rejection of gay people and their relationships within the Jewish mainstream.

Kimelman wants to shape an antigay public policy across denominational lines, something that a halachic opinion could not accomplish. Thus he avoids any direct reference to the sexual prohibitions in the book of Leviticus that might hamper his efforts to appeal to a liberal conscience. With the family at risk, many Jewish liberals can be counted on to join the opposition to gay rights in America and within the Jewish community.

The family-values argument reveals a preoccupation with the family that has itself become dangerous to Jewish continuity. As important as family is to the historic enterprise of the Jewish people, it is after all not the goal of our efforts but a means of accomplishing it. It is a potent but imperfect and sometimes unwieldy tool employed in the service of the covenant. The goals of the Torah are wide and deep, universal and particular, public and private. Many of these goals cannot be accomplished exclusively in or through the family, and some can be in tension with it.

Family as a goal in itself directs our attention away from the widow and the orphan, the unmarried and the divorced. The inappropriate preoccupation with family encourages parents to funnel the lion's share of their Jewish energy into their children and to ignore their own Jewishness.

Reprinted from TIKKUN MAGAZINE, A BI-MONTHLY JEWISH CRITIQUE OF POLITICS, CULTURE, AND SOCIETY. Subscriptions are $31.00 per year from TIKKUN, 251 West 100th Street, 5th floor, New York, NY 10025.

Kimelman's narrow conception of Judaism helps him portray any challenge to the normative family as a grave danger to Judaism. Instead, he employs a number of inaccurate analogies and confusing metaphors to support his case. For example, he fails to demonstrate, how the acceptance of homosexual commitments endangers heterosexual marriage. Kimelman claims that a "Gresham's Law" operates in relation to sex. Nonprocreative, or, as he calls it, "bad" sex, would tend to drive "good' sex out of the social system.

This boggles the mind. First, nonprocreative sex is not bad sex—not for Jews, anyway. While procreation is clearly an important value, sexual pleasure does not lose its legitimacy in nonprocreative settings. For Jews, sexual expression is not merely an appetite, but a central means to affirm and celebrate each other as images of God. Sex as a communication of loving has enormous power to affirm human dignity.

Second, what does Gresham's Law have to do with sex? Will easy access to one kind of sex really drive the other out of circulation? Kimelman argues that homosexual sex is less demanding and easier to enjoy because it has no generative consequences. Kimelman apparently believes that lazy heterosexuals might find gay life more comfortable, more hassle-free. Does he think that straight people who don't want the bother of having or raising children would prefer to try homosexuality rather than use a condom? Sexual desire alone no longer imposes marriage or family upon us. With birth control widely available childbearing is increasingly—and among Jews almost exclusively—an act of choice.

Parents raise their children, despite the difficulties, amid great love and satisfaction. My friends and relatives who have become fathers and mothers talk of the births of their children as the most incredible moments of their lives, a joy that connects them to the mystery of life itself. Professor Kimelman does not know the pain most gay people experience in the routine exclusion from this chapter of life.

Most straight people underestimate this loss for gay people: "If it is so important to be a father, then get married." When we respond that it is just not possible, we are again misunderstood. "Oh, that's because sex is too important to you." No again! For most of us, the contortion is too great. We know that we will not be adequate mates for spouses of the opposite sex, not because we cannot function sexually, but because we are not able to love and be loved in a way that is fully mutual and deep. We will constantly disappoint and be disappointed. Everyone wants sexual fulfillment, but many, if not most, people live in good relationships with much less sexual fulfillment than they might like. What couples need to feel, whether or not the sex is great, is that they belong in each other's arms.

Although it is surely politically incorrect, in at least one way I see gayness as a handicap, and not only in regard to the social milieu. For those who want to raise a family, gayness is a sterility of sorts, experienced in some similar ways as a bodily impediment to making a family. Heterosexuals are blessed with a loving that is ordinarily generative. Being gay, then, is a problematic quirk of fate in regard to family that challenges me to make it work anyway. In the tradition, life always finds a way.

In ancient Israel, the desire for life was so strong that sexual taboos were put aside for the sake of life. Sexual relations between a brother and sister-in-law were strictly forbidden in ordinary circumstances. But if a cruel fate took a young man's life before the birth of even one child, his brother was asked to marry his widow and raise children in the deceased brother's name.

The levirate duty supersedes the law in Leviticus. What was prohibited becomes obligatory. The power of life and memory overcomes both the prohibition and the punishment: barrenness is turned into hope. If only symbolically, a wife and brother reverse the fate of their husband and brother by becoming agents of new life. This is indeed not a normative family, yet death is conquered and new life born.

There are numerous biblical examples of this principle. Lot's daughters, at the edge of the maelstrom, thought the world had ended with the destruction of Sodom, and that life itself would cease with them. The Torah relates that they made their father drunk and then, on successive nights, slept with him to sustain life. Moab is born of one of these incestuous encounters. Ruth is a Moabite woman, returning from Moab with her mother-in-law, Naomi, to Israel. Both are widows and childless. Ruth discovers a relative of Naomi, an older man who might redeem them both from poverty and even childlessness. She steals into his chamber at night and uncovers his legs, or perhaps his genitals. He awakes to find her at his feet. Why does the tradition praise Ruth for this seduction? Because she wished to sustain life against the odds.

Tamar is widowed and childless. Her brother-in-law, Onan, marries her but defies the intent of the levirate duty. He sleeps with Tamar, but not wanting to sire children in his brother's name, spills his seed on the ground. Onan dies childless and Tamar is now left waiting for her father-in-law, Judah, to arrange for his third son, Shelah, to complete the levirate duty. Time passes, Judah's wife dies, and Tamar decides she must take matters into her own hands. She veils herself and waits by the roadside where Judah will pass. Judah takes her as a roadside prostitute, sleeps with her, and leaves her with pieces of his memory and identity, his signet ring, cord, and staff. Later, when she becomes pregnant, she is accused of adultery, being betrothed, as it were, to Shelah. At first, it seems she has violated a sexual taboo and must die. By the end we learn that it is Judah and his sons who have selfishly violated taboos. Tamar is vindicated because only she is truly dedicated to life and to memory.

The family lines in the Bible are interrupted by death and contorted by the intricacies of sexual mores and desire. Lot's daughter, Tamar, and Ruth all carry and renew life in this crazy, unpredictable world. Through them the king messiah, David, is born. David is the symbol of the final redemption, which is like David himself, just a shred of life, fragile and flawed, finding its way to Jerusalem.

Many gay people today have found ways to create families despite the physical challenges and social barriers. In San Francisco's outreach synagogue to gays and lesbians, Sha'ar Zahav, there have been six babies born within the last six months. One of the proud fathers is a good friend who for many years has wanted to become a father. Two years ago he met a wonderful lesbian woman who shared his desire for parenthood. After a number of months they developed an agreement that spelled out all the details of their family arrangement, including a large section on the Jewish upbringing of their child. Elijah David was born two months ago.

In a nearby community, a Jewish family struggled to accept their two gay sons. The younger one was lost to AIDS five years ago. The older brother recently adopted a baby boy, and I helped to arrange for a *brit milah* (circumcision ceremony). As this man held his child and pronounced the name he chose for his son—the name of his brother—there was not a dry eye to be found. Is this not life finding a way, Professor Kimelman? Isn't this what families do?

Although there is little if any justification to support the family-values argument, the images of [a] gay threat to the family are used effectively, if uncritically, as a key element in antigay rhetoric. The gay subculture unfortunately provides an ample supply of shocking countercultural images to whet the appetite of any conservative defender of the family and douse the flames of the most ardent liberal.

But the truth is that the gay subculture is not descriptive of the vast majority of gay people. Homosexuality defines no single lifestyle. It carries with it no set of behaviors or habits, no specific mannerisms or political views, no religious outlooks or sexual mores. Most homosexuals want what anyone would want: a comfortable place to live, a rewarding occupation, lasting friendships, a committed love, a community, and even a family.

In his recent book, *A Place at the Table,* Bruce Bawer, a gay journalist, lambastes the highly vocal and visible minority of gays who equate gayness with promiscuity, political correctness, and exhibitionism. He claims that they seriously misrepresent gay life. This is true partly because most gays who lead mainstream, often closeted, lives have kept out of the public eye and the debate. After two decades of the gay liberation movement, we have not even begun to communicate who we are.

The great majority of homosexuals have no desire to destroy institutions. We just want to be part of them. And it is no different in the Jewish community. The majority of gay Jews, even after much rejection, want to be part of Jewish families, Jewish communities.

Kimelman and the others who share his fears have shaped a set of demands that work as a double-bind. Family-values advocates attribute the rejection of gays to gay promiscuity, exhibitionism, and a vague array of countercultural values that threaten the normative family. Ironically, when gay people wish to join synagogues as couples, celebrate committed relationships, and build families there is even a greater public outcry. Professor Kimelman seems to suggest that gay people who establish committed relationships and make families are a deeper threat to family values than the gays whose lifestyle he condemns.

Rabbis and communal leaders need to understand that the young gay person is terribly confused. The gay subculture offers a hypersexual and/or hyperpolitical identity which in either case revolves around sexual desire. Gay sexual desire in itself is not a moral problem, but a life focused around sex is. If our communal and religious institutions ignore the gay youth, lock him out, push her away, these young people will have no haven but the one available in the gay subculture.

Indeed, if the Jewish community were truly family oriented, gay people would be offered communal services to aid them in family making. The Jewish community provides family services that help sterile heterosexual couples adopt children. Why not offer the same service to gay couples who are committed to each other and to raising Jewish children? If the Jewish community is invested in making Jewish singles into Jewish families, why not make gay couples into Jewish families in just the same or similar ways? Instead we are told, "Live in the closet or in the Village, but not among us."

While the family-values argument fails logically, it succeeds emotionally. What the argument conveys faithfully are the fears people harbor in regard to gayness in general, and gay visibility in particular. And because its central image is family, it speaks to parents whose fears in regard to their children are magnified.

Gayness is frightening to parents because they do not want their children to have to face the hardships that gay people must face today: the hatred, the exclusion, the struggle to find love. Worst of all, parents are powerless to protect their children from being gay. It is easier to feign control than to admit vulnerability. Thinking of gayness as a sickness that one can catch, or a taste that one can acquire rather than a given aspect of identity is comforting. But such a perception casts gay people either as infected lepers, or as missionaries seeking converts. In either case, we are safer kept away, out of sight, and out of the reach of young and impressionable children.

Beyond the generalized worry parents have for their kids, there are two kinds of sexual fear our public presence seems to generate. What we threaten, I think, is not the family per se, but the great certainties associated with the "world of the family." Families tend to keep the lines that divide men and women neat and clean. As a conservative institution, the family helps us to order and limit what otherwise might be a chaotic array of possibilities. It makes us comfortable to know what to expect of ourselves and others. For many heterosexuals, that world is made volatile and unpredictable by the intrusion of same-sex desire. We speak of children being in the "spitting image" of their parents. When families construct belonging in limited ways, it is easy for the mirror to break; for many parents, the news of their child's gayness shatters the mirror of parent-child resemblance.

Gay people are fearsome in one other important way. Somehow we have come to represent to white middle-class America the boundary-smashing power of sexuality. Having taken our sexual otherness into the streets, we have come to symbolize or even to embody sex itself. This is why frightened heterosexuals want to keep us in the closet. Our public presence seems to raise old, hitherto settled questions about how to manage the power of sexuality, how to attend to it, or to turn away from it.

Being outside the norms has some benefit for thinking through the moral and emotional intricacies of sexuality. The view from outside the heterosexual world reveals, among other things, the imbalance of power between the sexes that needs to be healed.

But being outside the norms means that we have none. We possess a sexuality that is essentially culturally unfettered. Gay liberation has expanded the human repertoire for loving, but having thrown off oppressive sexual mores gay people have been hesitant to accept any standards of sexual propriety. Too often, the gay community has condoned and even celebrated an obsessive preoccupation with the sexual. We have neither accepted straight norms, nor have we fully shaped our own.

Every society makes rules and patterns of behavior to domesticate the sex drive. We are just beginning to develop the cultural, spiritual, and intellectual frameworks to manage a different sexuality. In part, it is the lack of these institutional frameworks, so available to heterosexuals, that makes gay desire so fearsome. Family is just one of those institutional frameworks that we can now employ to move from freedom to holiness.

The family is always a subset of a world. And since the Jewish people [have] traversed many worlds, we have constructed many kinds of families. The biblical family and many of the models of Jewish family throughout history have varied greatly from the narrow institution called the modern nuclear family. Gay and lesbian families thus signal a return to a more expansive understanding of family which enhances rather than undermines family's most important lesson: We all become better human beings inside of dependable, loving relationships.

Selected Bibliography

Bawer, Bruce. *A Place at the Table: The Gay Individual in American Society.* New York: Simon & Schuster, 1994.

LeVay, Simon. *The Sexual Brain.* Cambridge, Mass.: MIT Press, 1993.

McNeil, John J. *The Church and the Homosexual.* 4th ed. Boston: Beacon Press, 1993.

Melton, J. Gordon, ed. *The Churches Speak on Homosexuality: Official Statements from Religious Bodies and Ecumenical Organizations.* Detroit: Gale Research, Inc., 1991.

Nicolosi, Joseph. *Reparative Therapy of Male Homosexuality: A New Clinical Approach.* Northvale, N.J.: Jason Aronson, Inc., 1991.

Pronk, Pim. *Against Nature? Types of Moral Argumentation Regarding Homosexuality.* Grand Rapids, Mich.: William B. Eerdmans Publishing Company, 1993.

Ruse, Michael. *Homosexuality: A Philosophical Inquiry.* New York: Basil Blackwell, Inc., 1988.

Gramick, Jeannine, and Robert Nugent, eds. *The Vatican and Homosexuality: Reactions to the "Letter to the Bishops of the Catholic Church on the Pastoral Care of Homosexual Persons."* New York: The Crossroad Publishing Company, 1988.

Shilts, Randy. *Conduct Unbecoming: Lesbians and Gays in the U.S. Military, Vietnam to the Persian Gulf.* New York: St. Martin's Press, 1993.

Swidler, Arlene, ed. *Homosexuality and World Religions.* Valley Forge, Pa.: Trinity Press International, 1993.

Wells-Petry, Melissa. *Exclusion: Homosexuals and the Right to Serve.* Washington, D.C.: Regnery Gateway, 1993.

White, Mel. *Stranger at the Gate: To be Gay and Christian in America.* New York: Simon & Schuster, 1994.

Contributors

R. D. Adair is a Major in the United States Army, currently assigned to the Defense Attaché's Office in Venezuela.

Les Aspin (1938–1995) was United States Secretary of Defense from 1993 to 1994.

Michael Bailey is assistant professor of psychology at Northwestern University.

Bruce Bawer is a literary critic and author of *A Place at the Table*.

Paul Duke is pastor of Kirkwood Baptist Church, Kirkwood, Missouri.

John Finnis is a professor of law at Oxford University.

Steven Goldberg is chair of the Department of Sociology, City College of New York.

Barry Goldwater is a former United States Senator from Arizona and Republican nominee for president in 1964.

William A. Henry III (1950–1994) was a Pulitzer Prize-winning drama critic for *Time* magazine.

John J. Jeffries, Jr., is a former law clerk of Justice Lewis F. Powell, Jr., and member of the faculty at University of Virginia Law School.

Stanton L. Jones is chair of the Psychology Department, Wheaton College.

Reuven Kimelman is associate professor of Jewish Studies at Brandeis University.

Yaakov Levado is a pseudonym.

Simon LeVay is a neuroanatomist at the Salk Institute and author of *The Sexual Brain.*

Carlyle Marney served as pastor of Baptist churches in Texas and North Carolina and was founder and director of Interpreter's House, Lake Junaluska, North Carolina. He died in 1978.

Joseph C. Myers is a Captain in the United States Army, currently assigned to the Defense Attaché's Office in Venezuela.

Joseph Nicolosi is a psychologist in private practice.

Martha Nussbaum is a professor of philosophy and classics at Brown University.

Richard Pillard is associate professor of psychiatry at Boston University's School of Medicine.

John R. Quinn is archbishop of San Francisco.

Joseph Cardinal Ratzinger is Cardinal Prefect for the Congregation of the Doctrine of the Faith in Rome.

Darrell Yates Rist is a co-founder of the Gay & Lesbian Alliance Against Defamation and author of *Heartlands: A Gay Man's Odyssey Across America.*

Randy Shilts (1951–1994) was a journalist, a gay rights activist, and the author of *And the Band Played On* and *Conduct Unbecoming: Lesbians and Gays in the Military, Vietnam to the Persian Gulf.*

Robert Stone is a writer whose most recent novel is *Outerbridge Reach.*

Stuart Taylor, Jr., is a senior writer for *The American Lawyer.*

Margaret Susan Thompson is an associate professor of history at Syracuse University.

Lindsy Van Gelder is a contributing editor to *Ms.* magazine.

George M. Weaver is a member of the England, Weaver & Kytle Law Firm in Atlanta, Georgia.